CH00796330

New Testament Studies. I. Luke the Physician

You are holding a reproduction of an original work that is in the public domain in the United States of America, and possibly other countries.You may freely copy and distribute this work as no entity (individual or corporate) has a copyright on the body of the work.This book may contain prior copyright references, and library stamps (as most of these works were scanned from library copies).These have been scanned and retained as part of the historical artifact.

This book may have occasional imperfections such as missing or blurred pages, poor pictures, errant marks, etc. that were either part of the original artifact, or were introduced by the scanning process. We believe this work is culturally important, and despite the imperfections, have elected to bring it back into print as part of our continuing commitment to the preservation of printed works worldwide. We appreciate your understanding of the imperfections in the preservation process, and hope you enjoy this valuable book.

o

CROWN THEOLOGICAL LIBRARY

XX.

VOL. ~~XIX~~

HARNACK'S LUKE THE PHYSICIAN

Crown Theological Library

WORKS ALREADY PUBLISHED

Descriptive Prospectus on Application.

𝔑𝔢𝔴 𝔗𝔢𝔰𝔱𝔞𝔪𝔢𝔫𝔱 𝔖𝔱𝔲𝔡𝔦𝔢𝔰

I

LUKE THE PHYSICIAN

THE AUTHOR OF THE THIRD GOSPEL
AND THE ACTS OF THE APOSTLES

BY

ADOLF HARNACK

PROFESSOR OF CHURCH HISTORY IN THE
UNIVERSITY OF BERLIN

TRANSLATED BY

THE REV. J. R. WILKINSON, M.A.

LATE SCHOLAR OF WORCESTER COLLEGE,
OXFORD, AND RECTOR OF WINFORD

EDITED BY

THE REV. W. D. MORRISON, LL.D.

WILLIAMS & NORGATE

14 HENRIETTA STREET, COVENT GARDEN, LONDON

NEW YORK: G. P. PUTNAM'S SONS

1907

AUG 26 1907
Divinity School.

BS
2275
. 4 .713
v. 1

Printed by BALLANTYNE & Co. LIMITED
Tavistock Street, London

AUTHOR'S PREFACE

It was my original intention that the following treatise should be included in the third part of my " History of Early Christian Literature." However, it grew under my hands to such an extent that I now publish it in a separate volume. It must form the first of a few other treatises on the subject of Introduction to the New Testament which will appear shortly, for some of the cardinal problems of this branch of Biblical study are still far from being set in so clear a light as to permit of their being dismissed in a short essay.

The genuine epistles of St. Paul, the writings of St. Luke, and the history of Eusebius are the pillars of primitive Christian history. This fact has not yet been sufficiently recognised in the case of the Lukan writings; partly because critics are convinced that these writings are not to be assigned to St. Luke. And yet, even if they were right in their supposition, the importance of the Acts of the Apostles at least still remains fundamental. However, I hope to have shown in the following pages that critics have gone astray in this question, and that the traditional view holds good. The Lukan writings thus recover their own excelling value as historical authorities; for they are written by a Greek who was a fellow worker of St. Paul, and companied with Mark, Silas, Philip, and James the brother of the Lord.

Ten years ago, in the preface to the first volume of the second part of my " History of Christian Literature," I stated that the criticism of the sources of primitive Christianity was gradually returning to the traditional standpoints.   My friends have taken offence at this statement of mine, although I ˉhad already in part established its truth.   I now offer them a new proof, and I beg for their impartial criticism.   With my opponents, on the other hand, my statement has fared much more sadly.   I saw myself suddenly brought forward as a witness to testify that in historical criticism we are returning to the conservative point of view.   I am not responsible for this misapprehension of my position; indeed, in that very preface I took care to guard myself against it—as it seems, to no purpose.   Let me, therefore, now express my absolute conviction that historical criticism teaches us ever more clearly that many traditional positions are untenable and must give place to new and startling discoveries.   We do, of course, recover something of the old ground, in that we can now more accurately circumscribe the home and the time of the formation of the most primitive and fundamental Christian tradition.   We can now assert that *during the years 30–70* A.D., *and on the soil of Palestine —more particularly in Jerusalem—this tradition as a whole took the essential form* which it presents in its later development, and that the only other factor which has played an important part in this formation is the influence of Phrygia and Asia, with their populations so strongly intermixed with Jewish elements. This result of research is becoming clearer day by day, and is steadily replacing the earlier "critical" hypothesis which assumes that the fundamental development of Christian tradition extended over a period of some one hundred years, and that in its formation the whole Diaspora played a part as important as that of the Holy Land and its primitive churches.

In regard to the chronological framework, the majority of the leading personages who are named, and the scene of action, the report of ancient tradition stands firm; but when we proceed further—i.e., when we attempt to realise historical situations—we are thrown back upon our own groping judgment, and are often unable to accept the conceptions and explanations of the primitive annalists. Indeed, the problems which present themselves are rendered the more difficult by the shortening of the period of fundamental development and by the weight which must be assigned to the testimony of persons who still belong to the first generation. If, for instance, St. Luke and not some other unknown compiler is the author of the third gospel and the Acts, we are then left with a psychological and historical problem of extraordinary difficulty—scarcely less difficult, indeed, than that which the author of the fourth gospel presents when he includes in his narrative both the Miracle at Cana and the Final Discourses.

The method which I have followed in this book is little in accord with the impressionalism that is the ruling fashion in the Biblical criticism of to-day. I am also far from wishing to commend it in every case; but the problem before us—whether the author of the so-called "we" sections is identical with the author of the whole work—can be really mastered by a method which comprises close and detailed examination and discussion of vocabulary and style. It is possible to carry this examination further than I have done—for instance, one might investigate the use of λέγειν and λαλεῖν or of σύν and μετά in the "we" sections and in the whole work—with always the same result, namely, that the author of both is one and the same person.

A. H.

Berlin, *May* 17, 1906.

PREFACE TO THE ENGLISH EDITION

I HAVE looked through this book with a view to its translation into English. I have corrected it in a few places, and have amplified the last Appendix (St. Luke and St. John). Otherwise the book remains unaltered. I gladly seize the opportunity of expressing my thanks to the English scholars Hawkins, Hobart, and Plummer for all that I have learnt from their works.

A. H.

BERLIN, *January* 10, 1907.

CONTENTS

APPENDICES

§₀

CHAPTER I

GENERAL INVESTIGATION

THE great historical work, which has come down to us in two parts, the third gospel and the Acts of the Apostles, is anonymous, but the unanimous report of ecclesiastical tradition, which ascribes it to an author Luke by name, can be traced back to the middle of the second century. In fact, there is no justifiable reason for doubting that Justin already regarded the third gospel as the work of St. Luke ("Dial." 103). Indeed, a further step backwards is permissible; for those who first formed the collection of four gospels—and this was done before the middle of the second century, perhaps long before—gave this gospel the inscription *KATA ΛOTKAN*. It is therefore probable that Marcion, who assailed the other gospels while he accepted and edited the third gospel, was already acquainted with the name Luke as the name of its author. This, however, does not admit of stringent proof,[1] and one must therefore

---

[1] In proof of Marcion's knowledge of the name of Luke we may bring forward the fact that Marcion in his text of Col. iv. 14 has erased the words ὁ ἰατρὸς ὁ ἀγαπητός, and thus seems to have had some interest in St. Luke (he could not have been a physician, for

rest satisfied with the knowledge that the Lukan authorship has been universally accepted since the years
140–150 A.D.

Of necessity the gospel which begins with a prologue
must have contained in its title the name of its author.
If St. Luke was not the author, then the real author's
name must have been purposely suppressed either when
the book was combined with the three other gospels or
at some previous time. Such a suppression or substitution of names is, of course, quite possible, yet the
hypothesis of its occurrence is by no means simple.
Anonymous compilations in the course of tradition
easily acquire some determining name, and it is easy to
imagine an author writing under a pseudonym; but in
the case of a writing determined by a prologue and a
dedication we require some very definite reasons for a
substitution of names, especially when this is supposed
to occur only one generation after the date of publication.[1]

That the " Luke " whose name is so closely connected
with the third gospel and the Acts is the Luke mentioned
in the Pauline epistles has never been questioned.

---

care of the body is irreligious); but we may not build much upon
this. If Iren. III. i. depends upon the authority of Papias, the latter
also described the third gospel as Lukan; but the source of Irenæus'
information is uncertain.

[1] The substituted name ought to be that of some recognised
authority. But " Luke" was not this, so far as we know. On this
very account, ever since the end of the second century these historical
writings were carefully brought into such close connection with the
Apostle St. Paul that the name " Luke " lost all importance. The
name, therefore, was not authoritative enough at that time.

According to these epistles (Col. iv. 14; Philem. 24; 2 Tim. iv. 11), he was (1) a Hellene by birth,[1] (2) a physician,[2] (3) a companion of St. Paul, (4) a fellow-worker with St. Paul.[3] This Luke is first mentioned in those epistles of the Apostle which were composed in Rome (or Cæsarea ?), but this does not exclude the conjecture that he came into connection with St. Paul at an earlier period. It is not, however, probable that he was with the Apostle at the time of the composition of the epistles to the Thessalonians, to the Corinthians, and to the Romans; for in this case we should expect some mention of his name. It is therefore improbable that he was personally, or at all events intimately, acquainted with the Christian communities of Thessalonica, Corinth, and Rome (before St. Paul visited that city).[4] According to 2 Tim. iv. 11, he continued to the end in the company of the Apostle, while Demas, Crescens, and Titus had left him.

[1] Compare Col. iv. 10 ff. with iv. 12 ff.

[2] And also the physician of St. Paul ; for this is implied in the words Λουκᾶς ὁ ἰατρὸς ὁ ἀγαπητός. As "the beloved son "="my son," so also the beloved physician=my physician. St. Paul would not have given such emphasis to the special profession of his companion in travel if he himself had not derived benefit therefrom.

[3] This follows from Philemon 24, where Luke—together with Mark Aristarchus, and Demas—is described by the Apostle as "my synergos." He thus shared in the work of the mission. On the other hand, he is never mentioned as a fellow-prisoner of St. Paul like Aristarchus (Col. iv. 10) and Epaphras (Philem. 23) ; he therefore lived in freedom in Rome.

[4] No conclusions may be drawn from Galatians and Philippians, because St. Paul in these epistles makes no mention of individuals who send greeting.

The report of tradition concerning St. Luke, apart
from these references to him in the writings of St.
Paul, is probably not altogether untrustworthy, though
it will not here claim our attention. One statement,
however, deserves to be regarded as specially reliable.[1]
Both Eusebius[2] and the ancient " Argumentum evangelii
secundum Lucan" agree in describing him as a native
of Antioch. The style of the language used by both
authorities is the same (Λουκᾶς τὸ μὲν γένος ὢν τῶν ἀπ᾿
Ἀντιοχείας, τὴν ἐπιστήμην δὲ ἰατρός, τὰ πλεῖστα
συνγεγονὼς τῷ Παύλῳ, καὶ τοῖς λοιποῖς δὲ οὐ παρέργως
τῶν ἀποστόλων ὡμιληκώς—" Lucas Syrus natione An-
tiochensis, arte medicus discipulus apostolorum, postea
Paulum secutus "); but Eusebius is scarcely dependent
upon the "Argumentum," since he defines the relations of
St. Luke with the original Apostles more accurately
than the latter. Rather we are here compelled to
assume a common source, which must therefore be of
very early date.[3] The fact that this record tells us

1 The "Argumentum evangelii secundum Lucan," which belongs at
the latest to the beginning of the third century (Corssen., " Monarch-
ianische Prologe. Texte u. Unters." Bd. 15, I. s. 7 ff.), asserts that he
remained unmarried, that he died seventy-four years old in Bithynia,
and that he composed his gospel in Achaia. This is probably correct.
Tne statement that St. Luke was one of the seventy disciples of our
Lord is quite untrustworthy.

2 " Hist. Ecc." iii. 4, 6.

3 See also Julius Africanus (" Mai. Nova. Patr. Bibl." IV. 1, p. 270):
ὁ δὲ Λουκᾶς τὸ μὲν γένος ἀπὸ τῆς βοωμένης Ἀντιοχείας ἦν. It is not
quite certain that these words—together with the following account
that St. Luke was better acquainted with Greek science than with
Hebrew—go back to Africanus. We may have here only the words
of Eusebius.

nothing of the place of composition, but simply fixes St. Luke's native city, speaks in favour of its reliability; for in ancient times we find that a famous man's place of origin is generally noted, while records of the places where he composed his writings are much more rare. Nor can we assign any weight to a late tradition found in the pseudo-Clementine "Recognitions" (x. 71), that the Theophilus to whom St. Luke addressed his work was the principal citizen of Antioch; for this report could have been easily manufactured from a combination of the prologue of the third gospel with the tradition that St. Luke was a native of Antioch. The latter tradition, however, could scarcely have arisen from the Acts itself; for though it is evident, as we shall see later, that this book has a special interest in Antioch, this interest is nevertheless not so directly expressed as to lead at once to the conclusion that the author was a native of Antioch.[1] And since the tradition seems to have no ulterior motive it may well pass for trustworthy.

Can it be possible that Luke the Greek physician of Antioch, the companion and fellow-worker of St. Paul, composed the third gospel and the Acts of the Apostles? "If the gospel were the only writing ascribed to his authorship," writes a recent critic,[2] we should probably raise no objection against this record

---

[1] It is, however, possible that the noteworthy gloss in Acts xi. 28 (συνεστραμμένων ἡμῶν) already presupposes the tradition that St. Luke was an Antiochean. The supposition is not, however, necessary.

[2] J. Weiss, "Die Schriften des N. T.'s, das Lukas-Evang.," 1906, s. 378.

of ancient tradition ; for we have no sufficient reasons
for asserting that a disciple of St. Paul could not have
composed this work." The difficulty, therefore, is
assumed to lie in the Acts of the Apostles. This book
must be subjected to a separate and stringent examination—so the critics demand ; but this examination, so
they say, is already completed, and has led to the certain
conclusion that tradition here is in the wrong—the
Acts cannot have been composed by a companion and
fellow-worker of St. Paul. This is the judgment of
Hilgenfeld, Holtzmann, Overbeck, Hansrath, Weizsäcker, Wendt, Schürer, Pfleiderer, von Soden, Spitta,
Jülicher, J. Weiss, Knopf, Clemen, and others, following
the lead of Königsmann, De Wette, Baur, and Zeller.
In spite of the opposition of Credner,[1] B. Weiss,
Klostermann, Zahn, Renan, Hobart, Ramsay, Hawkins,
Plummer, Vogel, Blass, and others, the indefensibility
of the tradition is regarded as being so clearly estab-
lished· that nowadays it is thought scarcely worth
while to reprove this indefensibility, or even to notice
the arguments of conservative opponents.[2] Indeed,

[1] Credner, "Einleit. in d. N. T." i. s. 153 f. : " There is no sufficient
reason for throwing doubt, with De Wette, upon the unanimous
tradition of the Church which makes Luke the author of our gospel ;
at least the way that faults in the Church are reproved by this
author does not justify such doubts. He was at all events of the
Pauline school, and for several years a companion of St. Paul—the
supposition that the ' we ' sections belong to a diary from another
hand, which he has incorporated in his work, is disproved by the
homogeneity of vocabulary and style throughout the book ; this of
itself is enough to prove the indefensibility of those doubts, which
are not at all removed by a change of names."

[2] I have indicated my attitude towards this problem in the year

it seems that there exists a disposition to ignore
the fact that such arguments still exist. Jülicher
(Introduction, 447 ff.) feels compelled to regard the
ascription of the book to St. Luke as a "romantic
ideal."[1] So quickly does criticism forget its true
function, with such bigoted obstinacy does it cling to
its hypotheses.[2]

And yet we find that even critics, in spite of their
verdict, have actually made, and are still making,

1892 ("Texte u. Unters." Bd. 8, H. 4, s. 37 ff.). Since that date my
continued studies have rendered it possible for me to speak more
positively.

[1] On the contrary, Plummer ("Commentary on St. Luke," p. xii.)
writes : "It is perhaps no exaggeration to say that nothing in
Biblical criticism is more certain than the statement that the author
of the Acts was a companion of St. Paul." This, of course, is saying
too much, but the exaggeration is nearer the truth than Jülicher's
opinion.

[2] Even criticism has for generations its freaks and fancies. Very
often one notices that, when some comprehensive critical theory has
been in fashion for a long time and then has been refuted, particular
fragments thereof still cling obstinately to men's minds although
they have no intellectual basis. The critical school of Baur, in
order to prove that the name Luke in connection with these writings
was a forgery, used only one argument—i.e., the work is not Pauline
but conciliatory in its tendency, hence it belongs to a late period in
the second century. Baur's method is now demolished ; and yet some
planks of his critical structure still float upon the surface of the
devastating flood. Seeing how one critic trustfully rests upon the
authority of another, we may congratulate ourselves that some
accident has prevented Scholten's hypothesis—that the third gospel
and the Acts have different authors—from finding its way into the
great stream of criticism and so becoming a dogma in these days.
This might very easily have happened, for a difference in the authorship of the third gospel and the Acts can be alleged with much more
plausible reasons than a difference in the authorship of the Acts as a
whole and the "we" sections.

considerable strides towards a compromise with tradition. Certain passages are found in the Acts where the
author introduces himself into the narrative with the
word "we." The more than rash hypothesis that this
"we" is a literary forgery has been renounced long
ago,[1] and nowadays scarcely a voice is raised even
against the hypothesis that this "we" proceeds from
the pen of St. Luke, the companion of St. Paul.[2]

We hear no more of those theories that would assign
the authorship of these sections to Timothy or Titus
or Silas, or some other companion of St. Paul. Indeed,
the compromise goes still further : passages of considerable length in those chapters of the second part
of the Acts in which the "we" does not occur must
now be regarded as proceeding from St. Luke. The
critics are not, of course, agreed on this point, but it is
quite clear that there is a growing tendency to assign
the greater part of chapters xvi.–xxviii. (and even of
chapters xi.–xv.) to the Lukan source.[3] But—say the

---

[1] So Schrader, B. Bauer, Havet; so also the assumption, com-
mended by Overbeck, that the "we" is, as a rule, authentic, but has
been forged in some places by the author of the complete work.
Neither has Zeller's theory—that the author allowed the "we" to
stand in order that he might pass for a companion of the Apostle—so
far as I know, found any champions in these days.

[2] Jülicher speaks on this point with hesitation (Introd. 447 ff.) ;
according to him the hypothesis that St. Luke is the author of the
"we" sections can only be regarded as probable ; so also Weizsäcker.
Holtzmann, for example ("Einleit.," 1892, s. 395), has given a distinct
vote for St. Luke.

[3] It is certain that the "we" record, if it was a source of the Acts,
does not coincide only with the sum of those verses in which the
"we" occurs ; it must have been more extensive.

critics—this must not be regarded as anything more than a source of the whole work.[1] Some anonymous writer, the author of the gospel, has used this excellent and most valuable source for the second part of his historical work, transforming it somewhat to suit his own purposes. If it be at once objected that it is improbable that so practised a writer should not have removed the " we " which he found in his source, it is answered that it is no less strange that an author should introduce himself abruptly, in the midst of his narrative, with an indefinite " we," and should then fall back again into narrative in the third person, only to appear afresh just as abruptly in the first person. The paradox in either case is not, of course, equally great, and it is mere perversity to describe the two hypotheses as equally difficult. The author who wrote in the first instance for the " excellent " Theophilus was not unknown to his correspondent. If he, then, in the midst of his text introduced himself with a " we," *after he had begun his book with an " I "* (chap. i. 1), Theophilus would at once know where he was; it would scarcely be fresh news to him that the man who dedicated his book to him was once himself a companion of St. Paul. Under these circumstances the literary fault of neglecting to make special mention of

---

1 It does not seem to have been realised how precarious the whole hypothesis becomes if we (*e.g.*, with Pfleiderer and von Soden) assign almost all in chapters xi., xiii., xiv., xvi.–xxviii. to this source. There then remains for the anonymous writer to Theophilus, the author of the gospel, only the substructure of the Acts, the history of the mission in Jerusalem and Palestine.

this fact at the right place [1] would be quite pardon-
able; indeed, one might say that this modest expedient
for introducing oneself into the course of one's narrative
is entirely in harmony with the general objectivity of
our author's style throughout his history. If, on the
other hand, the author was not a companion of St. Paul
and yet allowed this " we " to appear so abruptly in his
narrative, the negligence is so great that it is difficult
to avoid the suspicion that the author was influenced
by some motive that was not altogether honourable
(so Zeller). Such motives, of course, may possibly have
existed, so that we may not at present accept the
hypothesis of very insignificant negligence in preference to one of much greater negligence—it is, indeed
often the improbable that really happens—but we are
nevertheless bound to lay our finger upon a difficulty
which it is usual to pass over far too cursorily.[2]

---

[1] We must notice besides that the author of the Acts is upon other
occasions careless in introducing persons. In xvii. 5 he speaks of a
certain Jason as if he were already known. The introduction of
Sosthenes in xviii. 17 is awkward, and still more awkward that of
two exorcists out of the number of the seven sons of Sceva in xix. 16.
It is not at once clear why Gaius and Aristarchus are mentioned at
all in xix. 29; Weiss and others ingeniously conjecture that they
formed the author's authority for his narrative. Also in xix. 23
Alexander is very feebly brought upon the scene of action. Instances in which other writers use " we " abruptly in the course of
their narrative because they are copying the writing of an eye-
witness have been sought for in the whole literature of the world.
Some few have been discovered, and these not exactly analogous to
the instance in point.

[2] Renan presents the correct view ("Die Apostel," German
edition, s. 10): "One might perhaps understand such negligence
[allowing the " we " to stand] in some clumsy compilation; but the

There are accordingly two literary difficulties in which "criticism" is involved, and which are not so easily disposed of—first, that the author of this book, who otherwise shows himself a skilful writer, carried over into long passages of his narrative an uncorrected "we" from one of his sources, and thus, *volens aut nolens*, has given the impression that he was an eye-witness; next, that in the course of a few decades his name was forgotten by tradition and was replaced by the name of the author of the source, although the real author had never in his book mentioned this name, and although, so far as we know, this name was not one that carried any special authority. Two literary paradoxes at once—this is rather too much !

Where, then, lie the difficulties which absolutely forbid us to follow tradition and to accept St. Luke as the author of the Acts ? According to the critical view they are twofold. The critics hold it for impossible that a companion of the Apostle St. Paul should have said and should have refrained from saying about him what is now found and not found in the Acts, and they hold it for just as incredible that a man who lived in the apostolic age could have given the account which this author gives of the Apostles and the early history of the Church at Jerusalem. They point, moreover, to several instances of unevenness and want of clearness in the author's presentation of his facts, and, besides, to

third gospel and the Acts form a work which is very well composed. . . . We could not understand an editor committing so glaring an error . . . the author is the same person as he who has used the 'we' in several places."

many historical blunders. The question is thus one which belongs to the sphere of the higher historical criticism. In the face of these objections we must first investigate whether the "lower" criticism does not make the identity of the authorship of the Acts and the "we" source so evident that the "higher" criticism must hold its peace, and next we must find out whether the difficulties which higher criticism professes to find do not vanish with a franker and wider appreciation of the actual circumstances.   I must refrain from entering closely into the truly pitiful history of the criticism of the Acts; but in the following investigation I hope that I shall not be found to have overlooked anything of importance.

If we test what we know of St. Luke (*vide* p. 3) by the historical work which bears his name, we obtain the following results: (1) St. Luke is never mentioned in the Acts, which is just what we should expect if he himself was the author of the book. On the other hand, Aristarchus is mentioned three times—the man who is named with St. Luke in the epistles of St. Paul ! What reason, then, can we give for the omission of St. Luke's name in the Acts?[1]   (2) St. Luke was a Greek

[1] The mention of Aristarchus in the Acts may be at once employed as a not inconsiderable argument for its Lukan origin. In the Pauline epistles he appears twice (only in greetings), and *that in company with St. Luke.* The Acts makes no mention of so important a companion of St. Paul as Titus, and yet it mentions Aristarchus, and that twice ! The latter of these references shows that St. Paul on his last voyage had, besides Aristarchus, only one companion, namely, the author of the Acts (or of the "we" account, which hypothesis must be for the moment left open). Who, then, was this

by birth.—The gospel and the Acts show—there is, indeed, no need of a proof—that they were composed not by a Jew by birth, but by a Greek.[1] (3) St. Luke was a physician, and thus belonged to the middle or higher plane of contemporary culture.—To this plane we are directed not only by the prologue of the gospel, but by the literary standard attained in the whole work. The man who could compose speeches like those of St. Paul in the Acts—to mention only the most important point—who also possessed gifts of style and narrative like those of this writer, who knew so well how much to say and could so well arrange his material in accordance with the purpose of his work, this man possessed the higher culture in rich measure. But there is a still more striking coincidence : it is as good as certain from the subject-matter, and more especially from the style, of this great work that its author was a physician by profession. Of course, in making such a statement one still exposes oneself to the scorn of the critics,[2] and

author? Scarcely Demas, though he too is not mentioned in the Acts, of whom it is, however, said in 2 Tim. iv. 10 that "he loved this present world."

[1] Whether the author was a Jewish proselyte before he became a Christian cannot be definitely decided. No conclusion can be drawn from his mention of proselytes in the Acts. His masterly knowledge of the Greek Bible can well have been gained when he had become a Christian. οἱ βάρβαροι in xxviii. 2, 4 is in itself sufficient evidence of his Greek origin.

[2] Jülicher, Introd., s. 407 f.: "The discovery that the Acts, and here and there also the gospel, but more particularly the "we" sections, are so full of medical technical terms as to afford strong reasons for suspecting the authorship of St. Luke the physician, will have little weight with those who perceive the elementary nature of these terms.

yet the arguments which are alleged in its support are simply convincing. These would have had much more influence if the man who devoted his life to the task of proving from the work itself the medical profession of its author had not gone too far with his evidence and had not brought forward much that has neither force nor value. Accordingly his book [1] has had quite the opposite effect to that he intended, especially with those who have read it cursorily. Those, however, who have studied it carefully will, I think, find it impossible to escape the conclusion [2] that the question here is not one of merely accidental linguistic colouring, but that this great historical work was composed by a writer who either was a physician or was quite intimately acquainted with medical language and science. And, indeed, this conclusion holds good not only for the " we " sections, but for the whole work. While I refer the reader to my special treatment of this question in Appendix I., may I here specially mention the following points which have escaped the notice even of Hobart?

Must we because of 1 Thess. v. 3 infer that St. Paul was a gynæcologist?"

[1] Hobart, "The Medical Language of St. Luke. A Proof from Internal Evidence that ' the Gospel according to St. Luke' and 'the Acts of the Apostles' were written by the same Person, and that the Writer was a Medical Man" (Dublin, 1882, 305 pp.). Compare also Campbell, "Crit. Studies in St. Luke's Gospel, its Demonology and Ebionitism" (Edinburgh, 1891).

[2] So Zahn and Hawkins. I subscribe to the words of Zahn ("Einleit." ii. s. 427): "Hobart has proved for every one who can at all appreciate proof that the author of the Lukan work was a man practised in the scientific language of Greek medicine—in short, a *Greek physician.*"

In the " we " sections, as is well known, the author distinguishes very carefully between the " we " and St. Paul. Wherever he possibly can do so he modestly allows the " we " to fall into the background and gives St. Paul the honour, and thus the " we " here and there partakes of a somewhat shadowy character, and we are often left in doubt how far the narrator was an eyewitness. In chap. xxviii. 8–10 he, however, writes as follows : ἐγένετο τὸν πατέρα τοῦ Ποπλίου πυρετοῖς καὶ δυσεντερίῳ συνεχόμενον κατακεῖσθαι, πρὸς ὃν ὁ Παῦλος εἰσελθὼν καὶ προσευξάμενος, ἐπιθεὶς τὰς χεῖρας αὐτῷ ἰάσατο αὐτόν. τούτου δὲ γενομένου καὶ οἱ λοιποὶ οἱ ἐν τῇ νήσῳ ἔχοντες ἀσθενείας προσήρχοντο καὶ ἐθεραπεύοντο, οἳ καὶ πολλαῖς τιμαῖς ἐτίμησαν ἡμᾶς. In this narrative, which is also noteworthy for the precise medical definition πυρετοῖς καὶ δυσεντερίῳ, [1] we are struck by the concluding words : " *we* were honoured with many honours." It follows that the numerous sick folk (we

[1] The plural πυρετοί (here only in the N. T.) in combination with dysentery describes the illness with an accuracy which we can scarcely imagine in a layman. Besides, Hobart shows that συνέχεσθαι also is used in the technical sense (pp. 3 f). In illustration of the plural πυρετοί Hobart has collected instances from Hippocrates, Aretæus, and Galen. With πυρετοῖς καὶ δυσεντερίῳ he compares : Hippocr. " Judicat." 55 : ὅσοις ἂν ἐν τοῖς πυρετοῖς τὰ ᾦτα κωφωθῇ τουτέοισι μὴ λυθέντος τοῦ πυρετοῦ μανῆναι ἀνάγκη, λύει δ' ἐκ τῶν ῥινῶν αἷμα ῥυὲν ἢ δυσεντερίη ἐπιγενομένη. L.c. 56 : λύει δὲ καὶ πυρετὸς ἢ δυσεντερίη. Hippocr. " Prædic." 104 : αἱ δυσεντερίαι ξὺν πυρετῷ μὲν ἢν ἐπίωσιν. Hippocr. " Aer." 283 : τοῦ γὰρ θέρεος δυσεντερίαι τε πολλαὶ ἐμπίπτουσιν καὶ . . . πυρετοί. Hippocr. " Epid." 1056 : λύει δὲ καὶ πυρετὸς καὶ δυσεντερίη ἄνευ ὀδύνης. L.c. 1207 : ὁ Ἐριστολάου δυσεντερικὸς ἐγένετο καὶ πυρετὸς εἶχε. L.c. 1247 : ἀνάγκῃ τοῦ θέρεος πυρετοὺς ὀξεῖς καὶ ὀφθαλμίας καὶ δυσεντερίας γίνεσθαι.

hear nothing of any who were " possessed ") were healed
not only by St. Paul, but also by his companion, the
writer of the narrative. If St. Paul had been the sole
agent upon this occasion, the author would not have
written simply ἐθεραπεύοντο, but would have added ὑπὸ
Παύλου. This undefined ἐθεραπεύοντο prepares, as it
were, the way for the ἡμᾶς which follows. Now of
course it can be objected that the author need not
therefore have been a regular physician; he could, like
St. Paul, have healed by means of prayer. We cannot
with certainty refute this objection, but taken in connection with the exact description of the illness it has
not much force. Faith-healers are seldom wont to
trouble themselves about the real nature of an illness.
The author was certainly no professional philosopher,
nor a rhetorician or advocate [1]—with all these profes-
sions his acquaintance is only that of a man of culture.
In matters of navigation he only shows the lively
interest of the average Greek. If, then, we would classify
the man, who certainly belonged to some liberal profession, all indications seem to point to his having been a
physician. Moreover, I would here draw attention to
another point. Just as the author at the end of his

---

[1] Philosophical reflections or demonstrations, dialectical proofs,
&c., are not his business. In respect to the latter, St. Luke shows a
self-restraint which is strange in an educated Greek. Of interest in and
knowledge of literature there are only faint traces ; these things, at
all events, formed no essential element in the mental life of the
author. In legal matters alone his interest seems strongly marked ;
these, however, both in the gospel and the Acts, are closely bound
up with the general aim of the work, nor does St. Luke even here
betray special technical knowledge.

great historical work clearly and yet unconsciously declares himself a physician, so also in a passage towards the beginning he employs a medical metaphor—at the commencement of his description of the preaching of Jesus (I omit for the moment the consideration of the prologue). He is here the only evangelist who puts into the mouth of our Lord the words (chap. iv. 23), πάντως ἐρεῖτέ μοι τὴν παραβολὴν ταύτην· ἰατρέ, θεράπευσον σεαυτόν. The incident is in itself striking ; but it is still more striking when one perceives that the words do not fit into the context, but are, as it were, forced into it (cf. Vogel, "Charakteristik des Lukas," 1899, s. 28 : "The manner in which the proverb is introduced can scarcely be regarded as happy "). We may well believe that our author was better acquainted with the proverb than was our Lord, and that he could scarcely have received it from tradition, at least in its present form and context. It is, in fact, an anticipation of St. Mark xv. 31 : ἄλλους ἔσωσεν, ἑαυτὸν οὐ δύναται σῶσαι (see also St. Luke xxiii. 35, St. Matthew xxvii. 42), and is especially characteristic of the disposition of the unbelieving Jewish people towards Jesus at the end of His ministry, though it is quite out of place at the beginning. The thought finds an evident parallel in Galen ("Comm." iv. 9 ; "Epid." vi. [xvii. B. 151]): ἐχρῆν τὸν ἰατρὸν ἑαυτοῦ πρῶτον ἰᾶσθαι τὸ σύμπτωμα καὶ οὕτως ἐπιχειρεῖν ἑτέρους θεραπεύειν.

(4) St. Luke was a companion of St. Paul.—In the Acts, from chapter xvi. to the end of the work, the author throughout long stretches of his narrative concerning St. Paul writes as an eye-witness (using a " we "). The

objection, which has been already mentioned, that he is here using foreign material and has either carelessly or of set purpose allowed the "we" to stand, will be investigated in the next chapter. The most natural conclusion is that behind this "we" stands the author of the whole work. There is yet another circumstance which supports such a conclusion. We notice that the author of this work begins by laying for himself a broad foundation and seems to set himself the task of describing the victorious progress of the Gospel from Jerusalem to Rome through the operation of the mighty power of God indwelling in the Apostles, and that yet in the last quarter of his book he loses himself in the history of St. Paul, and herein seems utterly to forget his aim in his detailed description of the final voyage. Who, if not one who was a companion of St. Paul, can be regarded as responsible for what we must describe as a glaring fault in the composition of a work of this kind? Even in a companion of the Apostle such a fault is sufficiently astounding, but in a later writer of high literary gifts, personally unacquainted with St. Paul, it is absolutely unintelligible. And, further, it has been already noticed (p. 8) that St. Luke was probably not with St. Paul when the epistles to the Thessalonians, to the Corinthians, and to the Romans were written, and that he was not personally, or at all events not intimately, acquainted with the Churches of Thessalonica and Corinth. Turning to the Acts, we find no "we" either in the passages which deal with Thessalonica or in those dealing with Corinth. On the other hand, we have evidence to show that St. Luke was in Rome with St. Paul, and accordingly in this city we fall in with the author of the Acts (or of the "we" sections) in the company of the Apostle, with whom he had made the voyage thither. Finally, wherever St. Luke is mentioned in the Pauline epistles St. Mark is mentioned with him. We should therefore expect that the author of the third gospel and the Acts would show himself intimately acquainted with St. Mark. Now we find that he has incorporated practically the whole gospel of St. Mark into his own gospel, and is so far acquainted with that evangelist that he is actually able to tell us the name of his mother's maid-servant !

(5) St. Luke was not only a companion but also a fellow-worker with St. Paul.—The author of the Acts writes (chapter xvi. 10) : ὅτι προσκέκληται ἡμᾶς ὁ θεὸς εὐαγγελίσασθαι αὐτούς, and (chapter xvi. 13) : καθίσαντες ἐλαλοῦμεν ταῖς συνελθούσαις γυναιξίν. He also, with St. Paul, was therefore a missionary preacher.[1]

---

[1] This fact becomes still more clear from the consideration of the great discourses scattered throughout the Acts. Such discourses (especially those of chapters. xiii. and xvii.) can only have been composed by a missionary practised in the work of evangelisation. To learn that this missionary was a disciple of St. Paul it suffices to read but one passage (chapter xiii. 38 f.) : γνωστὸν ἔστω ὑμῖν, ὅτι διὰ Ἰησοῦ Χριστοῦ ὑμῖν ἄφεσις ἁμαρτιῶν καταγγέλλεται [καὶ] ἀπὸ πάντων ὧν οὐκ ἠδυνήθητε ἐν νόμῳ Μωϋσέως δικαιωθῆναι ἐν τούτῳ πᾶς ὁ πιστεύων δικαιοῦται (cf. also the discourse at Miletus, xx. 28 : ... τὴν ἐκκλησίαν τοῦ Θεοῦ ἣν περιποιήσατο διὰ τοῦ αἵματος τοῦ ἰδίου). Whether St. Paul's doctrine is here correctly reproduced or whether theologumena are to be found in the book which differ from those of the Pauline theology is a matter of indifference—he who wrote this passage was a near disciple of St. Paul. The relative Paulinism of the author of the Acts—and this is all we need establish—can be proved from his

(6) St. Luke was most probably a native of Antioch.—
In the Acts the author never describes himself as an

vocabulary (*cf.* Hawkins, "Horæ Synopticæ," 1899, pp. 154 ff.). It
will suffice for our purpose to neglect the much more numerous
coincidences in vocabulary between the ten Pauline epistles and the
Acts, and to draw our instances from the gospel alone :

St. Matt. and St. Paul have twenty-nine words in common which
are not to be found elsewhere in the gospels, St. Mark and St. Paul
have twenty such words in common, St. John and St. Paul seventeen
words ; St. Luke (gospel) and St. Paul, however, have eighty-four
such words in common which are not to be found elsewhere in the
gospels.

St. Paul and St. Matt. : ἀκαθαρσία, ἀκέραιος, ἀκρασία, ἅμα, ἀμέριμνος,
ἀναπληροῦν, ἀπάντησις, ἀπέναντι, δειγματίζειν, δῆλος, ἐκτός, ἐλαφρός,
ἐξαιρεῖν, ἐπίσημος, κεραμεύς, μύριοι, μωρός, νῖκος, ὁδηγός, ὀδυρμός, ὀκνηρός,
ὅλως, ὀφειλή, ὀφείλημα, παρεκτός, πλατύνειν, τάφος, ψευδομάρτυς, ὡραῖος
(thus only four verbs).

St. Paul and St. Mark : ἀββά, ἀλαλάζειν, ἁμάρτημα, ἀποστερεῖν, ἀφρο-
σύνη, ἀχειροποίητος, εἰρηνεύειν, ἐξαυτῆς, ἐξορύσσειν, εὐκαιρεῖν, εὐσχήμων,
ἡδέως, περιφέρειν, προλαμβάνειν, προσκαρτερεῖν, πώρωσις, συναποθνήσκειν,
τρόμος, ὑποδεῖσθαι, ὑστήρησις (thus ten verbs).

St. Paul and St. John : ἀνατρέφειν, ἀνέρχεσθαι, διδακτός, ἐλευθεροῦν,
Ἑλλην, Ἰσραηλείτης, μαίνεσθαι, ὁδοιπορία, ὅμως, ὅπλον, ὀσμή, παραμυθεῖ-
σθαι, περιτομή, πηλός, πόσις, συνήθεια, ψῦχος (thus five verbs).

St. Paul and St. Luke (gospel) : ἄδηλος, αἰφνίδιος, αἰχμαλωτίζειν,
ἀναζῆν, ἀνακρίνειν, ἀναλύειν, ἀναπέμπειν, ἀνόητος, ἀνταπόδομα, ἀνταπο-
κρίνεσθαι, ἀντίκεισθαι, ἀντιλαμβάνεσθαι, ἀπειθής, ἀποκρύπτειν, ἀπολογεῖσθαι, ἄρα, ἀροτριᾶν, ἀσφάλεια, ἀτενίζειν, ἄτοπος, βιωτικός,[1] δεκτός,
διαγγέλλειν, διαιρεῖν, διερμηνεύειν, δόγμα, ἐγγράφεσθαι, ἔνδοξος, ἐνκακεῖν,
ἐξαποστέλλειν, ἐξουσιάζειν, ἐπαινεῖν, ἐπαναπαύεσθαι, ἐπέχειν, ἐργασία,
εὐγενής, ἐφιστάναι, ἡσυχάζειν, κατάγειν, καταξιοῦσθαι, κατευθύνειν,
κατηχεῖν, κινδυνεύειν, κραταιοῦσθαι, κυριεύειν, μέθη, μεθιστάναι, μεθύ-
σκεσθαι, μερίς, μεταδιδόναι, μήτρα, οἰκονομία, ὀπτασία, ὁσιότης, ὀψώνιον,
παγίς, πανοπλία, πανουργία, πληροφορεῖν, πρεσβύτης, προκόπτειν, σιγᾶν,
σκοπεῖν, σπουδαίως, στεῖρος, συναντιλαμβάνεσθαι, συνεσθίειν, συνευδοκεῖν,
συνκαθίζειν, συνελεῖν, συνοχή, συνχαίρειν, σωτήριον, ὑποστρέφειν, ὑπω-
πιάζειν, ὑστέρημα, φόρος, φρόνησις, χαρίζεσθαι, χαριτοῦν, ψαλμός. Among
these there are no less than forty-nine verbs which are found
only in St. Luke and St. Paul and not in St. Matthew, St. Mark, and

Antiochean (for we need not pay attention to the gloss chap. xi.28—*vide supra*, p. 5, *note* 1, and "Sitzungsber.d. K. Preuss. Akad. d. Wissensch.," April 6, 1899), but the book nevertheless shows a distinct affinity to this city. When reading the first part of the Acts the conscientious historian in some passages breathes freely and feels firm ground under his feet. *Every time that this happens* (chap. xii. excepted) *he finds himself in Antioch or concerned with a narrative which points his attention to that city.* This happens for the first time in the account of the choice of the Seven (chap. vi.). The names of these seven Hellenists are all given, but only in the case of one of them—and that not Stephen, as might be expected—are we told his native place : " Nicholas, a proselyte of Antioch." And, moreover, the whole account distinctly points towards Antioch ; for the choice of the Seven, with all its attendant circumstances, is narrated because of St. Stephen ; the history of Stephen leads on to the persecution, the persecution to the dispersion, the dispersion to the mission, the mission to the planting of Christianity in Antioch, which city forthwith becomes, as it were, a second Jerusalem. This is the whole gist of chap. xi. 19 ff : οἱ μὲν οὖν διασπαρέντες ἀπὸ τῆς θλίψεως τῆς γενομένης ἐπὶ Στεφάνῳ διῆλθον ἕως

St. John. We may, then, speak without hesitation of a lexical affinity between St. Paul and the gospel of St. Luke—even when, as is the case here, we neglect the Acts, in which thirty-three of the eighty-four words are also found, besides many others which this book has in common with St. Paul (Colossians and Ephesians in particular show a close affinity to the vocabulary of the Acts). After St. Luke the next nearest of the evangelists to St. Paul is St. Mark, but there is a wide gap between him and St. Luke.

Φοινίκης καὶ Κύπρου καὶ Ἀντιοχείας, μηδενὶ λαλοῦντες
τὸν λόγον εἰ μὴ μόνον Ἰουδαίοις. ἦσαν δέ τινες ἐξ αὐτῶν
ἄνδρες Κύπριοι καὶ Κυρηναῖοι, οἵτινες ἐλθόντες εἰς
Ἀντιόχειαν ἐλάλουν καὶ πρὸς τοὺς Ἕλληνας, εὐαγγελι-
ζόμενοι τὸν κύριον Ἰησοῦν. καὶ ἦν χεὶρ κυρίου μετ'
αὐτῶν, πολύς τε ἀριθμὸς ὁ πιστεύσας ἐπέστρεψεν ἐπὶ
τὸν κύριον. Certainly this interest in Antioch is
intelligible merely from the actual course of events; [1]
but the record that those who first preached to the
Gentiles in that city were men of Cyprus and Cyrene
presupposes local information. Also the verses which
follow (chap. xi. 22–27) give us many similar details of
information (among others that in Antioch the believers in Jesus were first called Christians). The
continuation of the story in chap. xiii. 1 f. is of a
similar character. Here the five prophets and teachers
of the Antiochean Church are enumerated. By the
phrase κατὰ τὴν οὖσαν ἐκκλησίαν they are definitely
distinguished from the prophets which had come to
Antioch from Jerusalem (chap. xi. 27). The enumera-
tion of all five by name (and especially the distinguish-
ing additions to the names) could have been interesting
only to Antiocheans, or can be explained only from the
interest it had for an Antiochean writer; for Symeon,
surnamed Niger, Lucius of Cyrene, and Manaën, who
had been brought up with Herod the Tetrarch, remained

---

[1] One ought not, however, to forget that the Church of Antioch
plays no part in the epistles of St. Paul—is, indeed, only once mentioned (Gal. ii. 11), though, of course, on a most important occasion.
The emphasis with which this Church is mentioned in the Acts is
not, therefore, to be explained simply from the facts themselves.

obscure people.[1] The great missionary journey of
St. Paul and St. Barnabas (chap. xiii. s.) appears as an
Antiochean undertaking ; in Antioch (xv. 2) the burning
question concerning circumcision is brought to a crisis
by the Church in this city, which sends its representa-
tives to the council at Jerusalem. Compare, moreover,
chap. xiv. 26 (εἰς Ἀντιόχειαν ὅθεν ἦσαν παραδεδομένοι
τῇ χάριτι τοῦ θεοῦ εἰς τὸ ἔργον ὃ ἐπλήρωσαν), chap.
xv. 23 (κατὰ τὴν Ἀντιόχειαν καὶ Συρίαν καὶ Κιλικίαν),
chap. xv. 35 (notice μετὰ ἑτέρων πολλῶν, which has no
parallel in any other part of the book), and the mention of Antioch in chap. xviii. 23.[2]   All these instances
surely permit the conclusion that the testimony of the
Acts is not only not opposed to the tradition that its
author was a native of Antioch, but even admirably
accommodates itself thereto. The book does not, indeed,
suggest that its author was a member of the Church in
Antioch (nor is this asserted by tradition), but that he
took special interest in, and had special knowledge of,
the affairs of that community. Negative grounds in

---

[1] No Cypriote is mentioned by name, though the Antiochean
Church is said to have been founded by men of *Cyprus* and Cyrene.
But in chap. xxi. 16 (a " we " section) Mnason, a Cypriote, with whom
St. Paul and his companion lodged in Jerusalem is described as an
old disciple having intimate relations with the brethren of Cæsarea.
May he not perhaps have been the Cypriote missionary of Antioch ?
This would well explain the interest which St. Luke takes in him.
At all events, according to chap. xiii. 1, the Cypriote missionary of
Antioch had left that community when Barnabas and Saul were sent
thither, while the missionary from Cyrene still remained.

[2] Let it be mentioned, only by the way, that Wellhausen describes
the συμφωνία of St. Luke xv. 25 (here only in the New Testament)
as an Antiochean musical instrument. I do not, of course, know what
grounds he has for this assertion.

support of tradition are also to be found both in the
gospel and the Acts.—The author is certainly not a
native of Palestine, nor does he write for natives of that
district, for he has no clear understanding of the geographical relations of Palestine (see the gospel);
-neither does he write for Macedonians (see Acts xvi. 11).
On the other hand, in addition to Antioch and the
coastland of Phœnicia and Palestine (especially
Cæsarea), he knows Asia well (see Ramsay on this
point). To Jerusalem he came as a stranger; nor
does it appear how long he abode there (chap. xxi.
15, 17).[1]

(7) The time of the composition of this great
historical work has been fixed (" Chronologie," Bd. I. s.
246 ff.) without reference to the question of authorship.
It is limited to the years 78–93 A.D. The book must
have been written before the persecution of Domitian,
before the epistles of St. Paul had been widely
circulated, before the name " Christians " had firmly
established itself in Christian phraseology (see 1 Peter and
the Ignatian epistles), before the canonising of the idea
ἐκκλησία (see below), before the use of the word μάρτυς in
the special sense of " martyr," but some time after the
destruction of Jerusalem.[2] The tradition that the

---

[1] Local information concerning Jerusalem is given in Acts i. 12,
Acts iii. 2, 10. See also St. Luke xxiv. 13. It should not be overlooked that the force of the typical discourse at Nazareth, with
which the author of the gospel begins his presentation of the teaching
of our Lord, culminates in the mention of Naaman the *Syrian*. This
discourse begins with a medical metaphor and closes with a reference
to the Syrian who was preferred to the Chosen People. Can this be
accidental ?

[2] The time of Josephus need not be taken into consideration ; for

author was a companion of St. Paul fits in with this hypothesis. He could thus have been a man of fifty or sixty years of age when he wrote his book.

So far, then, it seems that the result of our investigation is that, according to all the rules of criticism, the tradition of the Lukan authorship is in a great measure accredited. We have by no means confined ourselves to the " we " sections, but have taken into equal consideration practically all parts of the work.

Nevertheless we must still ask ourselves the questions, (1) Whether the " we " sections (with greater or smaller context) cannot be separated as a source from the rest of the Acts ?[1] (2) Whether the subject-matter of the Acts (more especially of chaps. i.-xii., xv.) does not oppose insuperable difficulties to the hypothesis that the book is the work of St. Luke?

the theory that the author of the Acts had read that historian is quite baseless. From St. Luke xxi. 32 it conclusively follows that we must not go beyond the time of Domitian. Wellhausen, of course, asserts that this utterance, simply taken from St. Mark, no longer suits the situation of St. Luke. That, however, is just the question. The arguments adduced above—we may notice also that οἱ ἅγιοι as *term. techn.* for Christians, though used four times by St. Luke, is plainly dying out—make it seem absolutely impossible to push forward the composition of the gospel and the Acts into the second century. Indeed, in the face of these arguments it is to me very improbable that the date was much later than 80 A.D. He who assigns the work to 80 A.D. will about hit the mark.

[1] In this case the considerations which seem to favour St. Luke's authorship of the whole work must be accounted as due to accident —an hypothesis which is, indeed, difficult enough.

CHAPTER II

SPECIAL INVESTIGATION OF THE SO-CALLED "WE" ACCOUNT OF THE ACTS OF THE APOSTLES

It has been often stated and often proved that the "we" sections in vocabulary, in syntax, and in style are most intimately bound up with the whole work, and that this work itself (including the gospel), in spite of all diversity in its parts, is distinguished by a grand unity of literary form.[1] Klostermann[2] has given a splendid demonstration of this unity, dealing more particularly with the "we" sections. B. Weiss, in his concise, instructive commentary (1893), has done the best work in demonstrating the literary unity of the whole work. Vogel also ("Zur Charakteristik des Lukas," 2 Aufl., 1899) has made admirable contributions to the treatment of the subject. Finally Hawkins ("Horæ Synopticæ," 1899), after a yet more careful and minute investigation, has proved the identity of the author of the "we" sections with

---

[1] Strongly emphasised by Zeller, "Die Apostelgeschichte," 1854.

[2] "Vindiciæ Lucanæ," 1866.

the author of the whole work. But all this valuable labour has not attained its purpose because it was not accurate nor detailed enough and because it seemed to prove too much.[1] Seeing that the prologue of the gospel, and still more the relation of this book to the gospel of St. Mark, show clearly that the gospel depends upon written sources, and seeing that it is therefore *a priori* probable that similar sources lie behind the Acts of the Apostles, it is obvious that a general proof that the whole work forms a literary whole is quite irrelevant to the question concerning sources. In every case—*i.e.*, in every considerable passage—it must be found out whether, in spite of traits which betray the pen of the author of the whole work, an earlier source is not employed. Happily we possess the gospel of St. Mark, and therefore in respect to a source of considerable content we are in a position to ascertain the manner in which the author of the whole work has employed it.

Before, however, we enter upon a linguistic investigation of the problem presented by the " we " sections we must by comparison discover the relationship in which the facts related in the " we " sections and the interests of their author stand to those of the author of the whole work.

The narrative of the " we " sections runs somewhat as follows :

---

[1] This is not true of Hawkins. The valuable work of this scholar is not so widely known as it deserves.

I. Sojourn and Work of Evangelisation in Philippi
(xvi. 10–17)

a. A vision in Troas, which causes us to migrate to Europe.

b. A list of halting-places on the journey from Troas to Philippi.

c. We proceed on the Sabbath day to the Jewish place of prayer (this place of prayer is the scene of the activity of the evangelists, of whom the narrator is one—he is not a mere companion).

d. The conversion and baptism of Lydia, the purple seller of Thyatira, a Jewish proselyte, together with all her house.

e. We are constrained by Lydia to lodge with her.

f. The exorcism by St. Paul of the "spirit" of a female ventriloquist, a slave who was exploited as a prophetess by her masters. This "spirit" had recognised the evangelists (Παῦλον καὶ ἡμᾶς), and had described them as messengers of the Most High God which preach the "Way of Salvation."

II. Sojourn and Activity in Troas
(xx. 5 [4]–15)

a. A notice concerning the companions of St. Paul.

b. The journey from Philippi to Troas, with exact dates.

c. An assembly of the Church (object in the first place κλάσαι ἄρτον) in the upper story of a house, which lasts from evening to midnight—indeed, even until dawn. St. Paul is the preacher; the narrator appears as a listener with the rest.[1]

d. A youthful listener, Eutychus, overcome by sleep, falls down from the upper story. He is called back to life by St. Paul, who stretches himself upon him. St. Paul then, as if nothing had happened, proceeds with his discourse.

e. The journey from Troas to Miletus, with exact data.

III. The Journey from Miletus to Jerusalem
(xxi. 1–18)

a. The voyage from Miletus to Tyre, with exact data.

b. Sojourn with the "disciples" (of Jesus) in Tyre; these warn St. Paul "διὰ πνεύματος" not to go to Jerusalem.

---

[1] There are grounds for questioning whether a definite Church was already in existence at Troas, and whether the assembly was not thus confined to the numerous companions of St. Paul and a few other believers or inquirers; for brethren in Troas are not expressly mentioned, but are certainly included in the ἡμῶν of xx. 7, especially as an αὐτοῖς follows. (Many not very trustworthy authorities read, for intelligible reasons, μαθητῶν for ἡμῶν.) We notice also that there is no mention of a leave-taking in Troas (xx. 11). The whole situation has light thrown upon it by 2 Cor. ii. 12 : Ελθὼν δὲ εἰς τὴν Τρῳάδα εἰς τὸ εὐαγγέλιον τοῦ Χριστοῦ, καὶ θύρας μοι ἀνεῳγμένης ἐν κυρίῳ, οὐκ ἔσχηκα ἄνεσιν τῷ πνευματί μου τῷ μὴ εὑρεῖν με Τίτον τὸν ἀδελφόν μου ἀλλ' ἀποταξάμενος αὐτοῖς ἐξῆλθον εἰς Μακεδονίαν. St. Paul had thus broken off his mission in Troas before it had scarcely begun. The two passages thus admirably support and explain each other.

c. Sojourn in " Ptolemais " with the brethren.

d. Arrival in Cæsarea; we take up our abode in the house of the evangelist Philip, " one of the seven," who has three virgin daughters, prophetesses. No further reference is, however, made either to the father or the daughters.

e. The prophet Agabus comes out of Judæa to Cæsarea. He prophesies, with symbolic action, the binding of St. Paul by the Jews in Jerusalem, and his delivery into the hands of the Gentiles.

f. Both his companions in travel and the brethren of Cæsarea try to persuade St. Paul not to go to Jerusalem; but St. Paul will not be persuaded; he declares himself ready even to die in Jerusalem for the name of the Lord Jesus. The brethren—the narrator includes himself and his companions with the brethren of Cæsarea—cease their petition with the words, " The will of the Lord be done."

g. Journey to Jerusalem; certain brethren of Cæsarea journey with us, taking with them an old disciple, Mnason, a Cypriote, with whom we should lodge. (This man must therefore have been one in whom they had special confidence.)

h. The brethren in Jerusalem receive us gladly.

i. On the very next day Paul goes with us to James, with whom all the Elders are present (with a view to a conference).

IV. Journey from Cæsarea to Rome
(xxvii. 1—xxviii. 16)

a. St. Paul and some other prisoners [altogether about seventy-six persons] are delivered to Julius, a centurion of the σπεῖρα Σεβαστή, for transport to Italy (in a ship of Adramytium bound for Asia).

b. "With us" was Aristarchus, a Macedonian of Thessalonica ("we" here means only St. Paul and the writer).

c. At Sidon the officer Julius treated St. Paul with kindness and allowed him to refresh himself among his friends in that town.

d. Description of the voyage to Myrrha; there they embark on board an Alexandrian ship bound for Italy (there are as yet no Christians in Myrrha, nor, indeed, at Lasea in Crete, nor in Malta, Syracuse, and Rhegium).

e. A detailed description of the unlucky voyage and of the storm up to the complete wreck of the ship (accompanied here, as before, by geographical data).

f. St. Paul proves himself an experienced sailor who foretells the disastrous voyage (perhaps supernatural knowledge is implied; yet this is improbable).

g. St. Paul prophesies the destruction of the ship, with, however, no loss of life. He says that he had that night seen in a vision the angel of the Lord, who had told him that he would appear before Cæsar and that God had granted him the lives of all that sailed with him.

h. St. Paul hinders the sailors from forsaking the sinking ship, declaring that if this happened they and all the rest would perish.

i. St. Paul rouses the spirits of all, and, in order to restore confidence, in the midst of the storm he breaks and eats bread with thanksgiving; the rest follow his example.

k. At the moment that the ship is threatening to break up the soldiers propose to slay the prisoners, fearing lest they should escape.   Julius forbids this because he wishes to save St. Paul.   All save themselves either by swimming or upon planks from the ship, and reach land on an island (Malta).

l. The " Barbarians" receive all with kindness, and light a fire for them on the sea-shore, so that they may warm themselves.

m. A snake which had crept out of the faggots bites St. Paul in the hand [encircles his hand?]; he shakes it off without receiving any hurt.   The Maltese regard him first as a murderer whom Dike suffers not to live, then as a god.

n. St. Paul heals the father of Publius, the principal magistrate on the island, who was suffering from attacks of gastric fever, by laying his hands upon him.   Publius had hospitably received us into his house.

o. Other sick folk of the island also came and were healed.   They honoured us with many honours and provided us with provision for our further voyage.

p. The voyage from Malta to Puteoli (by Syracuse and Rhegium) in an Alexandrian ship bearing the name of the *Dioskuri*. At Puteoli we find brethren, who entertain us.

q. The journey to Rome on foot. The Roman brethren who had heard of our arrival, came to meet us as far as Forum Appii and the Three Taverns. As he saw them Paul gave thanks to God and took courage.

r. St. Paul was allowed to hire a private dwelling, living there under the guardianship of a soldier.

The " we" sections thus contain narratives of an exorcism, of the healing by laying on of hands of a man stricken with fever, of a miraculous deliverance from the effects of snake-bite. They include also a summary account of many cases of healing, they tell of one who was raised from the dead, of prophecies delivered by brethren in Tyre, of a prophecy of the prophet Agabus, of the prophesying daughters of Philip, of several prophecies of St. Paul himself, of the appearance of an angel to St. Paul in the ship, and of a vision in Troas. Could one wish for more miracles within the compass of so few verses?[1] *The author shows himself just as fond of the miraculous—and in particular just as deeply interested in miracles of healing, in manifestations of the " Spirit," and in appearances of angels—as the author of the third gospel and the Acts.* So far as regards the subject-matter of the narrative, the relationship could scarcely be closer than it is;[2] consider more especially the part played by the "Spirit" in both cases. Vain efforts

---

[1] The detailed investigation of points of coincidence with the whole work is left to the reader. *Cf.*, *e.g.*, xx. 12 with ix. 41.

[2] Compare how St. Paul in xxviii. 6 is regarded as a god, just as at Lystra.

have been made to show that the author of the " we "
sections paints the miraculous " in less miraculous
colours " than the author of the Acts and the gospel.
But Eutychus is, as the author believes, really dead (not
merely seemingly dead),[1] and even if St. Paul was not
bitten by the serpent (which is by no means certain—indeed, is improbable) [2] his preservation from the bite is,
according to the author, just as miraculous as his deliverance from its fatal effects.   A noteworthy coincidence is
also shown in the fact that the evil spirit, who in the
gospel is the first to recognise Jesus as the Son of the
Most High God (St. Luke viii. 28 : τί ἐμοὶ καὶ σοί, Ἰησοῦ
υἱὲ τοῦ Θεοῦ τοῦ ὑψίστου), here also at Philippi first proclaims the evangelists as δοῦλοι τοῦ Θεοῦ ὑψίστου.

In particular I would draw attention to the following
important points of similarity : As in the Acts (and,
mutatis mutandis, in the gospel), St. Paul, with his
companions, betakes himself in the first place to the
synagogue (or to the place of prayer) ; converts are baptised "with their whole house "; St. Paul teaches " the
Way of Salvation," or " the Way "; in Christian assemblies " the bread is broken "; a college of Elders exists
in the Church at Jerusalem ; St. James appears
at the head of that Church (xv. 13, but xii. 17 is still
more striking) ; Christians use the expression, " the will
of God be done " (see St. Luke xxii. 42) ; St. Paul is

---

[1] St. Paul's stretching himself upon Eutychus is only a stronger
measure than the laying on of hands, which is always found in
St. Luke's accounts of healing. In St. Luke vii. 14 the touch-
ing of the bier has the same significance. The only exception is
Acts ix. 40.

[2] Hobart, *l.c.* p. 288, and *infra* in Appendix I.

ready to die "for the name of the Lord Jesus"; a classical reminiscence appears in xxviii. 4 (ἡ Δίκη ζῆν οὐκ εἴασεν), an Homeric in the word ἀσμένως; likewise a word (θάρσος)[1] occurs which is used by Homer and the tragedians; St. Paul heals by means of laying on of hands;[2] and we can trace no strong interest in what is purely ecclesiastical.[3] Wherever comparison

[1] Also ὕβρις and βάρβαροι should be mentioned. The classical reminiscences to be found in the Acts, outside the "we" sections, are well known (the quotation from Aratus [Cleanthes], δεισιδαίμων, Διοπετές, Ζεύς, Ἄρτεμις, Stoics, Epicureans, and many others). In the gospel also may be found similar instances; compare, for instance, Wellhausen on St. Luke xvi. 3.

[2] Also the somewhat sentimental expression (xxi. 13), τί ποιεῖτε κλαίοντες καὶ συνθρύπτοντές μου τὴν καρδίαν, fits in marvellously with many instances of sentimentality in the third gospel and the Acts (see ix. 39: παρέστησαν πᾶσαι αἱ χῆραι κλαίουσαι καὶ ἐπιδεικνύμεναι χιτῶνας καὶ ἱμάτια ὅσα ἐποίει ἡ Δορκάς; cf. also xx. 19, 23, 25, 31, 37, 38). These coincidences in feeling seem to me of special importance. St. Mark and St. Matthew speak only of the bitter tears of St. Peter; but there is much weeping in St. Luke; our Lord Himself weeps over Jerusalem, and beatifies those that weep. We find the same trait in St. John, but not so strongly marked; it is Hellenic in character.

[3] Wellhausen has rightly emphasised this trait in the third gospel ("Luk.," s. 72). It is a remarkable coincidence that the author of the "we" sections never uses the word "Church." He individualises the Christians in Tyre, Ptolemais, Cæsarea, Jerusalem, Sidon, and Puteoli, and calls them "disciples," "brethren," "friends" (unless in this case special friends are intended, which, however, is less probable, for in this case their names would most likely have been given). In St. Luke, as is well known, the word ἐκκλησία never occurs; on the other hand, it is found twenty-three times in the Acts. But (1) the Acts uses the word both for Jewish and heathen assemblies (vii. 38; xix. 32, 39, 41), and by this shows that the word had not yet gained for the author of the Acts a sacred significance; (2) of the other nineteen instances, in fifteen the reference is to the Church in general and to the communities of Jerusalem and Antioch. Of the remaining four occur-

is at all possible, we therefore find complete agreement.[1]

Indeed, no difference worthy of mention can be discovered. It is true that in the account of the shipwreck the personality of St. Paul is presented in fresher colours, and more vividly impresses us with the sense of its grandeur than anywhere else in the book ; but is this strange ? The author was upon this occasion an admiring eye-witness of the Apostle's heroic behaviour in an anxious and dangerous situation ! We cannot be

rences, in three instances the word is used in the plural, for the Churches in Europe and Asia (xiv. 23, xv. 41, xvi. 5), and once for the Church in Ephesus. In this point, therefore, there is no noteworthy difference between the Acts and the " we " sections, for the latter also uses ἀδελφοί and μαθηταί—though not ἐκκλησία—in a technical sense : ἀδελφοί, i. 15 ; ix. 30 ; x. 23 ; xi. 1 (οἱ ἀπόστολοι καὶ οἱ ἀδελφοὶ οἱ ὄντες κατὰ τὴν Ἰουδαίαν) ; xi. 29 (οἱ ἐν τῇ Ἰουδαίᾳ ἀ.) ; xii. 17 (Ἰάκωβος κ. οἱ ἀ.) ; xiv. 2 ; xv. 1, 3, 22 ; xv. 23 (twice οἱ α. οἱ ἐξ ἐθνῶν) ; xv, 32, 33, 36, 40 ; xvi. 2, 40 ; xvii. 6, 10, 14 ; xviii. 18, 27 ; and μαθηταί, vi. 1, 2, 7 ; ix. 1, 10, 19, 25, 26, 38 ; xi. 26 (here we see that it is the proper technical expression) ; xi. 29 ; xiii. 52 ; xiv. 20, 22, 28 ; xv. 10 ; xvi. 1 ; xviii. 23, 27 ; xix. 1, 9, 30 ; xx. 1, 30. In the Acts the Christians are called οἱ ἅγιοι only in chap. ix. (twice) and in xxvi. 10 ; it is not, therefore, remarkable that this designation is wanting in the " we " sections. Of οἱ πιστοί (πιστός) = Christians there are three examples in the Acts. One stands in the first half (x. 45), one in the second (xvi. 1), and one in the " we " sections (xvi. 15).

[1] We may also notice such traits as the interest displayed in those persons with whom St. Paul lodged in the various cities. The " we " sections mention Lydia in Philippi, Philip in Cæsarea, Mnason in Jerusalem, Publius in Malta. It is unnecessary to quote the numerous passages in the Acts of a similar kind ; think only of Simon in Joppa, Jason in Thessalonica, &c. It is most remarkable that the " we " sections share in the same by no means casual variation between Ἱεροσόλυμα and Ἱερουσαλήμ which characterises the Acts. In xxi. 4, 15, 17 we find Ἱεροσόλυμα, and in xxi. 11, 12, 13 Ἱερουσαλήμ. Good reasons may be assigned for the variation.

too thankful to him for this narrative; for, apart from what we learn from the Apostle's own writings, this is the only record we possess which shows us how St. Paul by constant self-discipline had gained inward and outward peace for his own soul, and thus power over the souls of others.   But the discussion of this point belongs to a later chapter.   Here only one point must be mentioned —namely, that the interest in travelling and halting-places which is displayed in the "we" sections is by no means absent in the author of the Acts.   He could not give such strong expression to this interest in other parts of his work, because he is there writing not as a fellow-traveller and an eye-witness, but from the report of others.   But one need only refer to Acts xiv. 21–26, viii. 26, 40, ix. 32, 35, 36, 43, and x. 1 to recognise that in this point also the two works are not quite out of relationship to one another.

Finally, we have above (pp. 3 ff.) investigated the conditions which must be satisfied if the third gospel and the Acts of the Apostles are to be assigned to the authorship of the Luke who is named and characterised by St. Paul, and (apart from the "higher" criticism) we have found these conditions fulfilled in the work itself.   In the same way, also, on the hypothesis of the identity of the authors of the Acts and the "we" sections, we may deduce from the latter (apart from the conformities we have already noticed) certain conditions, and may find out whether they are satisfied in the book as a whole. In order to avoid repetition I refrain from dealing with these conditions at present (the question will be fully dealt with later), and confine myself to two points:

(1) One passage of the " we " sections may be adduced
which might seem to suggest that the author is to be distinguished from the writer of the whole work. In xxi.
10 Agabus is introduced as if he had not been before
named, and yet he is already mentioned in xi. 28—and
that in a remarkably similar situation. The conclusion
drawn is that the author of the complete work carelessly
copied this passage (xxi. 10) from his source, in which,
of course, nothing was known of an earlier appearance of
Agabus. To this conclusion we would oppose the
following considerations : In the first place, Aristarchus
is introduced (xxvii. 2) in such a way as to lead one to
believe that he is here mentioned for the first time, and
yet he has already appeared in xix. 29 and xx. 4
[the latter passage cannot possibly be separated from
the " we " narrative]. And, in the second place, we
would only point out that the occurrence of the name
" Agabus " in xi. 28 is doubtful, and is probably due to
an ancient interpolation from xxi. 10. In xi. 28, as we
read κατῆλθον ἀπὸ ʽΙεροσολύμων προφῆται εἰς
ʼΑντιόχειαν· ἀναστὰς δὲ εἶς ἐξ αὐτῶν—ὀνόματι ῎Αγαβος
—ἐσήμαινεν διὰ τ. πνεύματος, κ.τ.λ., we are not led to expect the mention of the name of an individual prophet.
In xxi. 10, however, we read κατῆλθέν τις ἀπὸ τῆς
ʼΙουδαίας [and thus certainly not from Jerusalem]
προφήτης ὀνόματι ῎Αγαβος καὶ εἰσελθὼν πρὸς ἡμᾶς καὶ
ἄρας τὴν ζωνὴν τ. Παύλου, κ.τ.λ. How easily it would
occur to any one to complete the former passage by adding
the name from the latter ! At all events, we cannot argue
from one slight discrepancy, which admits of several

explanations, so long as no gap in the narrative and no rough edge in the style can be traced at the points of junction of the " we " sections with the rest of the work. (2) On the other hand, we may point to one striking instance of inward relationship between the " we " sections and the first half of the Acts. In the " we " sections (xxi. 8) the author relates that he had fallen in with Philip the Evangelist at Cæsarea, and with distinct reference to chap. vi. he speaks of him as " one of the seven." This reference is quite in order—in fact, just what we might expect. But it is most strange, or rather it is only to be explained from identity of authorship, that in viii. 40 the account concerning this Philip concludes with the words, " But Philip was found at Azotus ; and passing through he preached the gospel to all the cities, till he came to Cæsarea " [and nothing further is said of him]. If the two authors were not identical, how in the wide world can it be explained that the author of the whole work displays such interest in the residence of Philip at Cæsarea without telling us what he did there ? The narrative admits only of the ideal conclusion : " there I met him at a later time " [not " there he was met by someone else whose diary I shall later on incorporate in my work "]. Nor even in xxi. 8 are we told anything more concerning this Philip than that he with his four daughters dwelt in Cæsarea. Thus the information given concerning him in x. 40 is simply purposeless if the author of the complete work is not speaking in xxi. 8. But this information is both intelligible and natural under the hypothesis of identical authorship; it betrays the interest of the author of the whole work and of the "we" sections in a personal acquaintance which was made in Cæsarea.

We now proceed to our linguistic investigation. I have chosen the first and last passages of the "we" sections for detailed consideration. To go through the whole ninety-seven verses in similar fashion would simply impose a useless burden upon the reader. And, besides, chap. xxvii. has been excellently, though not thoroughly, treated by Klostermann.

(xvi. 10) ὡς δὲ τὸ ὅραμα εἶδεν, εὐθέως ἐζητήσαμεν ἐξελθεῖν εἰς (τὴν?) Μακεδονίαν, συμβιβάζοντες ὅτι προσκέκληται ἡμᾶς ὁ θεὸς (ὁ κύριος?) εὐαγγελίσασθαι αὐτούς.

The interpolated recension — according to Blass it is the earlier—reads somewhat as follows (Blass, 1896): διεγερθεὶς οὖν διηγήσατο τὸ ὅραμα ἡμῖν, καὶ ἐνοήσαμεν ὅτι προσκέκληται ἡμᾶς ὁ θεὸς εὐαγγελίσασθαι τοὺς ἐν τῇ Μακεδονίᾳ.

Νοεῖν is found in St. Matthew, St. Mark, and St. John, but not in St. Luke; διεγείρειν

This temporal ὡς is never found in St. Matthew and St. Mark, but it occurs about forty-eight times in St. Luke (gospel and Acts), and that in all parts of the work.

τὸ ὅραμα appears eleven times in the Acts; elsewhere in the whole New Testament it is only found once (St. Matthew xvii. 9).—τὸ ὅραμα εἶδεν occurs x. 17 and xi. 5—with βλέπειν xii. 9, ὤφθη xvi. 9—(εἶδεν) ἐν ὁράματι ix. 10; ix. 12; x. 3.

ἐζητήσαμεν ἐξελθεῖν]. ζητεῖν is not characteristic, since it is of constant occurrence in all four gospels and the Acts; yet see St. Luke xiii. 24: ζητήσουσιν εἰσελθεῖν. St. Matthew has a different version here. For ζητεῖν with the infin. vide Acts xiii. 8, xvii. 5, xxi. 31. ἐξελθεῖν εἰς]. Acts xi. 25; xiv. 20.

συμβιβάζοντες]. Wanting in the gospels, but found in two other places

does not occur else-
where in the Acts
(once in St. Luke viii.
24).

in the Acts : ix. 22, συμβιβάζων ὅτι
οὗτός ἐστιν ὁ Χριστός ; xix. 33, συνε-
βίβασαν Ἀλέξανδρον. Also only in
St. Luke ἐμβιβάζειν (xxvii. 6) and
ἐπιβιβάζειν (St. Luke x. 34, xix. 35;
Acts xxiii. 24).

προσκέκληται (ὁ θέος)]. This word
is used of God only in the Acts—
vide Acts xiii. 2, εἰς τὸ ἔργον ὃ προ-
σκέκλημαι αὐτούς, and ii. 39. Also
the perfect middle is only found in
xiii. 2 and in this passage.

εὐαγγελίσασθαι αὐτούς]. This
idiom does not occur in St. Matthew,
St. Mark, and St. John, but is found
in St. Luke's gospel eight times and
in the Acts fifteen times. εὐαγ-
γελίζεσθαι τινά : Acts viii. 25, 40,
xiii. 32, xiv. 15, 21.

There are numerous examples in
the Acts of the construction ὡς εἶδεν
... ἐζητήσαμεν ἐξελθεῖν ... συμβιβάζοντες.

[It is to the point to note that
according to this verse St. Paul's companion who writes here was not simply
a fellow-traveller, but also a missionary together with the Apostle.]

(xvi. 11) ἀν-
αχθέντες δὲ (οὖν?)
ἀπὸ Τρῳάδος εὐ-
θυδρομήσαμεν εἰς
Σαμοθρᾴκην, τῇ
δὲ ἐπιούσῃ εἰς
Νέαν πόλιν.

ἀνάγεσθαι = navem solvere is exclusively Lukan; it occurs eleven
times in the " we " sections, and elsewhere in St. Luke viii. 22 and Acts
xiii. 13, xviii. 21.

τῇ ἐπιούσῃ is found in the New
Testament only in the Acts (five

The interpolated recension reads somewhat as follows (Blass, *l.c.*): τῇ δὲ ἐπαύριον ἀναχθέντες ἀ. τ. εὐ. εἰς Σ., καὶ τῇ ἐπιούσῃ ἡμέρᾳ εἰς Ν. τ.

The expression τῇ ἐπαύριον is frequent in the Acts.

(xvi. 12) κἀκεῖθεν εἰς Φιλίππους, ἥτις ἐστὶν πρώτη τῆς μερίδος τῆς Μακεδονίας πόλις, κολωνία. ἦμεν δὲ ἐν ταύτῃ τῇ πόλει διατρίβοντες ἡμέρας τινάς.

Blass, following earlier scholars, proposes to read πρώτης μ·ρίδος because the usual reading does not coincide with facts. Interpolations: κεφαλή for πρώτη (D.), *diebus multis* (Gigas).

times)—*vide* xvii. 26, xx. 15, xxi. 18, xxiii. 11. In the first passage it is accompanied by ἡμέρᾳ, in the last by νυκτί.

[It is not true to say that interest in the stages of journeys is only displayed in the "we" sections. The same trait is found elsewhere in the book—*cf.* xiii. 4, xiii. 13, xiv. 19-26, (xvi. 6-8), xviii. 18-23. Of course we do not find dates indicated so closely as in the "we" sections.]

κἀκεῖθεν—*vide* Acts vii. 4, xiii. 21, xiv. 26, xx. 15, xxi. 1, xxvii. 4, xxviii. 15. It does not occur elsewhere in the whole New Testament.

ἥτις]. Used for ἥ on the same ground (perhaps because it is Attic) as in verses 16 and 17 and vii. 53, x. 41, xiii. 31. St. Luke is fond of these compound relatives. With the feminine *cf.* v. 58.

πρώτη]. πρῶτος in this secondary sense is a favourite word with St. Luke only—*vide* St. Luke xix. 47: οἱ πρῶτοι τ. λαοῦ, Acts xiii. 50: τοὺς πρώτους τ. πόλεως, xvii. 4: γυναικῶν πρώτων, xxv. 2: οἱ πρῶτοι τῶν Ἰουδαίων, xxviii. 7: ὁ πρῶτος τ. νήσου ("we" section); xxviii. 17: τῶν Ἰουδαίων πρώτους. Elsewhere only once—St. Mark vi. 21: οἱ πρῶτοι τῆς Γαλιλαίας.

μερίδος]. Wanting in St. Matthew, St. Mark, and St. John. On the

other hand, it is found in St. Luke
x. 42, Acts viii. 21.

διατρίβοντες]. The word is specifically Lukan. It occurs eight times
in the Acts, elsewhere in the whole
New Testament only once (St. John
iii. 22). It is accompanied by the
accusative of duration of time also in
xiv. 3 (ἱκανὸν χρόνον), xx. 6 (ἡμέρας
ἑπτά), xxv. 6 (ἡμέρας οὐ πλείους
ὀκτώ), xxv. 14 (πλείους ἡμέρας).
The construction of the participle
with ἦν (ἦσαν,·&c.) is found about a
hundred times in St. Luke (gospel
and Acts), and in all the other
writings of the New Testament together about sixty times.

ἡμέρας τινάς]. An expression
characteristic of the Acts—vide ix.
19, x. 48, xv. 36, xxiv. 24, xxv.
13; wanting in St. Matthew and
St. Mark. ἡμέραι πλείονες is also
characteristic of the Acts, and is
found twice in the "we" sections
(xxi. 10, xxvii. 20), twice in the
remaining chapters (xiii. 31, xxiv.
11), and nowhere else in the New
Testament. Lastly, also ἡμέραι
ἱκαναί is peculiar to the Acts. It
occurs once in the "we" sections
(xxvii. 7), and elsewhere only in Acts
ix. 23, 43, xviii. 18.

[The author does not presuppose
in his readers any knowledge of
Macedonia; that he himself is not
a Macedonian is clear from
xxvii. 2.]

(xvi. 13) τῇ τε ἡμέρᾳ τῶν σαββάτων ἐξήλθομεν ἔξω τῆς πύλης παρὰ ποταμόν, οὗ ἐνομίζομεν προσευχὴν εἶναι, καὶ καθίσαντες ἐλαλοῦμεν ταῖς συνελθούσαις γυναιξίν.

Blass conjectures, in my opinion on insufficient grounds, ἐνόμιζεν ἐν προσευχῇ εἶναι. Interpolations: ἐδόκει προσευχὴ εἶναι (D.), συνεληλυθυίας (D.).

τῇ ἡμέρᾳ τῶν σαββάτων]. Wanting in St. Matthew and St. Mark, but occurring in St. Luke iv. 16, xiv. 5 (τοῦ σαββάτου in both these passages), Acts xiii. 14.

τε]. There is no trace of this use of τε in St. Matthew, St. Mark, and St. Luke; it is, however, found in Acts i. 15, ii. 33, 37, 40, iv. 13, 14, 33, v. 19, xiii. 52, and in many other passages.

παρὰ ποταμόν]. Just as in x. 6: οἰκία παρὰ θάλασσαν; x. 32: ξενίζεται ἐν οἰκίᾳ Σίμωνος παρὰ θάλασσαν.

οὗ]. Wanting in St. Mark and St. John, found twice (three times) in St. Matthew and fourteen times in St. Luke (nine of these in the Acts, in all parts of that book).

ἐνομίζομεν]. νομίζειν is wanting in St. Mark and St. John; in St. Matthew it is found three times, in St. Luke (gospel and Acts) ten (nine) times. In St. Matthew, however, it is always followed by ὅτι, but in St. Luke by the accusative with infinitive. Only in Acts xxi. 29 does it take ὅτι (because of attraction).

καθίσαντες]. Vide Acts xiii. 14: ἐλθόντες εἰς τὴν συναγωγὴν τῇ ἡμέρᾳ τῶν σαββάτων ἐκάθισαν.

ἐλαλοῦμεν]. Without object (with the dative of the person), as in vii. 38, 44, ix. 27, x. 7 (x. 32), xi. 20, &c.

τ. συνελθούσαις γ.]. Peculiar to the

Acts—*vide* i. 6 : οἱ συνελθόντες, i. 21 : τῶν συνελθόντων ἀνδρῶν, x. 27 : συνεληλυθότας πολλούς. Besides, *cf.* ii. 6, v. 16, xix. 32, xxi. 22, xxv. 17, xxviii. 17.

[In connection with ἐλαλοῦμεν, *vide* verse 10, concluding note.]

[Notice the correct variation of tenses—imper. aorist and perfect— in verses 12-15, just as is found in other parts of the Acts.]

(xvi.14) καί τις γυνὴ ὀνόματι Λυδία, πορφυρόπωλις πόλεως Θυατείρων, σεβομένη τὸν θεόν, ἤκουεν, ἧς ὁ κύριος διήνοιξεν τὴν καρδίαν προσέχειν τοῖς λαλουμένοις ὑπὸ Παύλου.

Interpolations: τῆς πολ. (D.), ἤκουσεν (D¹al.), *audiebat verbum* (gpw).

καί τις γυνὴ ὀνόματι Λ.]. *Vide* ix. 10 : ἦν δέ τις μαθητὴς ὀνόματι 'Ανανίας, xiv. 8 : καί τις ἀνήρ, St. Luke, xi. 27 : ἐπάρασά τις φωνὴν γυνή, Acts xviii. 7 ; ἦλθεν εἰς οἰκίαν τινὸς ὀνόματι Τιτίου 'Ιούστου σεβομένου τὸν θεόν. The expression τίς ἀνήρ or ἀνήρ (γυνή) τις is not found in St. Matthew, St. Mark, and St. John ; on the other hand, it is of constant occurrence in St. Luke (*vide*, besides the passages mentioned, St. Luke viii. 27, Acts iii. 2, v. 1, viii. 9, x. 1, xvi. 9, xxi. 10, xxv. 14). This ὀνόματι is found only once in each of the gospels of St. Matthew and St. Mark, but in St. Luke (gospel and Acts) about thirty times, and in several places the construction is exactly the same as it is here.

πόλεως Θ.]. Often in St. Luke, never in St. Matthew and St. Mark. *Cf.* Acts xi. 5 : ἐν πόλει 'Ιόππῃ, xxvii. 8 : πόλις Λασέα.

σεβομένη τ. θ.]. σέβεσθαι occurs
in the gospels only in quotations.
In the Acts it is found seven times,
and, indeed, as here, in the technical
sense—*vide* xiii. 43: τῶν Ἰουδαίων
καὶ τῶν σεβομένων προσηλύτων,
xiii. 50: τὰς σεβομένας γυναῖκας,
xvii. 4: τῶν σεβομένων Ἑλλήνων,
xvii. 17: τοῖς Ἰουδαίοις καὶ τοῖς
σεβομένοις, xviii. 7: Ἰούστου σεβομένου τὸν θεόν, xviii. 3: σέβεσθαι
τὸν θεόν (once besides in another
sense, xix. 27).

ἤκουεν]. Lukan—*vide* the concluding note on verse 13. The imperfect
ἤκουεν is never found in St. Matthew
and St. John; in St. Luke (gospel
and Acts) it is found eight times
(in St. Mark three times).

ἧς]. This continuation of the
period by means of a relative is
specially Lukan, and is not so common in Greek as in Latin—*vide, e.g.*,
Acts ii. 24, iii. 3, xi. 6, xxiii. 29,
xxv. 16, and other passages.

ὁ κύριος]. That the Ascended
Christ is represented as the actor in
such cases and that He is called
ὁ κύριος is characteristic of St. Luke
—*vide* Acts ix. 10 ff. and elsewhere.

διήνοιξεν]. Wanting in St.
Matthew and St. John, found once
in St. Mark (vii. 34); in St. Luke it
is found seven times—*cf.* St. Luke
xxiv. 31: διηνοίχθησαν οἱ ὀφθαλμοί,
xxiv. 32: οὐχὶ ἡ καρδία ἡμῶν καιομένη
ἦν, ὡς ἐλάλει ἡμῖν, ὡς διήνοιγεν

ἡμῖν τὰς γραφάς, xxiv. 45: διήνοιξεν αὐτῶν τὸν νοῦν τοῦ συνιέναι τὰς γραφάς ; Acts vii. 56, xvii. 3.

προσέχειν]. Wanting in St. Mark and St. John. In St. Matthew it occurs only in the sense of "take heed"; in this sense, moreover, it occurs often in St. Luke, but also in the sense "give heed" (as here)— Acts viii. 6, προσεῖχον οἱ ὄχλοι τοῖς λεγομένοις, and Acts viii. 10, προσεῖχον αὐτῷ.

τοῖς λαλουμένοις ὑ. Π.]. Just as in Acts xiii. 45: τοῖς ὑπὸ Παύλου λαλούμενοις. Vide also xvii. 19 : ἡ ὑπό σου λαλουμένη διδαχή, xiii. 42: εἰς τὸ μεταξὺ σάββατον λαληθῆναι αὐτοῖς τὰ ῥήματα ταῦτα. Cf. St. Luke ii. 33, τὰ λαλούμενα περὶ αὐτοῦ, and i. 45. It does not occur elsewhere in the gospels.

(xvi. 15) ὡς δὲ ἐβαπτίσθη, καὶ ὁ οἶκος αὐτῆς, παρεκάλεσεν λέγουσα· εἰ κεκρίκατέ με πιστὴν τῷ κυρίῳ εἶναι, εἰσελθόντες εἰς τὸν οἶκόν μου μένετε· καὶ παρεβιάσατο ἡμᾶς.

Interpolations: πᾶς ὁ οἶκος (Dw), [παρεκάλεσεν] Paulum et nos (p2w), θεῷ for κυρίῳ (D.),

ὡς δὲ]. Vide verse 10.

καὶ ὁ οἶκος]. The same construction as in xviii. 2.

οἶκος]. The mention of the house, and that in the sense of the family, is characteristic of St. Luke—vide x. 2, xi. 14, xvi. 31 (σωθήσῃ σὺ καὶ ὁ οἶκός σου), xviii. 8.

παρεκάλεσεν λέγουσα]. Vide ii. 40: παρεκάλει λέγων. παρακάλειν without an object also in ix. 38, xiii. 42, xiv. 22, xix. 31, xxi. 12, xxiv. 4, xxvii. 33. παρακάλειν = to entreat, as in xvi. 9.

εἰ . . . κεκρ.]. This unassuming εἰ

εἰσελόντες for εἰσελθόντες (D.).

very nearly = ἐπεί. The construction is just the same as in iv. 9, xi. 17.

κεκρίκατε]. Does not occur in this weakened sense in St. Matthew, St. Mark, and St. John; see, on the contrary, St. Luke vii. 43 (ὀρθῶς ἔκρινας), xii. 57, and several passages in the Acts—e.g., xv. 19, xvi. 4 (τὰ δόγματα τὰ κεκριμένα), xx.16(κεκρίκει ὁ Παῦλος), xxvi. 8, xiii. 46 (ἀξίους κρίνετε ἑαυτοὺς τῆς αἰωνίου ζωῆς).

πιστὴν τῷ κυρίῳ]. Vide x. 1 : υἱὸς γυναικὸς Ἰουδαίας πιστής, x. 45 : οἱ ἐκ περιτομῆς πιστοί. These are the only passages in the gospel and the Acts. For τῷ κυρίῳ, vide xviii. 8 : Κρίσπος ἐπίστευσεν τῷ κυρίῳ σὺν ὅλῳ τῷ οἴκῳ αὐτοῦ. St. Paul says : πιστὸς ἐν κυρίῳ.

εἰσελθόντες εἰς τ. οἶκον]. Vide ix. 17 : εἰσῆλθεν εἰς τὴν οἰκίαν ; xi. 12 : εἰσήλθομεν εἰς τὸν οἶκον. For "house" in the ordinary sense St. Luke varies between οἶκος and οἰκία.

μένετε] = "take up your abode," as in ix. 43, μεῖναι ἐν Ἰόππῃ παρά τινι Σίμωνι, and in xviii. 3, διὰ τὸ ὁμότεχνον εἶναι ἔμενεν παρ' αὐτοῖς. Μένειν is found three times in St. Matthew, twice in St. Mark, twenty-one times in St. Luke.

παραβιάσατο]. This word does not occur again in the New Testament except in St. Luke xxiv. 29, a passage which has a remarkable likeness to the one we are dealing with : καὶ παρεβιάσαντο αὐτὸν λέγον-

τες· μεῖνον μεθ' ἡμῶν . . . καὶ
εἰσῆλθεν τοῦ μεῖναι σὺν αὐτοῖς.

(xvi. 16) ἐγένετο δὲ πορευομένων ἡμῶν εἰς τὴν προσευχήν, παιδίσκην τινὰ ἔχουσαν πνεῦμα πύθωνα ὑπαντῆσαι ἡμῖν, ἥτις ἐργασίαν πολλὴν παρεῖχεν τοῖς κυρίοις αὐτῆς μαντευομένη.

πύθωνος, ἀπαντῆσαι given in some ancient authorities. Interpolation: διὰ τούτου μαντ.

Concerning the different constructions with ἐγένετο which St. Luke uses, vide Plummer's "Commentary on St. Luke," p. 45 f. The construction with the acc. and infin., which is very common in St. Luke (twelve times in the Acts), is wanting in St. Matthew, St. Mark, and St. John. For the temporal use of the gen. abs. vide St. Luke xi. 14: ἐγένετο τοῦ δαιμονίου ἐξελθόντος, Acts xxii. 17: ἐγένετο δὲ . . . προσευχομένου μου . . . γενέσθαι με ἐν ἐκστάσει.

πορευομένων]. A favourite word of St. Luke which is wanting in St. Mark. St. Luke says, πορεύεσθαι εἰς τ. οὐρανόν (Acts i. 10, 11), διὰ μέσου αὐτῶν ἐπορεύετο (St. Luke iv. 31), πορεύου εἰς τὸν οἶκον (St. Luke v. 24), &c.

παιδίσκην]. Vide Acts xii. 13.

ἔχουσαν πνεῦμα]. Often in St. Luke in the gospel and the Acts— vide St. Luke iv. 33, xiii. 11, Acts viii. 7, xix. 13. Wanting in St. Matthew and St. John.

ὑπαντῆσαι]. Not found elsewhere in the Acts, but vide St. Luke viii. 27, xiv. 31.

ἥτις]. For ἥ Lukan, as in verse 12.

ἐργασίαν πολλὴν παρεῖχεν]. ἐργασία (see also verse 19) is not found in St. Matthew, St. Mark, or St. John;

D

on the other hand, *vide* Acts xix. 24: παρείχετο τοῖς τεχνίταις ἐργασίαν οὐκ ὀλίγην, xix. 25 : ἐκ ταύτης τῆς ἐργασίας. It is found also in the gospel (but in another sense)— *vide* xii. 58 : δὸς ἐργασίαν. If this is a Latinism ("da operam," Wellhausen) it is not the only one in St. Luke. We may consider as Latinisms the constant use of the relative to conjoin clauses (*vide sup.*, on verse 14), and probably also the use of χρῆσθαι (xxvii. 3, 17). For παρέχειν *vide* παρέχειν κόπον (St. Luke xi. 7, xviii. 5), πίστιν (Acts xvii. 31), ἡσυχίαν (Acts xxii. 2), φιλανθρωπίαν (Acts xxviii. 2).

τοῖς κυρίοις]. Also in St. Luke xix. 33. With singular exactness stress is laid upon the fact that the πῶλος belonged to several masters.

(xvi. 17) αὕτη κατακολουθοῦσα τῷ Παύλῳ καὶ ἡμῖν ἔκραζεν λέγουσα· οὗτοι οἱ ἄνθρωποι δοῦλοι τοῦ θεοῦ τοῦ ὑψίστου εἰσίν, οἵτινες καταγγέλλουσιν ὑμῖν ὁδὸν σωτηρίας.

κατακολουθήσασα : with good authority, and probably correct (Blass).
Interpolation : εὐαγγελίζονται in

αὕτη]. This use of οὗτος to repeat the subject is very common in the Acts—*vide* viii. 26, ix. 36, x. 6, 32, 36, xiii. 7, xiv. 9, xviii. 25, 26, &c.

κατακολουθοῦσα]. The word is found only once again in the New Testament, namely, in St. Luke xxiii. 55 : κατακολουθήσασαι αἱ γυναῖκες. (N.B.—ἡμῖν here does not include St. Paul.)

ἔκραζεν λέγουσα]. *Vide* St. Luke iv. 41 : δαιμόνια κράζοντα καὶ λέγοντα; Acts xix. 28 : ἔκραζον λέγοντες.

οὗτοι οἱ ἄνθρωποι]. *Vide* Acts iv.

place of καταγγέλλουσιν (D.). D. also omits ἄνθρωποι.

16 : τοῖς ἀνθρώποις τούτοις, cf. v. 25 v. 38 (the same phrase); xvi. 20 : οὗτοι οἱ ἄνθρωποι, vi. 13 : ὁ ἄνθρωπος οὗτος, xxvi. 31, 32 (the same phrase), xxviii. 4 (the same phrase).

δοῦλοι τ. θεοῦ]. *Vide* Acts iv. 29 : δὸς τοῖς δούλοις σου, St. Luke ii. 29 : τὸν δουλόν σου (*scil.* " of God "). Wanting elsewhere in the Gospels.

τοῦ θεοῦ τοῦ ὑψίστου]. Except in a doubtful passage of St. Mark (v. 7) and in Hebrews vii. 1 this expression is found only in St. Luke out of all the writings of the New Testament (Gospel five times, Acts twice). It occurs as a rule without ὁ θεός, but *vide* St. Luke viii. 28, υἱὲ τοῦ θεοῦ τοῦ ὑψίστου. Also τὸ ὕψος as the place of the Deity and ὑψοῦσθαι of Christ occur only (each twice) in St. Luke.

οἵτινες]. *Vide* notes on verses 12 and 16. With the narrative here compare that of xix. 15, which is very similar.

καταγγέλλουσιν]. The word does not occur in the gospels, but eleven times in the Acts, and, indeed, in all parts of the book—*vide, e.g.,* iv. 2 (ἀνάστασιν), xiii. 5 and xv. 36 (τὸν λόγον), xiii. 38 (ἄφεσιν ἁμαρτ), xvi. 21 (ἔθη), xvii. 3, 23 (Ἰησοῦν).

ὁδὸν σωτηρίας]. *Vide* St. Luke i. 79 : ὁδὸς εἰρήνης (which is the same), xx. 21 : ὁδὸς τοῦ θεοῦ, Acts ii. 28 : ὁδοὺς ζωῆς, ix. 2, xiii. 10, xviii. 25 : ὁδος τοῦ κυρίου, xviii. 26 : ὁδὸς τοῦ θεοῦ, xix. 9, 23, xxii. 4, xxiv. 22. Σωτηρία is wanting in St. Matthew and St. Mark, and is found once in St. John; in St. Luke (gospel and Acts) it occurs ten times—*vide, e.g.*, Acts xiii. 26: ὁ λόγος τῆς σωτηρίας ταύτης, St. Luke i. 69: κέρας σωτηρίας, St. Luke i. 77: γνῶσις σωτηρίας. Besides, we find τὸ σωτηρίον τ. θεοῦ in St. Luke ii. 30, iii. 6, Acts xxviii. 28.[1]

After this demonstration those who declare that this passage (xvi. 10–17) was derived from a source, and so was not composed by the author of the whole work, take up a most difficult position. What may we suppose the author to have left unaltered in the source? Only the " we "? For, in fact, nothing else remains! In regard to

[1] To show that in what directly precedes and follows the same relations of style and vocabulary prevail we would also compare verses 9 and 18 (where no " we " occurs). Verse 9 : καὶ ὅραμα (*vide* note on verse 10) διὰ [τῆς] νυκτὸς (only in Acts v. 19, xvii. 10, xxiii. 31) τῷ Παύλῳ ὤφθη (*vide* note on verse 10) ἀνὴρ Μακεδών τις (this is Lukan—*vide* note on verse 15) ἦν ἑστὼς (*vide* note on verse 15) καὶ παρακαλῶν (*vide* note on verse 15) αὐτὸν καὶ λέγων· διαβὰς (elsewhere only St. Luke xvi. 26) βοήθησον ἡμῖν. Verse 18 : τοῦτο δὲ ἐποίει ἐπὶ πολλὰς ἡμέρας (duration of time with ἐπὶ and acc., St. Luke iv. 25, x. 35, xviii. 4; Acts iii. 1, iv. 5, xiii. 31, xvii. 2, xviii. 20, xix. 8, 10, 34, xx. 11, xxvii. 20 ; never in St. Mark and St. John; once in St. Matthew, but only ἐφ' ὅσον, ix. 15), διαπονηθεὶς (elsewhere in the New Testament only Acts iv. 2) καὶ ἐπιστρέψας (used as in Acts xv. 36) τῷ πνεύματι εἶπεν· παραγγέλλω (*vide* St. Luke viii. 29 : παρήγγ. τ. πνεύματι ἐξελθεῖν ἀπό ; never in St. John, in St. Matthew and St. Mark once or twice each, in St. Luke fifteen times) ἐν ὀνόματι Ἰησοῦ Χριστοῦ ἐξελθεῖν ἀπ' αὐτῆς· καὶ ἐξῆλθεν αὐτῇ τῇ ὥρᾳ ([ἐν] αὐτῇ τῇ ὥρᾳ is besides found in the New Testament only in St. Luke ii. 38 vii. 21, x. 21, xii. 12, xiii. 31, xx. 19, Acts xxii. 13).

vocabulary, syntax, and style he must have transformed everything else into his own language! As such a procedure is absolutely unimaginable, we are simply left to infer that the author is here himself speaking. We may even go a step further: It is quite improbable —at least, so far as this narrative is concerned—that this passage had been written down years ago in the author's " diary," and then had been simply copied into his work. Could he, when he was twenty or thirty years younger—for this time, approximately, may have elapsed between the occurrence of the events and the composition of the Acts—could he then have observed so closely the same rules of method and proportion, could he have written in so similar a style and with so similar a vocabulary as he did later? No! this passage was first written down together with, and in close connection with, the composition and writing of the whole work. No sensible person can judge otherwise. It may well have been that the author possessed short notes which refreshed his memory. Yet even this hypothesis is unnecessary here; it will come up for consideration in connection with later sections of the " we " account.

I now proceed with the section chap. xxviii. 1–16. In its contents it affords so few parallels to what has been before narrated that we should naturally be prepared for few or no instances of conformity with what has gone before. They are therefore the more striking and significant.

(xxviii. 1) καὶ διασωθέντες τότε   διασωθέντες]. *Vide* St. Luke vii. 3: διασώσῃ τὸν δοῦλον αὐτοῦ, Acts xxiii.

ἐπέγνωμεν ὅτι Μελίτη ἡ νῆσος καλεῖται.

24: διασώσωσι τὸν Παῦλον, xxvii. 43, 44, xxviii. 4. Wanting in St. Mark and St. John; found once in St. Matthew (xiv. 36).

τότε]. For this use see St. Luke xxi. 10, Acts i. 12, vi. 11, xxv. 12, xxvi. 1.

ἐπέγνωμεν]. In this construction wanting in St. Matthew and St. John, occurs once in St. Mark, in St. Luke (gospel and Acts) nine times—vide, e.g., Acts xix. 34: ἐπιγνόντες ὅτι Ἰουδαῖος, xxii. 19: ἐπιγνοὺς ὅτι Ῥωμαῖος, &c.

(xxviii. 2) οἵ τε βάρβαροι παρεῖχαν οὐ τὴν τυχοῦσαν φιλανθρωπίαν ἡμῖν· ἅψαντες γὰρ πυρὰν προσελάβοντο πάντας ἡμᾶς διὰ τὸν ὑετὸν τὸν ἐφεστῶτα καὶ διὰ τὸ ψῦχος.

δέ for τε in good authorities; likewise προσανελάμβανον. πάντας is wanting in some authorities.

τε]. Concerning this Lukan use of τε vide note on xvi. 13.

παρεῖχαν]. Vide note on xvi. 16.

οὐ τὴν τυχοῦσαν]. Vide xix. 11: δυναμεις οὐ τὰς τυχούσας. Τυγχάνειν is wanting in St. Matthew, St. Mark, and St. John, but is found six times in St. Luke (gospel and Acts). For the negative expression vide Acts xii. 18 and xix. 23: τάραχος οὐκ ὀλίγος, xix. 24: οὐκ ὀλίγην ἐργασίαν, xiv. 28: χρόνον οὐκ ὀλίγον, xv. 2: συζητήσεως οὐκ ὀλίγης, xvii. 4: γυναικῶν οὐκ ὀλίγαι, xvii. 12: ἀνδρῶν οὐκ ὀλίγοι, xxvii. 20: χειμῶνος οὐκ ὀλίγου. Also elsewhere in the Acts wherein a distinct preference is shown for such negative expressions, vide, e.g., xx. 12: παρεκλήθησαν οὐ μετρίως, xxi. 39: οὐκ ἀσήμου πόλεως, xiv. 17; St. Luke xv. 13 (οὐ πολύ); St. Luke vii. 6 (οὐ μακράν); Acts

i. 5 : οὐ μετὰ πολλὰς ταύτας ἡμέρας, xiv. 17: οὐκ ἀμάρτυρον, xxvii. 14: μετὰ οὐ πολύ. This litotes, which thus occurs in St. Luke at least seventeen times (four of these in the "we" sections), is as good as absent elsewhere in the New Testament.

ἅψαντες πυράν. Vide St. Luke xxii. 25 : ἀψάντων δὲ πῦρ.

προσελάβοντο]. Does not occur in this sense in the gospels. On the other hand, vide Acts xviii. 26 : Πρίσκιλλα καὶ Ἀκύλας προσελάβοντο αὐτόν.

ὑετὸν]. Wanting in the gospels (which use instead the vulgar βρέχειν, βροχή). But see Acts xiv. 17.

ἐφεστῶτα]. ἐφιστάναι is not found in St. Matthew, St. Mark, and St. John. On the other hand, it occurs eighteen times in St. Luke (gospel and Acts). Acts xxii. 20 : ἐφεστώς.

(xxviii. 3) συστρέψαντος δὲ τοῦ Παύλου φρυγάνων τι πλῆθος καὶ ἐπιθέντος ἐπὶ τὴν πυράν, ἔχιδνα ἀπὸ τῆς θέρμης ἐξελθοῦσα καθῆψεν τῆς χειρὸς αὐτοῦ.

συστρέψαντος]. This word occurs elsewhere in the New Testament (apart from two interpolations in the Acts) only in St. Matthew xvii. 22 (and this is doubtful). On the other hand, συστροφή is found in Acts xix. 40. and xxiii. 12.

πλῆθος]. Elsewhere used only of men, except here and St. Luke v. 6 : πλῆθος ἰχθύων.—With this use of τι cf. St. Luke xxiii. 8, xxiv. 41, Acts v. 2, viii. 36, xi. 5, xviii. 14, xxv. 19.

Within the New Testament it is characteristic of St. Luke.

ἀπό]. Weiss, and others with him, declare that ἀπό here = Attic ὑπό—vide St. Luke xxi. 26, Acts xi. 19, xii. 14, xx. 9, xxii. 11 ; but ἀπό here can be very well explained according to its fundamental sense. ἐξέρχεσθαι ἀπό is very rare in St. Matthew, St. Mark, and St. John (altogether about six times) ; in St. Luke's gospel it is found twelve times—vide Acts xvi. 18 (p. 52, note).

(xxviii. 4) ὡς δὲ εἶδον οἱ βάρβαροι κρεμάμενον τὸ θηρίον ἐκ τῆς χειρὸς αὐτοῦ, πρὸς ἀλλήλους ἔλεγον· πάντως φονεύς ἐστιν ὁ ἄνθρωπος οὗτος, ὃν διασωθέντα ἐκ τῆς θαλάσσης ἡ Δίκη ζῆν οὐκ εἴασεν.

ὡς δὲ]. Vide note on xvi. 10.

πάντως]. Is not found in St. Matthew, St. Mark, and St. John. On the other hand, vide St. Luke iv. 24 : πάντως ἐρεῖτέ μοι (Acts xviii. 21, δεῖ με πάντως τὴν ἑορτὴν ποιῆσαι) ; Acts xxi. 22 : πάντως δεῖ πλῆθος συνελθεῖν.

ὁ ἄνθρωπος οὗτος]. Vide note on xvi. 17 (Acts v. 28, vi. 13, xxii. 26, xxvi. 31).

With the whole sentence cf. xxvi. 32 : ἐλάλουν πρὸς ἀλλήλους λέγοντες ὅτι οὐδὲν θανάτου ἄξιον πράσσει ὁ ἄνθρωπος οὗτος.

ζῆν]. Vide xxv. 19 : ὃν ἔφασκεν Παῦλος ζῆν, xxv. 24 : μὴ δεῖν αὐτὸν ζῆν, St. Luke xxiv. 23 : οἳ λέγουσιν αὐτὸν ζῆν, Acts xxii. 22 : οὐ καθῆκεν αὐτὸν ζῆν. Peculiar to St. Luke.

εἴασεν]. Not found in St. Mark and St. John, once in St. Matthew (xxiv. 43), in St. Luke (gospel and

Acts) ten times (of these οὐκ ἐὰν four times).

(xxviii. 5) ὁ μὲν οὖν ἀποτινάξας τὸ θηρίον εἰς τὸ πῦρ ἔπαθεν οὐδὲν κακόν.

μὲν οὖν and μὲν οὖν ... δὲ are found in the Acts about twenty-eight times, in the gospel once (iii. 18); they are wanting in St. Matthew, St. Mark, and St. John. Notice that the occurrence of these narrative particles is equally spread over the Acts.

ἀποτινάξας]. In the New Testament this word is only found besides in St. Luke ix. 5; here St. Matthew and St. Mark use ἐκτινάσσειν.

οὐδὲν κακόν]. Similarly in the New Testament only in Acts xvi. 28: μηδὲν πράξῃς σοι κακόν.

(xxviii. 6) οἱ δὲ προσεδόκων αὐτὸν μέλλειν πίμπρασθαι ἢ καταπίπτειν ἄφνω νεκρόν. ἐπὶ πολὺ δὲ αὐτῶν προσδοκώντων καὶ θεωρούντων μηδὲν ἄτοπον εἰς αὐτὸν γινόμενον, μεταβαλόμενοι ἔλεγον αὐτὸν εἶναι θεόν.

οἱ δὲ]. As in xxi. 20, 32.

προσεδόκων]. Wanting in St. Mark and St. John; occurs only twice in St. Matthew (xi. 3, xxiv. 50), in St. Luke (gospel and Acts) eleven times.

μέλλειν]. Constructions with μέλλειν are very frequent in all parts of the Acts (thirty-five times).

καταπίπτειν]. In the New Testament only here and in xxvi. 14.

ἄφνω]. In the New Testament only here and in ii. 2, xvi. 26.

νεκρόν]. As in v. 10: εὗρον αὐτὴν νεκράν, and xx. 9: ἤρθη νεκρός.

ἐπὶ πολύ]. Vide xvi. 18: ἐπὶ πολλὰς ἡμέρας, xiii. 31: ἐπὶ ἡμέρας πλείους, xviii. 20 : ἐπὶ πλείονα χρόνον, xxvii. 20 : ἐπὶ πλείονας ἡμέρας, xvii. 2 : ἐπὶ σάββατα τρία, xix. 8 : ἐπὶ μῆνας τρεῖς, xix. 10 : ἐπὶ ἔτη δύο, xix. 34 : ἐπὶ ὥρας δύο, xx. 9 : ἐπὶ πλεῖον διαλεγομένου, xx. 11 : ἐφ᾽ ἱκανὸν ὁμιλήσας, xxiv. 4 : ἐπὶ πλεῖον σε ἐνκόπτω.   St. Luke alone of the New Testament writers uses ἐπὶ in a temporal sense.

ἄτοπον].   Wanting in St. Matthew, St. Mark, and St. John (κακόν used instead), but found also in St. Luke xxiii. 41 and Acts xxv. 5 (and, indeed, just as here : τὸ ἄτοπον). The construction of the sentence both in sense and grammar is just as bad as it is in xxii. 17 f. and xxi. 34 : μὴ δυναμένου αὐτοῦ ἐκέλευσεν.

εἰς αὐτ. γιν.].   γίγνεσθαι εἰς occurs only in St. Luke—vide St. Luke iv. 23 : γενόμενα εἰς τὴν Καφαρναούμ. Vide also St. Luke v. 17 : δύναμις ἦν εἰς τὸ ἰᾶσθαι αὐτόν. The participial use of γίγνεσθαι (except in determination of time) is also Lukan.

(xxviii. 7) ἐν δὲ τοῖς περὶ τὸν τόπον ἐκεῖνον ὑ- πῆρχεν χωρία τῷ πρώτῳ τῆς νήσου, ὀνόματι Ποπλίῳ, ὃς ἀναδεξάμενος ἡμᾶς ἡμέρας τρεῖς

τοῖς περὶ].   Wanting in St. Matthew ; vide St. Luke xxii. 49, Acts xiii. 13.

τόπον ἐκεῖνον].   Vide xvi. 3 : ὄντας ἐν τοῖς τόποις ἐκείνοις.

ὑπῆρχεν].   ὑπάρχειν is wanting in St. Matthew, St. Mark, and St. John ; is found thirty-three times

φιλοφρόνως ἐξέ-
νισεν.

in St. Luke (gospel and Acts); only twice besides with the dative—Acts iii. 6, iv. 37.

τ. πρώτῳ]. Vide xiii. 50 : τοὺς πρώτους τ. πόλεως, xxv. 2 : οἱ πρῶτοι τῶν Ἰουδαίων. See also the note on xvi. 12. Yet it ought to be mentioned that the title πρῶτος Μελιταίων (municipii Melitensium primus omnium) has the authority of inscriptions.

ὀνόματι Π.]. Vide note on xvi. 14.

ἐξένισεν]. ξενίζειν does not occur in the gospels; see, however, Acts x. 6, 18, 23 (αὐτοὺς ἐξένισε), 32, xvii. 20, xxi. 16.

(xxviii. 8) ἐγέ-
νετο δὲ τὸν πατέρα
τοῦ Ποπλίου πυ-
ρετοῖς καὶ δυσεν-
τερίῳ συνεχόμε-
νον κατακεῖσθαι,
πρὸς ὃν ὁ Παῦ-
λος εἰσελθὼν καὶ
προσευξάμενος, ἐ-
πιθεὶς τὰς χεῖρας
αὐτῷ, ἰάσατο αὐ-
τόν.

For ἐγένετο with acc. and inf. (Lukan) see the note on xvi. 16.

συνεχόμενον]. Combined with πυρετῷ, is found besides only in St. Luke iv. 38. The whole expression is of a distinctly medical character— vide p. 15. συνέχειν occurs nine times in Lukan writings, never in St. Mark and St. John, once in St. Matthew.

κατακεῖσθαι]. Vide Acts ix. 33 : κατακείμενον ἐπὶ κραβάττῳ.

πρὸς ὃν]. The narrative is continued by means of a relative clause (Lukan). See note upon xvi. 14.

εἰσῆλθεν πρὸς]. So also St. Luke i. 28, Acts x. 3, xi. 3, xvi. 40, xvii. 2. Wanting in St. Matthew and St.

John ; found in St. Mark only once
(xv. 43).

ἐπιθεὶς τὰς χεῖρας]. As Campbell
("Crit. Studies in St. Luke's Gospel,"
1891, p. 56) has shown, St. Luke in
this connection makes a sharp distinction : sick people are healed by
laying on of hands, demoniacs by
the word of exorcism. So it happens
here. Faith is not demanded on the
part of the one to be healed ; rather
it first arises as the result of the
miracle.

ἰάσατο]. The active middle is
wanting in St. Mark and St. Matthew
(in the latter it occurs only once, in
a quotation from the LXX.) ; in St.
Luke (gospel and Acts) it is found
eleven times (vide also St. John).

(xxviii. 9) τού-
του δὲ γενομένου
καὶ οἱ λοιποὶ οἱ
ἐν τῇ νήσῳ ἔχον-
τες ἀσθενείας
προσήρχοντο καὶ
ἐθεραπεύοντο.

οἱ λοιποὶ]. Wanting in St. Mark
and St. John ; occurring in St. Matthew three times, in St. Luke (gospel
and Acts) eleven times.

ἀσθενείας]. Wanting in St. Mark
and St. Matthew (in the latter it
occurs once, in a quotation from the
LXX.); found in St. Luke's gospel
four times—vide xiii. 11 : πνεῦμα
ἔχουσα ἀσθενείας, v. 15, viii. 2,
xiii. 12.—St. Luke xiii. 14 : ἐρχό-
μενοι θεραπεύεσθε, St. Luke v.
15 : συνήρχοντο ὄχλοι πολλοὶ θερα-
πεύεσθαι ἀπὸ τῶν ἀσθενειῶν αὐτῶν,
vi. 18, vii. 21. The passive θερα-
πεύεσθαι is not found in St. Mark,
but in St. Matthew once and in St.

Luke ten times. In the gospel a general statement of this kind is often attached to an account of a particular miracle.

(xxviii. 10) οἳ καὶ πολλαῖς τν μαῖς ἐτίμησαι ἡμᾶς καὶ ἀναγομένοις ἐπέθεντο τὰ πρὸς τὰς χρείας.

For ἡμᾶς p¹ reads αὐτόν.

οἳ]. The narrative is continued in a relative clause (Lukan); see notes on verse 8 and xvi. 14. For οἳ καὶ vide Acts xi. 30: ὃ καὶ ἐποίησαν, xxvi. 10: ὃ καὶ ἐποίησα, St. Luke x. 30: οἳ καὶ ἀπῆλθον.

τιμ. ἐτίμησαν]. This idiom is Lukan—vide Acts iv. 17: ἀπειλῇ ἀπειλησώμεθα, v. 28: παραγγελίᾳ παρηγγείλαμεν, St. Luke xxii. 15: ἐπιθυμίᾳ ἐπιθύμησα, xxiii. 46: φωνήσας φωνῇ (so also Acts xvi. 28). Cf. also St. Luke vi. 8: ἀναστὰς ἔστη, Acts v. 4: μένον ἔμενεν, St. Luke ii. 8: φυλάσσοντας φυλακάς. Compare besides βαπτισθέντες τὸ βάπτισμα, φορτία φορτίζειν, ἀστραπὴ ἀστράπτουσα, &c.

ἀναγομένοις]. Vide note on xvi. 11.

τὰ πρὸς]. Vide St. Luke xiv. 32: ἐρωτᾷ τὰ πρὸς εἰρήνην.

χρείας]. Not found in the plural in St. Matthew, St. Mark, and St. John; it nevertheless occurs in Acts xx. 24.

[Not St. Paul only, but his companions also were honoured (or received an honorarium?); it follows from this that they also took part in the work of healing (vide p. 15 f.), which conclusion, indeed, is not forbidden but rather suggested by the wording of verse 9. Blass, without sufficient grounds, holds it as probable that a change of subject is to be assumed in verse 10, and that these expressions of honour proceeded from the community in general. The simple sense is:—Those who were healed honoured us with many honours because we had healed them.]

(xxviii. 11) με-
τὰ δὲ τρεῖς μῆ-
νας ἀνήχθημεν ἐν
πλοίῳ παρακε-
χειμακότι ἐν τῇ
νήσῳ, Ἀλεξαν-
δρινῷ, παρασήμῳ
Διοσκούροις.

Blass thinks that the construction παρασ. Διοσκ. is quite impossible, and conjectures, therefore, ᾧ ἦν παράσημον Διοσκούρων.

ἀνήχθημεν]. See note on xvi. 11 (xxviii. 10).

(xxviii. 12) καὶ
καταχθέντες εἰς
Συρακούσας ἐπε-
μείναμεν ἡμέραις
τρισίν.

ἡμέρας τρεῖς in many authorities.

κατάγειν]. Wanting in St. Matthew, St. Mark, and St. John; found in St. Luke (gospel and Acts) eight times; combined with εἰς, Acts ix. 30, (xxi. 3), xxiii. 28, xxvii. 3.

ἐπεμείναμεν]. ἐπιμένειν is wanting in St. Matthew, St. Mark, and St. John, but is found six other times in the Acts (combined with ἡμέραι x. 48, xxi. 4, 10, xxviii. 14).

ἡμέραις]. Dative of time, as in St. Luke viii. 29, Acts viii. 11, xiii. 20.

(xxviii. 13) ὅθεν περιελθόντες κατηντήσαμεν εἰς ῾Ρήγιον, καὶ μετὰ μίαν ἡμέραν ἐπιγενομένου νότου δευτεραῖοι ἤλθομεν εἰς Ποτιόλους,

καὶ ἐκεῖθεν ἄραντες for ὅθεν περιελ. Gigas ?—περιελόντες according to ancient authorities.

περιελθόντες]. Wanting in St. Matthew, St. Mark, and St. John ; but see Acts xix. 13.

κατανταν]. Wanting in St. Matthew, St. Mark, and St. John ; occurring, however, nine times in the Acts (nearly always combined with εἰς—vide xvi. 1, xviii. 19, 24, xxi. 7, xxv. 13, xxvi. 7, xxvii. 21.

δευτεραῖοι]. Vide xx. 6 : πεμπταῖοι (but the reading is uncertain). For the construction see St. Luke xxiv. 22) γενόμεναι ὀρθριναὶ . . . ἤλθον.

(xxviii. 14) οὗ εὑρόντες ἀδελφοὺς παρεκλήθημεν παρ᾽ αὐτοῖς ἐπιμεῖναι ἡμέρας ἑπτά· καὶ οὕτως εἰς τὴν ῾Ρώμην ἤλθαμεν.

παρ᾽ αὐτοῖς, ἐπιμείναντες ? (some authorities, Blass).

οὗ]. Vide note on xvi. 13.
παρεκλήθημεν]. Vide note on xvi. 15.
παρ᾽ αὐτοῖς ἐπιμεῖναι]. Vide note on verse 12 ; μένειν παρά τινι is not found in St. Matthew, St. Mark, and St. Luke (gospel) ; see, however, Acts ix. 43, x. 6 (παρά τινι Σίμωνι), xviii. 3, (20), xxi. 7, 8 (παρ᾽ αὐτοῖς, αὐτῷ).
(καὶ) οὕτως]. Vide Acts vii. 8, xvii. 33, xx. 11, xxvii. 44.

(xxviii. 15) κἀκεῖθεν οἱ ἀδελφοὶ ἀκούσαντες τὰ περὶ ἡμῶν ἦλθαν εἰς ἀπάντησιν ἡμῖν ἄχρι Ἀπ-

κἀκεῖθεν]. Vide note on xvi. 12.
τὰ περὶ ἡμῶν]. Vide Acts i. 3, viii. 12, xix. 8 : τὰ περὶ τῆς βασιλείας, xviii. 25, xxviii. 31 : τὰ περὶ τοῦ κυρίου, xxiii. 11 : τὰ περὶ ἐμοῦ, xxiii. 15 : τὰ περὶ αὐτοῦ, xxiv. 10 :

πίου φόρου καὶ
Τριῶν ταβερνῶν,
οὓς ἰδὼν ὁ Παῦ-
λος εὐχαριστή-
σας τῷ θεῷ ἔλα-
βεν θάρσος.

τὰ περὶ ἐμαυτοῦ, St. Luke xxii. 37 :
τὰ περὶ ἐμοῦ, xxiv. 19 : τὰ περὶ
Ἰησοῦ, xxiv 27 : τὰ περὶ ἑαυτοῦ.
This idiom is wanting in St. Matthew,
St. Mark, and St. John. Thus in
three places in xxviii. 7-15 τά
stands before a preposition (7, 10,
15), a trait which is so characteristic
of St. Luke's style when compared
with that of the other evangelists.

ἄχρι]. Wanting in St. Mark and
St. John ; occurring *once* in St.
Matthew, in St. Luke (gospel and
Acts) twenty times, in all parts of
the two books.

ἰδὼν ... εὐχαριστήσας ... ἔλαβεν].
Lukan—*vide*, *e.g.*, Acts xvi. 19 :
ἰδόντες . . . ἐπιλαβόμενοι εἵλκυσαν,
xiv. 29, xvii. 6, xviii. 23 : ποιήσας
. . . ἐξῆλθεν . . . διερχόμενος . . .
στερίζων, xx. 22, 37. Many such
examples have been collected by
Klostermann (p. 59 f.).

(xxviii. 16) ὅτε
δὲ εἰσήλθομεν εἰς
Ῥώμην, ἐπετρά-
πη τῷ Παύλῳ
μένειν καθ' ἑαυτὸν
σὺν τῷ φυλάσ-
σοντι αὐτὸν στρα-
τιώτῃ.

ὅτε δὲ ἤλθομεν εἰς
Ῥώμην, ὁ ἑκατόνταρχος
παρέδωκε τοὺς δεσ-

ὅτε κ.τ.λ.]. *Vide* i. 13 : καὶ ὅτε
εἰσῆλθον.
εἰσήλθομεν εἰς]. *Vide* xxiii. 33 :
εἰσελθόντες εἰς τ. Καισαρείαν, ix. 6 :
εἴσελθε εἰς τ. πόλιν, xiv. 20 : εἰσῆλθεν
εἰς τὴν πόλιν.
ἐπιτρέπεσθαι]. Occurring elsewhere in the gospels and the Acts
only in Acts xxvi. 1.
μένειν]. *Vide* note on xvi. 15.
φυλάσσοντι]. *Vide* xii. 4: παραδοὺς

ιους τῷ στρατοπε- στρατιώταις φυλάσσειν αὐτόν, xxiii.
άρχῃ [-χῷ], τῷ δὲ 35.[1]
Παύλῳ ἐπετράπη μένειν
καθ᾽ ἑαυτὸν (ἔξω τῆς
παρεμβολῆς) σὺν
κ.τ.λ. — vide "Sit-
zungsber. d. K.
Preuss. Akad." d. W.
1895, p. 491 ff.

One sees that the position here is the same as in xvi.
10 ff.; there is absolutely nothing left which the author,

---

[1] Since those critics who separate the "we" account as a source
from the work as a whole assert that the surest justification of this
distinction lies in the contrast between xxviii. 1–16 and xxviii. 17 to
end, a contrast which is here peculiarly striking (this point will
be dealt with later), let us accordingly give a list of instances
wherein kinship in language, matter, and style is shown between
xxviii. 17 ff. and the "we" sections. It must not be forgotten in
this connection that in xxviii. 17 ff. we are dealing with only a few
verses, and that the "we" sections also consist only of ninety-seven
verses, and that the subject-matter in either case is quite different.

V. 17. μετὰ ἡμέρας τρεῖς as in xxviii. 7, 12 ; ἐγένετο with acc.
and infin. as in xxviii. 8 ; οἱ τῶν Ἰουδαίων πρῶτοι as in xxviii. 7
(xvi. 12) ; συνελθόντων as in xvi. 13 ; παρεδόθην εἰς τὰς χεῖρας τ.
Ῥωμαίων as in xxi. 11 : παραδώσουσιν εἰς χεῖρας ἐθνῶν (only here).

V. 18. διὰ τὸ with infin. as in xxvii. 4, 9 (five times elsewhere in
the Acts) ; ὑπάρχειν four times in the "we" sections.

V. 19. ὡς with the participle as in xxvii. 30 ; ἔχων τι κατηγορεῖν
as in xxi. 13 ἑτοίμως ἔχω ἀποθανεῖν.

V. 20. παρεκάλεσα (to beg) as in xvi. 15, xxi. 12, xxviii. 14 ;
ἐλπίς as in xvi. 19 and xxvii. 20 (five times elsewhere in the Acts).

V. 21. οἱ δὲ as in Acts xxviii. 6 ; παραγενόμενος as in Acts
xxi. 18.

V. 22. μέν without δέ as in Acts xxvii. 21.

V. 23. ἦλθον πρὸς αὐτὸν εἰς, thus only in xx. 6 : ἤλθομεν πρὸς αὐτοὺς
εἰς. For ξενίαν see xxviii. 7 (ἐξένισεν), xxi. 16. πλείονες as in
xxvii. 12 (οἱ πλείονες) ; elsewhere only in xix. 30. For the continuation with a relative clause (οἷς) vide xvi. 14. For the continuation with τε vide xvi. 13. For τε-καί vide xxi. 12, xxvii. 1.

E

if he copied or used a source, can have taken over from it unchanged. He must have clothed the contents of his source in a perfectly fresh narrative, for everywhere, where the subject-matter in the least allows of it, we hear the voice, we see the hand, and we trace the style of the author of the whole work. Nothing anywhere strikes us as strange; for the ἅπαξ-λεγόμενα are easily explained from the special character of the subject-matter. That the narrative is more vivid and trustworthy than in those parts of the book where no " we " is to be found is surely no matter for wonder. For many sections—as, for instance, for xxviii. 11–14, xx. 5, 6, 13–15, xxi. 1–8, but especially for xxvii.—the author must have possessed notes which refreshed his memory; [1] but more than this we may not say.

V. 24. ἐπείθοντο τοῖς λεγομένοις just as in xxvii. 11 (and here only): ἐπείθετο τοῖς λεγομένοις.

V. 25. πρὸς ἀλλήλους as in xxviii. 4 (three times elsewhere in the Acts) ; τὸ πνεῦμα τὸ ἅγιον ἐλάλησεν, vide xxi. 11. Now follows the long quotation and its application in verse 28 (the gospel as τὸ σωτήριον τοῦ θεοῦ, as in xvi. 17 as ὁδὸς σωτηρίας). V. 29 is an interpolation which is no longer printed in the better editions.

V. 30. ἐν ἰδίῳ μισθώματι, vide xxi. 6 ; ἀπεδέχετο as in xxi. 17.

V. 31. τὰ περὶ κυρίου as in xxviii. 15 : τὰ περὶ ἡμῶν.

These coincidences within the space of a few verses are by no means few ; nevertheless in themselves they do not as yet afford a convincing proof of identity of authorship.

[1] The theory which, indeed, first suggests itself is that which dispenses with the hypothesis of notes, and, in consequence, supposes the whole work to have been written soon after the arrival of St. Paul in Rome (xxviii. 30 f. would then be a note added by the author when his work was published). But this view, though it is otherwise attractive, and even to-day is upheld by many critics, must be rejected because of the gospel, which cannot well have been written before 70 A.D., and also because of Acts xx. 25, where it seems probable that the death of the Apostle is presupposed.

But in order to bring to a conclusion the proof of the identity of the author of the "we" sections with the author of the whole work, it is necessary to make a thorough investigation of the vocabulary of these sections. Statistics of words may be deceptive, and may lead to absurd conclusions if they are applied to objects of limited extent, or under false principles, or if the investigator is satisfied with doubtful results. Here, however, such imposing results have been gained on a wide basis of investigation that they may be called simply decisive.[1]

In what follows it must always be kept in view that we are dealing with only ninety-seven verses—the whole extent of the "we" sections.[2]

I. *Words which are found in the "we" sections and the Acts, but are wanting in St. Matthew, St. Mark, St. Luke, and St. John.*

(a) In the "we" sections [3] and only in the second half of the Acts: xiii., xiv., xvi.–xxviii.[4]

ἅμα with partic. [xxvii. 40]; xxiv. 26.
ἀνιέναι [xxvii. 40]; xvi. 26.

---

[1] Hawkins has already dealt with this question in great detail (see especially pp. 13 ff., 148 ff.). I shall give a short summary of his results below; they first came under my notice after I had finished my own studies on a different plan.

[2] The "we" sections form a small tenth part of the Acts, (97 : 1007).

[3] The passages from the "we" sections are set in square brackets.

[4] I give this division because chap. xv. seems to belong more closely to chaps. i.–xii.

ἀποπλεῖν [xx. 15; xxvii. 1]; xiii. 4; xiv. 26.[1]

διαλέγεσθαι [2] [xx. 7, 9]; xvii. 2, 17; xviii. 4; xix. 8, 9; xxiv. 12, 25.

διατρίβειν χρόνον or ἡμέρας [xvi. 12; xx. 6]; xiv. 3, 28; xxv. 6, 14.

διαφέρεσθαι [xxvii. 27]; xiii. 49.

δίκη, καταδίκη [xxviii. 4]; xxv. 15.

εἰ with optat. [xxvii. 12,39]; xvii. 11, 27; xxiv. 19; xxv. 20.

ἐκεῖσε [xxi. 3]; xxii. 5.

ἐξιέναι [xx. 7; xxvii. 43]; xiii. 42; xvii. 15.[3]

ἐπιβαίνειν [4] [xxi. 2, 4; xxvii. 2]; xx. 18; xxv. 1.

εὔθυμος [xxvii. 36]; xxiv. 10. Vide also εὐθυμεῖν [only xxvii. 22, 25].

εὔχεσθαι [xxvii. 29]; xxvi. 29.

καταντᾶν [xx. 15; xxi. 7; xxvii. 12; xxviii. 13]; xvi. 1; xviii. 19, 24; xxv. 13; xxvi. 7.

καταπίπτειν [xxviii. 6]; xxvi. 14.

καταφέρειν [xx. 9 twice]; xxv. 7; xxvi. 10.

μένειν = to await [xx. 5]; xx. 23.

(νῆσος) [xxvii. 26; xxviii. 1, 7, 9, 11]; xiii. 6.

περιέρχεσθαι [xxviii. 13]; xix. 13.

---

[1] The participle ἀσπασάμενος is not found in the gospels, but only in the " we " sections [xx. 1, xxi. 7], and in the second half of the Acts (xviii. 22, xxi. 19, xxv. 13); γίγνεσθαι εἰς Ἱερουσαλήμ [xxi. 17], xx. 16, xxv. 15.

[2] No account is here taken of the form διελέχθε (διελέχθησαν) which is found once in St. Mark (ix. 34), and perhaps once in the Acts (xviii. 19).

[3] Vide εἰσιέναι and τῇ ἐπιούσῃ (p. 70); ἀπιέναι in the New Testament only in Acts xvii. 10, συνιέναι only in St. Luke viii. 4.

[4] In the sense " to ride " ἐπιβαίνειν occurs once in St. Matthew xxi. 5, but only in a quotation from the LXX.

πιστεύειν τῷ θεῷ [xxvii. 25]; xvi. 34.

πλείονας ἡμέρας [xxi. 10; xxvii. 20]; xxiv. 11.

προσλαμβάνεσθαι = recipere [xxviii. 2]; xviii. 26.

οἱ σεβόμενοι [xvi. 14]; xiii. 43, 50; xvii. 4, 17; xviii. 7.

οὐ τὴν τυχοῦσαν [xxviii. 2]; xix. 11.

ὑετός [xxviii. 2]; xiv. 17 (in St. Matthew βροχή).

ὑπονοεῖν [xxvii. 27]; xiii. 25; xxv. 18.

αἱ χρεῖαι [xxviii. 10]; xx. 34.

It remains also to be noticed that the narrative of St. Paul's abode in Athens concludes with almost the same words as that of his abode in Troas [vide xvii. 33, οὕτως ὁ Παῦλος ἐξῆλθεν, and [xx. 11], οὕτως [ὁ Παῦλος] ἐξῆλθεν); further, that διό with imper. occurs only in [xxvii. 25] and xx. 31; finally, that the participle εἴπας is found only in [xxvii. 35], xxii. 24, and xxiv. 22.

(b) In the " we " sections and only in the first half of the Acts—Acts i.-xii., xv.

(ἀσμένως) [xxi. 17]; ii. 41 (but the reading is doubtful here).

ἀρχαῖος (of an earlier period in the history of the Gospel) [xxi. 16]; xv. 7.

εἰ in the sense of ἐπεί [xvi. 15]; iv. 9; xi. 17.[1]

ἐκπίπτειν [xxvii. 17, 26, 29, 32]; xii. 7.

---

1 In xxi. 13 ἀποθανεῖν εἰς Ἰερουσαλήμ (with ἐλθών omitted) is exactly parallel to viii. 40 : Φίλιππος εὑρέθη εἰς Ἄζωτον.—πλήν τινος is only found (disregarding a quotation from the LXX. in St. Mark) in [xxvii. 22], viii. 1, xv. 28.

ἐξωθεῖν [xxvii. 39]; vii. 45.

ἐπιμένειν [xxi. 4, 10; xxviii. 12, 14]; x. 48; xii. 16; (xv. 34).

ἕτερός τις [xxvii. 1]; viii. 34.

αἱ ἡμέραι τ. ἀζύμων [xx. 6]; xii. 3.

πειθαρχεῖν [xxvii. 21]; v. 29, 32.

διὰ πνεύματος [xxi. 4]; i. 2; iv. 25; xi. 28.

πρόθεσις = purpose [xxvii. 13]; xi. 23.

καθ' ὃν τρόπον [xxvii. 25]; xv. 11.

ὑπὲρ τοῦ ὀνόματος [xxi. 13]; v. 41; ix. 16; xv. 26.

ὑπερῷον [xx. 8]; Acts i. 13; ix. 37, 39.

ψυχαί=homines [xxvii. 37]; ii. 41, 43; vii. 14.

(c) In the " we " sections and only in both halves
of the Acts taken together.[1]

ἄφνω [xxviii. 6]; ii. 2; xvi. 26.

βία [xxvii. 41]; v. 26; xxi. 35; (xxiv. 7).

εἰσιέναι [xxi. 18]; iii. 3; xxi. 26.

ἐκπλέειν [xx. 6]; xv. 39; xviii. 18.

ἐλπίς [xxvii. 20]; ii. 26; xvi. 19; xxiii. 6; xxiv. 15; xxvi. 6, 7; xxviii. 20.

τῇ ἐπιούσῃ [xvi. 11; xx. 15; xxi. 18]; vii. 26; xxiii. 11.

ἡμέραι ἱκαναί [xxvii. 7]; ix. 23, 43; xviii. 18.

---

[1] We here omit the fairly numerous instances of words which are
often repeated in the " we " sections and the Acts, but are of rare
occurrence in the gospels—for instance, βούλεσθαι, which occurs only
six times in all the gospels taken together (twice in St. Luke), but is
found fourteen times in the Acts—four times in the first half, ten
times in the second half (once in the " we " sections, xxvii. 43). It
is also a rare word with St. Paul.

ἡμέρας τινάς [xvi. 12]; ix. 19 ; x. 48 ; xv. 36 ; xxiv. 24.

κἀκεῖθεν [xvi. 12 ; xx. 15 ; xxi. 1 ; xxvii. 4 ; xxviii. 15]; vii. 4 ; xiii. 21 ; xiv. 26.

καταγγέλλειν [xvi. 17]; iii. 24 ; iv. 2 ; xiii. 5, 38 ; xv. 36 ; xvi. 21 ; xvii. 3, 13, 23 ; xxvi. 23.

μέλλειν ἔσεσθαι [xxvii. 10]; xi. 28 ; xxiv. 15.

μεταλαμβάνειν [xxvii. 33, 34]; ii. 46 ; xxiv. 25 (in the first three passages combined with τροφῆς).

νεανίας [xx. 9]; vii. 58 ; xxiii. 17 (elsewhere νεανίσ-κος).

τὰ νῦν [xxvii. 22]; iv. 29 ; v. 38 ; xvii. 30 ; xx. 32.

ξενίζειν [xxi. 16 ; xxviii. 7]; x. 6, 18, 23, 32 ; xvii. 20.

ἐπὶ πλεῖον [xx. 9]; iv. 17 ; xxiv. 4.

λέγει (or a similar word) τὸ πνεῦμα (τὸ ἅγιον)˙ [xx. 23 ; xxi. 11]; viii. 29 ; x. 19 ; xi. 12 ; xiii. 2 ; xxviii. 25.

οἱ πρεσβύτεροι (Christian officials) [xxi. 18]; xi. 30 ; xiv. 23 ; xv. 2, 4, 6, 22, 23 ; xvi. 4 ; xx. 17.

προπέμπειν [xxi. 5]; xv. 3 ; xx. 38.

προσκαλεῖσθαι (of God) [xvi. 10]; ii. 39 ; xiii. 2.

συμβιβάζειν [xvi. 10]; ix. 22 ; xix. 33.

There are thus about sixty-seven words or phrases which are common to the "we" sections and the Acts of the Apostles, while they are wanting in the four gospels. Of course, some of these coincidences may be put down to accidental causes ; but the larger half at least are of great weight, and must be regarded as highly cha-racteristic of style, especially when we consider how

constant is the occurrence of particular words or
phrases in the above lists.

II. *Words which are found in the "we" sections, in the
Acts, and in St. Luke's gospel, but not in St.
Matthew, St. Mark, and St. John.*

ἀνάγεσθαι (of a ship) [xvi. 11; xx. 13; xxi. 1, 2;
xxvii. 4, 12, 21; xxviii. 10, 11]; St. Luke, viii. 22;
Acts xiii. 13; xviii. 21; xx. 3.

ἀποδέχεσθαι [xxi. 17]; St. Luke viii. 40; ix. 11;
Acts ii. 41; xviii. 27; xxiv. 3; xxviii. 30.

ἄστρον [xxvii. 20]; St. Luke xxi. 25; Acts vii. 43.

ἄτοπον [xxviii. 6]; St. Luke xxiii. 41; Acts xxv. 5.

ἄχρις οὗ [xxvii. 33]; St. Luke xxi. 24; Acts vii.
18.[1]

βουλή [xxvii. 12, 42]; St. Luke vii. 30; xxiii. 51;
Acts ii. 23; iv. 28; v. 38; xiii. 36; xx. 27.

διασῶσαι [xxvii. 43]; St. Luke vii. 3; Acts xxiii. 24
(the passive occurs besides three times in the "we"
sections and once in St. Matthew).

διατάσσεσθαι [xx. 13]; St. Luke iii. 13; xvii. 9, 10;
Acts vii. 44; xviii. 2; xxiii. 31; xxiv. 23.

ἐνώπιον (πάντων) [xxvii. 35]; in St. Luke twenty
times; in the Acts, excluding the "we" sections, fourteen times (ἐνώπιον πάντων only again in Acts xix.
19); occurs once, indeed, in St. John.

---

[1] It is noteworthy that ἄχρις is wanting in St. Mark and St. John,
and occurs once in St. Matthew (xxiv. 38), but that in St. Luke (gospel
and Acts) it occurs twenty times, four of which occurrences are in
the "we" sections.

ἑξῆς [xxi. 1; xxvii. 18]; St. Luke vii. 11; ix. 37; Acts xxv. 17.

ἐπί, with acc. of time [xx. 11; xxvii. 20]; St. Luke iv. 25; x. 35; xviii. 4; Acts iii. 1; iv. 5; xiii. 31; xvi. 18; xvii. 2; xviii. 20; xix. 8, 10, 34.

ἐργασία [xvi. 16]; St. Luke xii. 58; Acts xvi. 19; xix. 24, 25.

εὐαγγελίζεσθαί τι, τινά [xvi. 10]; St. Luke i. 19; ii. 10; iii. 18; iv. 18, 43; viii. 1; ix. 6; xx. 1; Acts v. 42; viii. 4, 12, 25, 35, 40; x. 36; xi. 20; xiii. 32; xiv. 7, 15, 21; xv. 35; xvii. 18.

ἐφιστάναι [xxviii. 2]; St. Luke ii. 9, 38; iv. 39; x. 40; xx. 1; xxi. 34; xxiv. 4; Acts iv. 1; vi. 12; x. 17; xi. 11; xii. 7; xvii. 5; xxii. 13, 20; xxiii. 11, 27 (ἐφεστώς, xxii. 20 and [xxviii. 2]).

τῇ ἐχομένῃ [xx. 15]; St. Luke xiii. 33; Acts xxi. 26.

ἡμέρα with γίγνεσθαι [xxvii. 29, 33, 39]; St. Luke iv. 42; Acts xii. 18; xvi. 35; xxiii. 12. αἱ ἡμέραι αὗται [xxi. 15]; St. Luke vi. 12; xxiii. 7; xxiv. 18; i. 24; Acts i. 15; vi. 1; xi. 27; i. 5; xxi. 15; v. 36; xxi. 38; iii. 24.

ἡσυχάζειν [xxi. 14]; St. Luke xiv. 4; xxiii. 56; Acts xi. 18.

κατάγειν [xxvii. 3; xxviii. 12]; St. Luke v. 11; Acts ix. 30; xxii. 30; xxiii. 15, 20, 28.

κατέρχεσθαι [xxi. 3, 10; xxvii. 5]; St. Luke iv. 31; ix. 37; Acts viii. 5; ix. 32; xi. 27; xii. 19; xiii. 4; xv. 1, 30; xviii. 5, 22.

κρίνειν (in the wider sense) [xvi. 15; xxvii. 1]; St. Luke vii. 43; xii. 57; Acts iv. 19; xiii. 46; xv. 19; xvi. 4; xx. 16; xx xxi. 25; v. 25; xxvi. 8.

τὰ λαλούμενα [xvi. 14]; St. Luke i. 45; ii. 33; Acts xiii. 45; (xvii. 19).

λατρεύειν [xxvii. 23]; St. Luke i. 74; ii. 37; iv. 8; Acts vii. 7, 42; xxiv. 14; xxvi. 7.[1]

μὲν οὖν [xxviii. 5]; St. Luke iii. 18; Acts viii. 4, 25; ix. 31; xi. 19; xii. 5; xiv. 3; xv. 3, 30; xvi. 5; xvii. 12, 17; (xviii. 14); xix. 38; xxiii. 18, 31; xxv. 4.

μερίς [xvi. 12]; St. Luke x. 42; Acts viii. 21.

μήν [xxviii. 11]; St. Luke i. 24, 26, 36, 56; iv. 25; Acts vii. 20; xviii. 11; xix. 8; xx. 3.

μόλις [xxvii. 7, 8, 16]; St. Luke ix. 39; Acts xiv. 18.

ὁμιλεῖν [xx. 11]; St. Luke xxiv. 14, 15; Acts xxiv. 26.

πάντως [xxviii. 4]; St. Luke iv. 23; Acts (xviii. 21); xxi. 22.

πείθεσθαι [xxi. 14; xxvii. 11]; St. Luke xvi. 31; xx. 6; Acts v. 36, 37, 40; xvii. 4; xxiii. 21; xxvi. 26; xxviii. 24.

τὰ περί τινος [xxviii. 15]; St. Luke xxii. 37; xxiv. 19, 27; Acts i. 3; (viii. 12); xviii. 25; (xix. 8); xxiii. 11, 15; xxiv. 10, 22; xxviii. (23), 31.

οἱ πλείονες (τὸ πλεῖον) [xxvii. 12]; St. Luke vii. 43; Acts xix. 32.

ποιεῖσθαι=ποιεῖν [xxvii. 18]; St. Luke v. 33; xiii. 22; Acts i. 1; xx. 24; xxv. 17.

πόλις, added to the name of the city [xvi. 14; xxvii. 8]; St. Luke ii. 4; Acts xi. 5.

μετ᾽ οὐ πολύ (μετ᾽ οὐ πολλὰς ἡμέρας) [xxvii. 14]; St. Luke xv. 13; Acts i. 5.

---

[1] Once in St. Matthew (iv. 10) in a quotation from the LXX.

προσάγειν [xxvii. 27]; St. Luke ix. 41; Acts xvi. 20.[1]

σταθείς [xxvii. 21]; St. Luke xviii. 11, 40; xix. 8; Acts ii. 14; v. 20; xi. 13; xvii. 22; xxv. 18.

συναρπάζειν [xxvii. 15]; St. Luke viii. 29; Acts vi. 12; xix. 29.

συνβάλλειν [xx. 14]; St. Luke ii. 19; xiv. 31; Acts iv. 15; xvii. 18; xviii. 27.

θέντες (θεὶς) τὰ γόνατα [xxi. 5]; St. Luke xxii. 41; Acts vii. 60; ix. 40; xx. 36.[2]

τυγχάνειν [xxvii. 3; xxviii. 2]; St. Luke xx. 35; Acts xix. 11; xxiv. 2; xxvi. 22.

ὑπάρχειν [xxvii. 12, 21, 34; xxviii. 7]; St. Luke vii. 25; viii. 41; ix. 48; xi. 13; xvi. 14, 23; in the Acts about twenty-two times, excluding the "we" sections.

ὑποστρέφειν [xxi. 6]; in St. Luke (gospel) about twenty-two times; Acts i. 12; viii. 25, 28; xiii. 13, 34; xiv. 21; xx. 3; xxii. 17; xxiii. 32.

χαρίζεσθαι [xxvii. 24]; St. Luke vii. 21, 42, 43; Acts iii. 14; xxv. 11, 16.

χρόνον ἱκανόν [xxvii. 9]; St. Luke viii. 27; xx. 9; xxiii. 8; Acts viii. 11; xiv. 3.[3]

---

1 σπεύδειν also should be added here [xx. 16, which may well belong to the "we" sections]. Cf. St. Luke ii. 16, xix. 5, 6; Acts xxii. 18.

2 τιθέντες τὰ γόνατα is found once in St. Mark (xv. 19).

3 ἐᾶν [xxvii. 32, 40, xxviii. 4] occurs elsewhere in the Acts five times, in St. Luke's gospel twice, is wanting in St. Mark and St. John, and is found once only in St. Matthew. ἔθος [xxviii. 17] occurs elsewhere in the Acts six times, in St. Luke three times, is wanting in St. Matthew and St. Mark, and is found once in St. John; τὰ ἔθη only occurs in the "we" sections and three times in the Acts.

This group of forty-four words and phrases is of still greater import than the former, for the gospel of St. Luke is here included. We at once learn that the " we " sections are somewhat more nearly allied to the second half of the Acts than to the first, and yet that they are also closely connected with this first half. With the first half of the Acts they have in common about sixty-seven words which are wanting in St. Matthew, St. Mark, and St. John ; with the second half about eighty-eight words, of which forty-five are the same in both cases.

III. *Words which are found in the " we " sections and in St. Luke's gospel, but not in St. Matthew, St. Mark, St. John, and the Acts of the Apostles.*

We must preface an observation of the first importance. In xxviii. 35 (a " we " section) we read : εἴπας (scil. ὁ Παῦλος) δὲ ταῦτα καὶ λαβὼν ἄρτον εὐχαρίστησεν τῷ θεῷ ἐνώπιον πάντων καὶ κλάσας ἤρξατο εσθίειν. This is a deliberate imitation of St. Luke xxii. 19: καὶ λαβὼν ἄρτον εὐχαριστήσας ἔκλασεν (*cf.* xxiv. 30: λαβὼν τὸν ἄρτον εὐλόγησεν καὶ κλάσας, κ.τ.λ.; *cf.* 1 Corinthians xi. 23: ἔλαβεν ἄρτον καὶ εὐχαριστήσας ἔκλασεν). The opinion of Wellhausen and others that the verses St. Luke xxii. 19-20 are not genuine is therefore scarcely tenable. We besides notice that ἐσθίειν only occurs here in the Acts, whilst it is found twelve times in St. Luke's gospel.

ἀναφαίνειν [xxi. 3] ; St. Luke xix. 11.
ἀνευρίσκειν [xxi. 4] ; St. Luke ii. 16.

ἀποσπασθῆναι ἀπό [xxi. 1]; St. Luke xxii. 41.

ἀποτινάσσειν [xxviii. 5]; St. Luke ix. 5.

ἅπτειν λύχνον vel πῦρ [xxviii. 2]; St. Luke viii. 16; xi. 33; xv. 8; xxii. 55.

διιστάναι [xxvii. 28]; St. Luke xxii. 59; xxiv. 51.

(ἐπιμέλεια) [xxvii. 3]; only St. Luke x. 34, 35; in xv. 8 are found ἐπιμελεῖσθαι and ἐπιμελῶς.

ἐπιφαίνειν [xxvii. 20]; St. Luke i. 79.

εὔθετος, ἀνεύθετος [xxvii. 12]; St. Luke ix. 62; xiv. 35.

κατακολουθεῖν [xvi. 17]; St. Luke xxiii. 55.

κατέχειν [xxvii. 40]; St. Luke iv. 42; viii. 15; xiv. 9.

θρὶξ ἐκ τῆς κεφαλῆς ἀπολεῖται [xxvii. 34]; St. Luke xxi. 18.

νότος [xxvii. 13, twice]; St. Luke xi. 31; xii. 55; xiii. 29.[1]

παραβιάζεσθαι [xvi. 15]; St. Luke xxiv. 29.

περιπίπτειν [xxvii. 41]; St. Luke x. 30.

πλεῖν [xxi. 3; xxvii. 2, 6, 24]; St. Luke viii. 23.

πλῆθος (of things) [xxviii. 3]; St. Luke v. 6.

τραχύς [xxvii. 29]; St. Luke iii. 5.[2]

μὴ φοβοῦ (with vocative) [xxvii. 24]; St. Luke i. 13, 30; xii. 32.[2]

This group of twenty words, taken together with the former group, is the most important of all. *In the "we" sections, as we see, no less than sixty-four words*

---

[1] In all these instances used of the wind; once in St. Matthew (xii. 42), βασίλισσα νότου.

[2] But only in a quotation from the LXX.

and phrases are found which also occur in St. Luke's gospel while they are wanting in St. Matthew, St. Mark, and St. John!

There are thus about 130 words (or phrases) [1] in 190 places (in the 97 verses) which the " we " sections have in common with the Acts or with St. Luke's gospel or with both together, and which are wanting in St. Matthew, St. Mark, and St. John; [2] *i.e., on an average we meet with two such words (or phrases) in every verse of the " we " sections.*

Let us now apply the following test, with very instructive results :

The " we " sections have in common with the Acts and St. Luke > St. Matthew, St. Mark, and St. John . 44 words

The " we " sections have in common with St. Luke > St. Matthew, St. Mark, St. John, and the Acts . . 20 words (in 23 places)

64 words

The " we " sections have in common with the Acts and St. Matthew > St. Mark, St. Luke, and St. John . 3 words [3]

[1] Proper names and numerals are, of course, omitted.

[2] About sixty-seven in common with the Acts, about twenty with St. Luke's gospel, about forty-three with both.

[3] ἐπιβαίνειν, ὅραμα, ἅμα.

The "we" sections have in common with St. Matthew > St. Mark, St. Luke, St. John, and the Acts . . . .   3 words[1] (in 3 places)

---

6 words

The "we" sections have in common with the Acts and St. Mark > St. Matthew, St. Luke, and St. John .   2 words[2]

The "we" sections have in common with St. Mark > St. Matthew, St. Luke, St. John, and the Acts . .   1 word[3] (in 1 place)

---

3 words

The "we" sections have in common with the Acts and St. John > St. Matthew, St. Mark, and St. Luke .   2 words[4]

The "we" sections have in common with St. John > St. Matthew, St. Mark, St. Luke, and the Acts . .   2 words[5] (in 2 places)

---

4 words

---

1 ἀπάντησις, πέλαγος, συστρέφειν (but with another significance).
2 διαγίγνεσθαι and διαλέγεσθαι.
3 πρύμνα.
4 διατρίβειν and the active middle ἰᾶσθαι.
5 σχοινίον, ψῦχος.

The " we" sections have, besides, one word, ἀποκόπτειν, in common with St. Mark and St. John, which is not found in St. Matthew, St. Luke, and the Acts; another, κῦμα, which is not found in St. Luke and the Acts, in common with St. Matthew and St. Mark ; and another, σπεῖρα, not in St. Luke, in common with the Acts and the other three gospels.

If one now considers that of the sixty-four words in common with St. Luke thirty-five are verbs (of the 110 in common with the Acts fifty-five are verbs)—verbs have always great weight in questions of this kind—while of the sixteen words in common with St. Matthew, St. Mark, and St. John only $2+2+2+1=7$ are verbs; if one further considers that we have here omitted all the numerous words and phrases of constant occurrence in the " we " sections and the two great Lukan writings in case they appear, though only rarely, in St. Matthew, St. Mark, and St. John ; if one finally considers that the case is the same with constructions [1] and numerous particles which are sought for in vain, or almost in vain, in those other writings (e.g., multiplication of particles, ὡς in temporal clauses, εἰ in the sense of ἐπεί, εἰ with optative, μὲν οὖν, τε connecting

---

[1] The reader will pardon me for not over-burdening him with details on this point as well as on the question whether the words in common are always used with the same significance. If, however, such an investigation should be considered necessary—for my part the dead weight of the facts disclosed in the lists seems conclusive enough—I am prepared to show that from this side also we meet with confirmation, not refutation, of our position. Meanwhile, the remarks I have made on these points in the notes on the " we " sections of chaps. xvi. and xxviii., and those of Klostermann (loc. cit.) on questions of syntax in chap. xxvii., may suffice.

a new sentence, the continuation of the narrative by means of a relative clause, ἐκεῖσε, καθ' ὃν τρόπον, ἄφνω, κἀκεῖθεν, τὰ νῦν, ἄχρις οὗ, ἐπί with acc. of time, μόλις, πάντως, τὰ περί τινος, &c., &c.)—surely one can only say that there is but one unquestionable verdict to be given: *the " we " sections and the Acts of the Apostles have one and the same author.* We cannot explain such constant coincidence as due to accident; nor can we suppose that some " source " has here been worked up by a later hand, for on this hypothesis the source must have been revised line by line, and even word by word, and yet the reviser actually allowed the " we " to stand! There is no basis even for the hypothesis that the " we " source includes the greater part of chaps. xiii., xiv., xvi.-xxviii.; for though the relationship of the " we " sections with Acts i.-xii., xv., and St. Luke's gospel is not so close as with xiii., xiv., xvi.-xxviii. (the proportion is 88 : 67) it is nevertheless close enough to remain unintelligible on such an hypothesis.[1]

The proof is thus complete;[2] nor can its conclusiveness be shaken by comparing the " we " sections

---

[1] That the relationship with the second half of the Acts should be closer than that with the first half and St. Luke's gospel is not astonishing, seeing that in the former case the subject-matter of each is more nearly allied.

[2] The internal evidence will be discussed later. I would here give a short sketch of the method of Hawkins in marshalling the linguistic evidence for the identity of authorship.

(1) At the beginning of his work he draws up lists of 86 words and phrases in St. Matthew, 37 in St. Mark, 140 in St. Luke, which very frequently occur in each of these writers, namely, 841 times, 314 times, 1435 and 1235 times respectively (the last number referring to

and the remaining parts of the Acts with the vocabulary
of St. Paul; for the relationship with the Pauline

the Acts apart from the "we" sections), while they are of much
rarer occurrence in the other two. Now in the "we" sections these
Lukan phrases occur in 110 passages, *i.e.*—very nearly as often as in
St. Mark, although the latter is just seven times as long. In
St. Matthew they occur only 207 times, although it is eleven times
the length of the "we" sections. On the other hand, the phrases
characteristic of St. Matthew occur only eighteen times in the "we"
sections, those characteristic of St. Mark only eight times. What a
contrast to the 110 occurrences of Lukan phrases! If, however, one
considers only the phrases themselves, apart from the frequency of
occurrence, we find of the 86 phrases characteristic of St. Matthew
only 10 in the "we" sections, of the 37 Markan only 6, but of the
140 Lukan 43! That is, $\frac{1}{8}$ (St. Matthew), $\frac{1}{6}$ (St. Mark), $\frac{1}{3}$ (St. Luke)!
Hawkins may well say (p. 160): "Such evidence of unity of author-
ship, drawn from a comparison of the language of the three synoptic
gospels, appears to me irresistible. Is it not utterly improbable that
the language of the original writer of the 'we' sections should have
chanced to have so very many more correspondences with the language of the subsequent 'compiler' than with that of Matthew or
Mark?"

Next Hawkins draws up a list of the words of the whole New
Testament (not only of the gospels and Acts, as we have done), which
are found only in the "we" sections and in the Acts. There are
21 words occurring 28 times in the "we" sections, 46 times in the
remaining chapters of the Acts. Then comes a list of the words
which are found only in the "we" sections and St. Luke's gospel
("with or without the rest of Acts"). There are 16 words (29
times in the "we" sections, 25 times in St. Luke, 23 times in the
rest of Acts). Then Hawkins, after giving another list of a great
number of words (and phrases) which are characteristic of the "we"
sections and the Lukan writings (though they occur rarely elsewhere
in the New Testament), concludes with the remark: "On the whole,
then, there is an immense balance of internal and linguistic evidence
in favour of the view that the original writer of these sections was
the same person as the main author of the Acts and of the third
gospel, and, consequently, that the date of those books lies within
the lifetime of a companion of St. Paul." An involuntary confirmation of these statements is given also by Vogel ("Charakteristik des

vocabulary is in the "we" sections not closer, but less close, than in the other chapters of the Acts.

Lukas," 2 Aufl. s. 61–68).   He has instituted a comparison of the vocabulary of St. Luke and the Acts *without paying separate attention to the "we" sections*.   He produces :

I. 57 words (in 92 passages of Acts) which occur elsewhere in the New Testament only in St. Luke's gospel.

II. 41 words (in 85 passages of Acts) occurring in St. Luke, but elsewhere in the New Testament of only isolated occurrence.

III. 33 words (in 50 passages of Acts) which are especially characteristic of St. Luke and the Acts.

Thus in all 131 *words in* 227 *passages*.   Of these words the "we" sections show under I. 13 words in 14 passages, under II. 5 words in 8 passages, under III. 4 words in 5 passages ; *thus altogether* 22 *words in* 27 *passages*.   As the "we" sections form a small tenth part of the Acts, we should expect 12 (13) words in 22 passages.   *The "we" sections, therefore, are in language more closely allied to St. Luke's gospel than are the remaining parts of the Acts*.   Finally Vogel has also gathered together a number of "favourite expressions" of St. Luke which are found in both his writings (far more than 100 occurrences in each), while they are rare in the other writings of the New Testament.   Again, he absolutely ignores the problem of the "we" sections, *and yet of these twenty most important words no less than twelve occur also in this part of the Acts*.   I myself have made a calculation which affords a yet more striking result.   St. Luke's gospel and the Acts have in common about 203 different words (a few phrases included) which are wanting in St. Matthew, St. Mark, and St. John ; of these 203 words no less than 63 occur in the "we" sections (20 exclusively here), although these sections comprise only a small tenth of the Acts.   Now no one denies the identity of the author of St. Luke with the author of the Acts ; *and yet the lexical and linguistic relationship between the "we" sections and St. Luke's gospel is supported by twice the amount of evidence that can be alleged for the relationship between the rest of the Acts and this gospel.   How can it, then, be denied that the author of the "we" sections and of the Acts is one and the same man !*   In the 480 verses of Acts i.–xii. and xv. there stand about 132 words in common with St. Luke's gospel which are not found in St. Matthew, St. Mark, and St.

I therefore refrain from considering the matter in detail.[1]

Against the proof of the identity of the author of the " we " sections with the author of the whole work [2] it is possible, so far as I can see, to raise the following objections : [3] (1) The ἅπαξ λεγόμενα are more numerous in the " we " sections than in other parts of the Acts ; (2) the author of the third gospel and the Acts has plainly used written sources for other passages of his great work, transforming them in accordance with his own style ; it is thus possible that, in spite of all arguments to the contrary, the case is the same with the so-called " we " sections.

As regards the first objection, the number of ἅπαξ λεγόμενα in the " we " sections is certainly very large. We can, indeed, point to about 111 words which are not found elsewhere in the Acts and St. Luke's gospel.

John, and in the 527 verses of Acts xiii., xiv., xvi.-xxviii., about 141 such words. *But in the 97 verses of the "we" sections there are about 63 such words, when, judging from proportion, we should only expect to find about 26.*

[1] We have above (pp. 19 ff.) described the relationship of St. Luke's gospel to St. Paul (so far as vocabulary is concerned) as compared with that of the other gospels. In order to illustrate the relationship of the " we " sections to the Apostle it may suffice to point out that of the 105 words of the " we " sections which are not found in the rest of the Acts and the gospel only 11 occur in the Pauline epistles.

[2] Attempts to weaken the force of too striking coincidences between the " we " sections and the remaining parts of the work by the hypothesis of interpolations are unavailing ; for in this case more than three-quarters, if not all, the verses of the " we " sections would have to be regarded as interpolated.

[3] I here for the moment neglect the objections raised by the Higher Criticism.

This proportion is much greater than in the remaining parts of the work. For example, in the 480 verses of i.–xii., xv., there are only 188 words which are wanting in the rest of the Acts and St. Luke.[1] According to this proportion, only 38 ἅπαξ λεγόμενα should occur in the " we " sections, while in reality there are nearly three times as many. We attain the same result by means of the following comparison : In the whole of the Acts there are about 657 words (proper names excluded) which are wanting in St. Luke. In the " we " sections, therefore, which form about one-tenth of the Acts, there ought to be about 67 such words ; but there are really 162—thus two and a half times as many as we should expect.

As soon as we turn to the subject-matter it is at once seen what treacherous ground is afforded by these statistics. The twenty-seventh chapter of the Acts, which comprises nearly half of the " we " sections (forty-four verses), and some other verses besides of the same sections, contain subject-matter of a peculiar kind such as finds no parallel in the rest of the book—narratives of voyages and of the shipwreck. Three-fifths of the ἅπ. λεγ. belong to the latter narrative,[2] and the wonder is

1 One must count upon a small error here, but I think that the numbers are right on the whole.

2 That is, about sixty-nine. They are as follows : ἄγκυρα, αἰγιαλός, ἀντικρύ, ἀντοφθαλμεῖν [τῷ ἀνέμῳ], ἀποβολή, ἀποκόπτειν, ἀπορρίπτειν, ἀποφορτίζεσθαι, ἀρτέμων, ἀσάλευτος, ἆσσον, ἀσιτία, ἄσιτος, αὐτόχειρ, βοήθεια, βολίζειν, βραδυπλοεῖν, γόμος, διανύειν [τὸν πλοῦν], διαπλεῖν, διθάλασσος, ἐκβολή, ἐκκολυμβᾶν, ἐνβιβάζειν, ἐπιγίγνεσθαι, ἐπισκευάζεσθαι, ἐπισφαλής, ἀποκέλλειν, ἐρείδειν, εὐθυδρομεῖν, εὐρακύλων, ζευκτηρία, ζημία, κολυμβᾶν, κουφίζειν, κῦμα, κυβερνήτης, λιμήν, λίψ, ναύκληρος, ναῦς, ναύτης, νησίον, ὀργυιά, παραβάλλειν, παραλέγεσθαι, παράσημος, παραχειμάζειν, παραχει-

not that their number is here so great, but rather *that, even in chapter xxvii., in spite of this new subject-matter, the accustomed style and vocabulary of the writer are verse by verse most clearly distinguishable.*

Subtracting these *termini technici*, there then remain in the " we " sections the following ἄπ. λεγ. : ἀναδέχεσθαι, ἀπάντησις, ἀπασπάζεσθαι, (ἀσμένως), αὐγή, οἱ βάρβαροι, βούλημα, δεσμώτης, δευτεραῖος, διατελεῖν, διαφεύγειν, δυσεντερία, οἱ ἐντόπιοι, ἐξαρτίζειν, τῇ ἑτέρᾳ, ἑτοίμως ἔχειν, (εὐαγγελιστής), εὐθυμεῖν, θάρσος, θέρμη, θυρίς, καθάπτειν, κορεννύναι, μαντεύεσθαι, μεταβάλλεσθαι, μετρίως, παραινεῖν, παρατείνειν, πεζεύειν, περιαιρεῖν, πίμπρασθαι, (πορφυρόπωλις), πρός with genit., (πυθών), πυρά, συνπεριλαμβάνειν, συνθρύπτειν, συστρέφειν, σφοδρῶς, (τρίστεγον), φιλανθρωπία, φιλανθρώπως, φιλοφρόνως, (φρύγανον), χρῆσθαι.

This number (39–45), in proportion to the number of ἄπ. λεγ. in the whole work, is no longer too large. Striking singularities, of course, still remain. Among these I reckon οἱ βάρβαροι, βούλημα, δεσμώτης, οἱ ἐντόπιοι, θάρσος, φιλανθρωπία, as also μετρίως and σφοδρῶς, and among verbs διατελεῖν, ἑτοίμως ἔχειν, εὐθυμεῖν κορεννύναι, παραινεῖν, παρατείνειν, χρῆσθαι, and lastly τῇ ἑτέρᾳ and πρός with genit.[1] But the number of these singularities is scarcely greater than that we

μασία, πέλαγος, περικρατής [τῆς σκάφης], πηδάλιον, πλοῦς, προσεᾶν, πρύμνα, πρώρα, σανίς, σκάφη, σκευή, σχοινίον, τυφωνικός, ὕβρις, ὑποζωννύναι, ὑποπλεῖν, ὑποπνέειν, ὑποτρέχειν, χειμάζεσθαι, χῶρος, ψῦχος. A few of these, although used here in connection with navigation, seem to have been borrowed from the vocabulary of medicine (*vide infra*).

1 πρός in this construction does not occur elsewhere in the whole New Testament.

find in every chapter of the Acts. It is therefore hopeless to build upon them the hypothesis of a separate written source, especially as no difference of style (construction and particles) exists between the " we " sections and the remaining chapters of the Acts.

As regards the question of the sources of the third gospel and the Acts, the subject is, as is well known, one of very strenuous controversy. But one fact stands fast: the third Evangelist copied the work of the second. Nearly three-fourths of the text of St. Mark appears again in St. Luke, and throughout almost exactly in the Markan order. We thus possess a source of considerable content, and are able to compare the copyist with the original. With what result? In spite of all the freedom with which the author of the third gospel treats his source,[1] the style, the syntax, and also the vocabulary of that source are still everywhere apparent (cf. the works of Wernle and Wellhausen on the synoptists), although comparison is rendered difficult by the fact that the Greek and the general literary style of St. Mark are more closely allied to St. Luke than are, for example, the styles of St. Paul and St. John. I take the following two sections at random :

---

1 The text of St. Mark is considerably edited by St. Luke in the interest of a more correct Greek style. It is in places amplified by comments and other corrections which the editor regarded as improvements. Moreover, in numerous sections it is combined with matter from other sources.

St. Mark i. 21 : καὶ εἰσπορεύονται εἰς Καφαρναούμ. καὶ εὐθὺς τοῖς σάββασιν ἐδίδασκεν εἰς τὴν συναγωγήν.

St. Luke iv. 30 f. : καὶ κατῆλθεν εἰς Καφαρναοὺμ πόλιν τῆς Γαλιλαίας. καὶ ἦν διδάσκων αὐτοὺς ἐν τοῖς σάββασιν.

κατῆλθεν]. Because Jesus comes from Nazareth, the singular also depends upon what precedes.—πόλ. τ. Γαλ.]. St. Luke presupposes in his readers no knowledge of Palestine.—εὐθύς]. St. Luke avoids, on artistic grounds, the repetition of this favourite word of St. Mark. See also iv. 33, 37.—αὐτούς]. St. Luke here avoids leaving διδάσκειν without an object.—ἦν διδάσκων]. From St. Mark i. 22.

(22) καὶ ἐξεπλήσσοντο ἐπὶ τῇ διδαχῇ αὐτοῦ, ἦν γὰρ διδάσκων αὐτοὺς ὡς ἐξουσίαν ἔχων καὶ οὐχ ὡς οἱ γραμματεῖς.

(32) καὶ ἐξεπλήσσοντο ἐπὶ τῇ διδαχῇ αὐτοῦ, ὅτι ἐν ἐξουσίᾳ ἦν ὁ λόγος αὐτοῦ.

Simplification of style ; the form and sense is improved by the insertion of ὁ λόγος.

(23) καὶ εὐθὺς ἦν ἐν τῇ συναγωγῇ αὐτῶν ἄνθρωπος ἐν πνεύματι ἀκαθάρτῳ, καὶ ἀνέκραξεν λέγων·

(33) καὶ ἐν τῇ συναγωγῇ ἦν ἄνθρωπος ἔχων πνεῦμα δαιμόνιον καὶ ἀνέκραξεν φωνῇ μεγάλῃ·

The indefinite αὐτῶν is erased, the Hebraic ἐν is replaced by ἔχων, the indefinite ἀκαθάρτῳ by δαιμόνιον, the weak λέγων by φωνῇ μεγάλῃ.

(24) Τί ἡμῖν καὶ σοί, Ἰησοῦ Ναζαρηνέ; ἦλθες ἀπολέσαι ἡμᾶς; οἶδά σε τίς εἶ, ὁ ἅγιος τοῦ θεοῦ.

(34) [ἔα], τί ἡμῖν καὶ σοί, Ἰησοῦ Ναζαρηνέ; ἦλθες ἀπολέσαι ἡμᾶς; οἶδά σε τίς εἶ, ὁ ἅγιος τοῦ θεοῦ.

(25) καὶ ἐπετίμησεν αὐτῷ ὁ Ἰησοῦς [λέγων]· Φιμώθητι καὶ ἔξελθε ἐξ αὐτοῦ.

(35) καὶ ἐπετίμησεν αὐτῷ ὁ Ἰησοῦς λέγων· Φιμώθητι καὶ ἔξελθε ἀπ' αὐτοῦ.

ἀπὸ for ἐξ is an improvement.

(26) καὶ σπαράξαν αὐτὸν τὸ πνεῦμα τὸ

καὶ ῥίψαν αὐτὸν τὸ δαιμόνιον εἰς τὸ μέσον

St. Luke replaces the vulgar σπαράξαν

ἀκάθαρτον καὶ φωνῆσαν φωνῇ μεγάλῃ ἐξῆλθεν ἐξ αὐτοῦ.	ἐξῆλθεν ἀπ᾽ αὐτοῦ μηδὲν βλάψαν αὐτόν. [Probably ἀνακραυγάσαν τε should be read in place of εἰς τὸ μέσον.]	by ῥίψαν, φων. φων. μεγ. by the better word ἀνακραυγ. The addition of μηδὲν βλαψ. αὐτ. seemed necessary to one who was a physician.
(27) καὶ ἐθαμβήθησαν ἅπαντες, ὥστε συνζητεῖν αὐτοὺς λέγοντας· Τί ἐστιν τοῦτο; διδαχὴ καινή· κατ᾽ ἐξουσίαν καὶ τοῖς πνεύμασι τοῖς ἀκαθάρτοις ἐπιτάσσει, καὶ ὑπακούουσιν αὐτῷ.	(36) καὶ ἐγένετο θάμβος ἐπὶ πάντας, καὶ συνελάλουν πρὸς ἀλλήλους λέγοντες· τίς ὁ λόγος οὗτος, ὅτι ἐν ἐξουσίᾳ καὶ δυνάμει ἐπιτάσσει τοῖς ἀκαθάρτοις πνεύμασιν καὶ ἐξέρχονται;	θαμβεῖσθαι never used by St. Luke, θάμβος only a few times.—The more refined ἅπαντες occurs perhaps twice in St. Mark ; in St. Luke it is found thirty-six times.—συλλαλεῖν is more precise than συζητεῖν.—ἐθαμβ. ὥστε is awkward, and is therefore corrected. In what follows St. Luke adds touches which give greater clearness and precision.
(28) καὶ ἐξῆλθεν ἡ ἀκοὴ αὐτοῦ εὐθὺς πανταχοῦ εἰς ὅλην τὴν περίχωρον τῆς Γαλιλαίας.	(37) καὶ ἐξεπορεύετο ἦχος περὶ αὐτοῦ εἰς πάντα τόπον τῆς περιχώρου.	The corrections themselves emphasise the vulgarisms of St. Mark.

The source is, as one sees, on the whole only slightly altered (some characteristic idioms and solecisms of St. Mark are nevertheless erased); moreover, its peculiar style here stands out clearly in comparison with those parts in which St. Luke could give himself freer rein, for it is evident that in chap. iii. s.s. he has kept as closely as possible to the already existing type of gospel narrative. Compare the καί beginning a new sentence ten times repeated (just as in the source, and quite in

opposition to his own style);[1] also the expressions
ὁ ἅγιος τοῦ θεοῦ and φιμοῦν, which are not found elsewhere in St. Luke.

St. Mark ii. 1	St. Luke v. 17	
St. Mark ii. 1: καὶ εἰσελθὼν πάλιν εἰς Καφαρναοὺμ δι' ἡμερῶν ἠκούσθη ὅτι ἐν οἴκῳ ἐστίν. (2) καὶ συνήχθησαν πολλοὶ ὥστε μηκέτι χωρεῖν μηδὲ τὰ πρὸς τὴν θύραν, καὶ ἐλάλει αὐτοῖς τὸν λόγον.	St. Luke v. 17: καὶ ἐγένετο ἐν μιᾷ τῶν ἡμερῶν καὶ αὐτὸς ἦν διδάσκων, καὶ ἦσαν καθήμενοι Φαρισαῖοι καὶ νομοδιδάσκαλοι οἳ ἦσαν ἐληλυθότες ἐκ πάσης κώμης τῆς Γαλιλαίας καὶ Ἰουδαίας καὶ Ἰερουσαλήμ· καὶ δύναμις κυρίου ἦν εἰς τὸ ἰᾶσθαι αὐτόν. [The structure of the clause has been probably corrupted in course of transmission.]	This καὶ ἐγένετο, although not a Greek literary idiom, is yet Lukan. St. Luke has purposely adopted this Biblical phrase. Elsewhere this passage does not afford points for comparison; note only that parts of St. Mark ii. 6 are transferred here quite appropriately, and are therefore wanting in St. Luke v. 21. St. Luke has thus considered the whole section before he transformed it in detail.
(3) καὶ ἔρχονται φέροντες πρὸς αὐτὸν παραλυτικὸν αἰρόμενον ὑπὸ τεσσάρων. (4) καὶ μὴ δυνάμενοι προσενέγκαι αὐτῷ διὰ τὸν ὄχλον ἀπεστέγα-	(18) καὶ ἰδοὺ ἄνδρες φέροντες ἐπὶ κλίνης ἄνθρωπον ὃς ἦν παραλελυμένος, καὶ ἐζήτουν αὐτὸν εἰσενεγκεῖν καὶ θεῖναι ἐνώπιον αὐτοῦ. (19) καὶ μὴ εὑρόντες ποίας εἰσενέγκωσιν αὐ-	καὶ ἰδού never found in St. Mark; in St. Luke καὶ ἰδού and ἰδού γάρ occur thirty times in the gospel and about a dozen times in the Acts—chaps. i., v., viii., ix., x., xi.,

[1] Vogel ("Charakteristik des Lukas," 2 Aufl., 1899, s. 32) has discussed St. Luke's various methods of beginning a sentence, but he
has not drawn the final conclusion. If we, with him, compare 100
beginnings of sentences in the gospel with a similar number in the
second part of the Acts we arrive at the following result :

	καί	δέ	τε	Other particles	Without particle
Gospel .	50	36	1	6	7
Acts .	16	51	9	16	8

Accordingly καί preponderates in the gospel by three times. If, however, one subtracts all the cases in which the καί is derived from St.
Mark, then the relation of καί to δέ is much the same in both writings.

σαν τὴν στέγην ὅπου
ἦν, καὶ ἐξορύξαντες
χαλῶσι τὸν κράβαττον
ὅπου ὁ παραλυτικὸς
κατέκειτο.

τὸν διὰ τὸν ὄχλον,
ἀναβάντες ἐπὶ τὸ δῶμα
διὰ τῶν κεράμων κα-
θῆκαν αὐτὸν σὺν τῷ
κλινιδίῳ εἰς τὸ μέσον
ἔμπροσθεν τοῦ Ἰησοῦ.

xii., xiii., xvi., xx., xxvii. ("we" section). φέροντες]. St. Luke has an objection to such subjectless verbs and supplies ἄνδρες, and also a substantive (ἄνθρωπον) as object. — παραλελ.]. So always for παραλυτικός, which is a vulgar idiom.—In verses 18 and 19 St. Luke has completely revised the text (the reason is probably correctly given by Wellhausen); the coincidences which remain are underlined.

(5) καὶ ἰδὼν ὁ Ἰησοῦς τὴν πίστιν αὐτῶν λέγει τῷ παραλυτικῷ· Τέκνον, ἀφίενταί σου αἱ ἁμαρτίαι.

(20) καὶ ἰδὼν τὴν πίστιν αὐτῶν εἶπεν· Ἄνθρωπε, ἀφέωνταί σοι αἱ ἁμαρτίαι σου.

ὁ Ἰησοῦς is deleted as superfluous; so also τῷ παραλυτικῷ. Τέκνον perhaps seemed too familiar. The addition of σοι is difficult to explain (see also verse 23).

(6) ἦσαν δέ τινες τῶν γραμματέων ἐκεῖ καθήμενοι καὶ διαλογιζόμενοι ἐν ταῖς καρδίαις αὐτῶν·
(7) τί οὗτος οὕτως λαλεῖ; βλασφημεῖ· τίς δύναται ἀφιέναι ἁμαρτίας εἰ μὴ εἷς ὁ θεός;

(21) καὶ ἤρξαντο διαλογίζεσθαι οἱ γραμματεῖς καὶ οἱ Φαρισαῖοι λέγοντες· τίς ἐστιν οὗτος ὃς λαλεῖ βλασφημίας; τίς δύναται ἁμαρτίας ἀφεῖναι εἰ μὴ μόνος ὁ θεός;

Vide the note on verse 17. ἐν τ. καρδ. is here omitted because it occurs again in verse 8 of St. Mark = verse 22. The jagged sentences are fitted together; the slovenly εἷς is changed into the more correct μόνος. At the beginning ἤρξαντο is inserted (not in accordance with St. Luke's own style, but with that Biblical style which he imitates).

(8) καὶ εὐθὺς ἐπιγνοὺς ὁ Ἰησοῦς τῷ πνεύματι αὐτοῦ ὅτι οὕτως διαλογίζονται ἐν ἑαυτοῖς λέγει αὐτοῖς· τί ταῦτα διαλογίζεσθε ἐν ταῖς καρδίαις ὑμῶν;	(22) ἐπιγνοὺς δὲ ὁ Ἰησοῦς τοὺς διαλογισμοὺς αὐτῶν ἀποκριθεὶς εἶπεν πρὸς αὐτούς· τί διαλογίζεσθε ἐν ταῖς καρδίαις ὑμῶν;	καὶ εὐθύς deleted (*vide supra*), likewise τ. πνεύμ. αὐτ. as quite superfluous; the objective clause is replaced by a simple substantive; ἀποκριθεὶς is inserted according to St. Luke's custom, giving a certain effect of solemnity; the awkward ταῦτα is omitted.
(9) τί ἐστιν εὐκοπώτερον, εἰπεῖν τῷ παραλυτικῷ· ἀφίενταί σου αἱ ἁμαρτίαι, ἢ εἰπεῖν· ἔγειρε καὶ ἆρον τὸν κράβαττόν σου καὶ περιπάτει;	(23) τί ἐστιν εὐκοπώτερον, εἰπεῖν· ἀφέωνταί σοι αἱ ἁμαρτίαι σου, ἢ εἰπεῖν· ἔγειρε καὶ περιπάτει;	τῷ παραλυτ. is omitted as superfluous, likewise καὶ ἆρ. τ. κράβ. σου. The Word of Jesus gains in force through this abbreviation; besides, these words occur in the following verse, where they are in a more suitable position.
(10, 11) ἵνα δὲ εἰδῆτε ὅτι ἐξουσίαν ἔχει ὁ υἱὸς τοῦ ἀνθρώπου ἐπὶ τῆς γῆς ἀφιέναι ἁμαρτίας, λέγει τῷ παραλυτικῷ· σοὶ λέγω, ἔγειρε, ἆρον τὸν κράβαττόν σου καὶ ὕπαγε εἰς τὸν οἶκόν σου.	(24) ἵνα δὲ εἰδῆτε ὅτι ὁ υἱὸς τοῦ ἀνθρώπου ἐξουσίαν ἔχει ἐπὶ τῆς γῆς ἀφιέναι ἁμαρτίας, εἶπεν τῷ παραλελυμένῳ· σοὶ λέγω, ἔγειρε καὶ ἄρας τὸ κλινίδιόν σου πορεύου εἰς τὸν οἶκόν σου.	The subject is placed first as so often with St. Luke. Note at the close the participial construction so constant with this author. κράβαττον is avoided as a vulgarism by St. Luke in the gospel. Neither does he care for ὕπαγε; this word is wanting in the Acts, and is rare in the gospel, while it is found twenty times in St. Matthew and fifteen times in St. Mark.

Here also the constant occurrence of καί at the beginning of sentences is for every careful reader of the Acts an evident proof that the author is following a source and not speaking in his own words. Otherwise the narrative is in detail (in style) so much altered and polished that the special character of the source is not immediately discernible. The broad style of the narrative, however, facilitates such corrections. In so far this passage can scarcely be compared with the concisely written " we " sections of the Acts ; but it must be evident to every one that the author who wrote St. Luke i. 1 ff. or the " we " sections or the discourse delivered upon Areopagus could not have written St. Luke v. 17–24 as it stands if he had not been following a " source."

It is most instructive to notice here and in dozens of other places how St. Luke, in his correction and revision of the Markan text, endeavours to imitate the phraseology of the Bible (or of St. Mark). As far as he can he patches the garment with cloth of the same material.

Besides St. Mark, we can distinguish a second source underlying the third gospel, whence are derived those sections which in subject-matter coincide with St. Matthew. In regard to extent and exact wording this source cannot be determined with certainty, yet for a number of sections it may be made out quite clearly and unmistakably. How has St. Luke used this source, which consists principally of sayings and discourses of our Lord ?

(St. Matthew vii. 3)	(St. Luke vi. 41)	Almost all the divergences of St. Luke from St. Matthew in this passage are evidently and clearly stylistic corrections.
τί δὲ βλέπεις τὸ κάρφος τὸ ἐν τῷ ὀφθαλμῷ τοῦ ἀδελφοῦ σου, τὴν δὲ ἐν τῷ σῷ ὀφθαλμῷ δοκὸν οὐ κατανοεῖς ;	τί δὲ βλέπεις τὸ κάρφος τὸ ἐν τῷ ὀφθαλμῷ τοῦ ἀδελφοῦ σου, τὴν δὲ δοκὸν τὴν ἐν τῷ ἰδίῳ ὀφθαλμῷ οὐ κατανοεῖς ;	
(4) ἢ πῶς ἐρεῖς τῷ ἀδελφῷ σου· ἄφες ἐκβάλω τὸ κάρφος ἐκ τοῦ ὀφθαλμοῦ σου, καὶ ἰδοὺ ἡ δοκὸς ἐν τῷ ὀφθαλμῷ σου ;	(42) πῶς δύνασαι λέγειν τῷ ἀδελφῷ σου· ἀδελφέ, ἄφες ἐκβάλω τὸ κάρφος τὸ ἐν τῷ ὀφθαλμῷ σου, αὐτὸς τὴν ἐν τῷ ὀφθαλμῷ σου δοκὸν οὐ βλέπων ; ὑπο-	
(5) ὑποκριτά, ἔκβαλε πρῶτον ἐκ τοῦ ὀφθαλ-μοῦ σου τὴν δοκόν, καὶ τότε διαβλέψεις ἐκβα-λεῖν τὸ κάρφος ἐκ τοῦ ὀφθαλμοῦ τοῦ ἀδελφοῦ σου.	κριτά, ἔκβαλε πρῶτον τὴν δοκὸν ἐκ τοῦ ὀφθαλμοῦ σου, καὶ τότε διαβλέψεις τὸ κάρφος τὸ ἐν τῷ ὀφθαλμῷ τοῦ ἀδελφοῦ σου ἐκβαλεῖν.	

ἀφιέναι occurs only twice in the Acts (in v. 38 ἐάσατε should probably be read), and is therefore to be regarded as a word which has come into the gospel, where it frequently occurs, as a rule from the sources. Also ἐκβάλλειν τὸ κάρφος would scarcely have been written by St. Luke if he had not found it in his authority. Ὑποκριτής is likewise quite alien to the Acts, and the very unusual word διαβλέπειν never again occurs in the gospel and the Acts. And so, even if St. Matthew were not in existence, we should conclude that our author here depends upon a written source.

Let us consider one other passage :

(St. Matthew viii. 8)	(St. Luke vii. 6)	μὴ σκύλλου as in St. Mark v. 35 = St. Luke viii. 49.
ἀποκριθεὶς δὲ ὁ ἑκατόν-ταρχος ἔφη· κύριε, οὐκ εἰμὶ ἱκανὸς ἵνα μου ὑπὸ τὴν στέγην εἰσέλθῃς· ἀλλὰ μόνον εἰπὲ λόγῳ, καὶ ἰαθήσεται ὁ παῖς μου.	ὁ ἑκατοντάρχης λέγων αὐτῷ· κύριε, μὴ σκύλ-λου· οὐ γὰρ ἱκανός εἰμι ἵνα ὑπὸ τὴν στέγην μου εἰσέλθῃς. (7) ἀλλὰ εἰπὲ λόγῳ, καὶ ἰαθήτω ὁ παῖς μου.	

(9) καὶ γὰρ ἐγὼ ἄνθρωπός εἰμι ὑπὸ ἐξουσίαν, ἔχων ὑπ' ἐμαυτὸν στρατιώτας, καὶ λέγω τούτῳ· πορεύθητι, καὶ πορεύεται, καὶ ἄλλῳ· ἔρχου, καὶ ἔρχεται, καὶ τῷ δούλῳ μου· ποίησον τοῦτο, καὶ ποιεῖ.	(8) καὶ γὰρ ἐγὼ ἄνθρωπός εἰμι ὑπὸ ἐξουσίαν τασσόμενος, ἔχων ὑπ' ἐμαυτὸν στρατιώτας, καὶ λέγω τούτῳ· πορεύθητι, καὶ πορεύεται, καὶ ἄλλῳ· ἔρχου, καὶ ἔρχεται, καὶ τῷ δούλῳ μου· ποίησον τοῦτο, καὶ ποιεῖ.	τασσόμενος]. A stylistic improvement.
(10) ἀκούσας δὲ ὁ Ἰησοῦς ἐθαύμασεν καὶ εἶπεν τοῖς ἀκολοθοῦσιν· ἀμὴν λέγω ὑμῖν, παρ' οὐδενὶ τοσαύτην πίστιν ἐν τῷ Ἰσραὴλ εὗρον.	(9) ἀκούσας δὲ ταῦτα ὁ Ἰησοῦς ἐθαύμασεν αὐτὸν καὶ στραφεὶς τῷ ἀκολοθοῦντι αὐτῷ ὄχλῳ εἶπεν· λέγω ὑμῖν, οὐδὲ ἐν τῷ Ἰσραὴλ τοσαύτην πίστιν εὗρον.	The insertion of the objects is Lukan. στραφείς is wanting in St. Matthew and St. Mark; with St. Luke it is found eight times in the gospel (similar words yet oftener). The foreign word ἀμήν is also elsewhere omitted by St. Luke. οὐδὲ ἐν τ. Ἰσρ. is simpler, better, and more nervous Greek.

The corrections of St. Luke have not obliterated the special characteristics of the source. Ἱκανὸς ἵνα is never used by St. Luke in the Acts, and even in the gospel we find only ἱκανὸς λῦσαι. Εἰσέρχεσθαι ὑπό is found nowhere else in the gospel and Acts, although εἰσέρχεσθαι is used about eighty-six times. Also, εἰπεῖν with the dative λόγῳ is an idiom foreign to St. Luke, as also ὑπὸ ἐξουσίαν. Καὶ γάρ occurs only once in the Acts (xix. 40); in the gospel it is more frequent, because derived from the sources.

There is no need to continue this comparison or sayings of our Lord which are common to St. Luke and St. Matthew. Wernle (*loc. cit.*, s. 81) has rightly perceived that all the alterations made by St. Luke—as

regards a definite, fairly large body of these sayings [1]—
are of a very slight nature, and testify rather to the
faithfulness with which, on the whole, these sayings
have been reproduced.[2] This faithfulness extends even
to the preservation of the style of the language ; so
that no one can fail to perceive that we here have to
reckon with a written source.

But, it is said, though in the gospel (iii.-xxiv.) the
linguistic character of the sources employed is clearly
preserved, yet St. Luke i. and ii. and Acts i.-xii., xv.,
are certainly based upon written sources, in spite of
the fact that the style and vocabulary of these chapters
is entirely and absolutely Lukan ; therefore it is.
possible that the " we " sections also, in spite of their
Lukan character, are based upon a written source. Let
us, then, first investigate St. Luke i. and ii. I begin
by stating the result of this investigation :

The vocabulary and style characteristic of St. Luke
i. and ii. are so absolutely Lukan that, in spite of all
conjectures that have been made, the hypothesis of
a Greek source is impossible, for there is almost nothing
left for it. Two things only are possible : either St.
Luke has here translated an Aramaic source, or he was
dependent for his subject-matter upon no written source
at all, but has followed oral tradition, with which he
has dealt quite freely, so far as form is concerned. Yet

---

[1] The case is, of course, different with some other sayings, but it is
to me doubtful whether these come from the same source. I conjecture, partly on the ground of Wellhausen's remarks, that St. Luke
also possessed an Aramaic source, which he translated himself.

[2] *Cf.* also Vogel, *loc. cit.*, s. 38.

these two hypotheses are not of equal probability; for the second alone is free from difficulty, while the first presupposes much that is hard to reconcile with the facts. At all events, the two great psalms of St. Luke i. and ii. were not handed down to the author (either in Greek or Aramaic), but were composed by himself.

I investigate i. 5-15.

(5) ἐγένετο ἐν ταῖς ἡμέραις Ἡρῴδου βασιλέως τῆς Ἰουδαίας ἱερεύς τις ὀνόματι Ζαχαρίας ἐξ ἐφημερίας Ἀβιά, καὶ γυνὴ αὐτῷ ἐκ τῶν θυγατέρων Ἀαρών, καὶ τὸ ὄνομα αὐτῆς Ἐλισάβετ.

It is well known how characteristic of St. Luke is this ἐγένετο. St. Matthew writes ἐν ἡμέραις Ἡρῴδου; St. Luke, however, adds the article here and in iv. 25 (ἐν ταῖς ἡμέραις Ἠλίου), xvii. 26 (ἐν ταῖς ἡμέραις Νῶε), xvii. 28 (ἐν ταῖς ἡμέραις Λώτ), Acts vii. 45 (ἕως τῶν ἡμ. Δαυείδ). ἱερεύς τις ὀνόματι]. St. Luke, and he only, presents this construction about a dozen times in the gospel and the Acts. θυγατέρων Ἀαρών without the article, like θυγατέρα Ἀβραάμ (xiii. 16). Compare for the style Acts xviii. 2: εὑρών τινα Ἰουδαῖον ὀνόματι Ἀκύλαν . . . καὶ Πρίσκιλλαν γυναῖκα αὐτοῦ.

(6) ἦσαν δὲ δίκαιοι ἀμφότεροι ἐναντίον τοῦ θεοῦ, πορευόμενοι . ἐν πάσαις ταῖς ἐντολαῖς καὶ δικαιώμασιν τοῦ κυρίου ἄμεμπτοι.

ἀμφότεροι wanting in St. Mark and St. John, occurring nine times in St. Luke (in St. Matthew three times). ἐναντίον and ἔναντι are found in the New Testament only in St. Luke (six times)—vide St. Luke xx. 26, xxiv. 19, Acts vii. 10, viii. 21, viii. 32. πορευεσθαι is a

G

favourite word of St. Luke. δικαί-
ωμα and ἄμεμτος are not found in
the gospels (yet compare St. Paul).

(7) καὶ οὐκ ἦν
αὐτοῖς τέκνον, κα-
θότι ἦν ἡ Ἐλι-
σάβετ στεῖρα, καὶ
ἀμφότεροι προβε-
βηκότες ἐν ταῖς
ἡμέραις αὐτῶν
ἦσαν.

καθότι occurs in the New Testament only in St. Luke—vide xix. 9,
Acts ii. 24, ii. 45, iv. 35, xvii. 31
(here in the discourse at Athens,
which was certainly composed by St.
Luke himself). With the concluding
words compare St. Luke xvii. 24:
ἐν τῇ ἡμέρᾳ αὐτοῦ—vide note on
verse 5.

(8, 9) ἐγένετο
δὲ ἐν τῷ ἱερατεύ-
ειν αὐτὸν ἐν τῇ
τάξει τῆς ἐφημε-
ρίας αὐτοῦ ἔναντι
τοῦ θεοῦ, κατὰ τὸ
ἔθος τῆς ἱερατείας
ἔλαχε τοῦ θυμιᾶ-
σαι εἰσελθὼν εἰς
τὸν ναὸν τοῦ
κυρίου.

ἐγένετο ἐν τῷ . . . ἔλαχε . . . .
εἰσελθών is one of the constructions
of the New Testament which is
specifically Lukan, though it is confined to the gospel. Concerning
ἔναντι, see note on verse 6 (exclusively Lukan). κατὰ τὸ ἔθος is
likewise exclusively Lukan—vide ii.
42 and xxii. 39; moreover, also, the
word ἔθος is found in St. Luke in all
ten times, elsewhere only in St. John
xix. 40 and Hebrews x. 25. Also
κατὰ τὸ εἰωθός is found only in St.
Luke (iv. 16, and Acts xvii. 2), and
κατὰ τὸ εἰθισμένον only in St. Luke
ii. 27.

(10) καὶ πᾶν τὸ
πλῆθος ἦν τοῦ
λαοῦ προσευχό-
μενον ἔξω τῇ ὥρᾳ
τοῦ θυμιάματος.

ἦν προσευχόμενον]. As is well
known, a favourite construction with
St. Luke, which occurs five times in
many chapters. πλῆθος twenty-five
times in St. Luke, elsewhere in the
gospels only twice in St. Mark and

twice in St. John. πᾶν (ἅπαν) τ. πλῆθος in St. Luke viii. 37, xix. 37 xxiii. 1, Acts vi. 5, xv. 12, xxv. 24 πλῆθος τοῦ λαοῦ]. This characteristic combination is also found in St. Luke vi. 17 (πλῆθος πολὺ τοῦ λαοῦ), xxiii. 27 (πολὺ πλῆθος τοῦ λαοῦ), Acts xxi. 36 (τὸ πλῆθος τοῦ λαοῦ), and nowhere else.

(11) ὤφθη δὲ αὐτῷ ἄγγελος κυρίου ἑστὼς ἐκ δεξιῶν τοῦ θυσιαστηρίου τοῦ θυμιάματος.

ὤφθη occurs once in both St. Matthew and St. Mark, in St. Luke (gospel and Acts) thirteen times. ἄγγελος κυρίου is also found in the Acts—vide v. 19, vii. 30, viii. 26, xii. 7, 23, xxvii. 23; it is wanting in St. Mark and St. John; in St. Matthew it is found at the beginning and end of that book. This angel is therefore quite a speciality of St. Luke, and is introduced by him into trustworthy narrative.

(12) καὶ ἐταράχθη Ζαχαρίας ἰδών, καὶ φόβος ἐπέπεσεν ἐπ' αὐτόν.

ἐταράχθη ἰδών, Lukan.—καὶ φόβος ἐπέπ. επ' αὐτόν]. Besides, only in Acts xix. 17: ἐπέπεσε φόβος ἐπὶ πάντας. Also ἐπιπίπτειν ἐπὶ is only found with St. Luke.

(13) εἶπεν δὲ πρὸς αὐτὸν ὁ ἄγγελος· μὴ φοβοῦ, Ζαχαρία, διότι εἰσηκούσθη ἡ δέησίς σου, καὶ ἡ γυνή σου Ἐλισάβετ γεννήσει

εἶπεν δέ and εἶπεν πρός very frequent with St. Luke; the latter is quite a characteristic of his style, and he often uses εἶπεν δέ when one would expect καί instead. μὴ φοβοῦ never occurs in St. Matthew, once in St. Mark, in St. Luke seven times: vide i. 30, ii. 10, viii. 50, xii. 32, Acts υἱόν σοι, καὶ καλέσεις τὸ ὄνομα αὐτοῦ Ἰωάννην.

xviii. 9, xxvii. 24 ("we" section !). That the name of the person addressed is added is an exclusively Lukan trait—*vide* i. 30, xii. 32, Acts xxvii. 24. διότι occurs in the New Testament only in St. Luke ii. 7, xxi. 28, Acts (x. 20), (xvii. 31), xviii. 10 (twice), xxii. 18. εἰσηκούσθη, of prayers, occurs besides only in Acts x. 31 : εἰσηκούσθη σου ἡ προσευχή (elsewhere in the gospels found only once in St. Matthew vi. 7). δέησις wanting in St. Matthew, St. Mark, and St. John ; see, however, St. Luke ii. 37, v. 33, Acts i. 14 (not certain). ἐγέννησεν, of the mother, only found besides in St. Luke i. 35, 57, xxiii. 29 : κοιλίαι αἳ οὐκ ἐγέννησαν. — σου . . . σοι]. As in St. Luke v. 20, 23.

(14) καὶ ἔσται χαρά σοι καὶ ἀγαλλίασις, καὶ πολλοὶ ἐπὶ τῇ γενέσει αὐτοῦ χαρήσονται.

ἀγαλλίασις wanting in St. Matthew, St. Mark, and St. John ; see, however, St. Luke i. 44, Acts ii. 46 ; ἀγαλλιᾶν four times in St. Luke (among these Acts xvi. 34), wanting in St. Mark, once in St. Matthew. χαίρειν ἐπὶ is found also in xiii. 17 and Acts xv. 31 (once in St. Matthew).

(15) ἔσται γὰρ μέγας ἐνώπιον κυρίου, καὶ οἶνον καὶ σίκερα οὐ μὴ πίῃ, καὶ πνεύματος ἁγίου πλησ-

μέγας]. *Cf.* Acts viii. 9 : εἶναι τινα ἑαυτὸν μέγαν. ἐνώπιον]. Wanting in St. Matthew and St. Mark ; found once in St. John ; occurs in St. Luke about thirty-six times, including one occurrence in the θήσεται ἔτι ἐκ κοιλίας μητρὸς αὐτοῦ. "we" sections (xxvii. 35, ἐνώπιον πάντων, nearly the same in Acts xix. 9). οὐ μή]. Occurs in the Acts, as here, exclusively in quotations from the LXX. πνεύμ. ἁγ. πλησθ. is exclusively Lukan—*vide* i. 41, i. 67, Acts iv. 8, iv. 31, ix. 17, xiii. 9 (πλησθῆναι in St. Luke twenty-two times, never in St. Mark and St. John, in St. Matthew once; πνεῦμα ἅγιον in St. Luke about fifty-three times, rare in the other writers). ἐκ κοιλίας μητρός is found once in St. Matthew, never in St. Mark and St. John, three times in St. Luke (*vide* Acts iii. 2, xiv. 8).

After these remarks there is, I think, no need for me to prove that St. Luke in the above passage has not copied from a Greek source, but has either translated from another language or else has reproduced oral information quite freely in his own literary form. The latter alternative, as every careful critic will allow, is the more probable.

In my paper on the "Magnificat" of Elizabeth ("Sitzungsberichte," 1900, May 17) I have, however, shown, according to the same method, and in great detail, that our author could not have been dependent on a Greek source for St. Luke i. 39-56, i. 68-79, ii. 15-20, ii. 41-52—passages which, verse by verse, betray his own style and vocabulary. I have, moreover, demonstrated, certainly in the case of the "Magnificat" and "Benedictus," that here at last all possibility of even an Aramaic source disappears, and that, apart from suggestions afforded by numerous verses of the Greek Old Testament, all is the creation of St. Luke himself.[1] Since, then, this has been proved for fifty-nine out of 128 verses, we may justly extend our result to the whole of the first two chapters, which form the prelude of St. Luke's gospel. We therefore assert that the hypothesis of a Greek source is impossible,[2] and that the hypothesis of an Aramaic source is, indeed, possible, but not probable, because not suggested by any dependible criteria.[3]

[1] In Appendix I. I have repeated this proof in a yet more detailed form.

[2] There is no force in the objection that the passages which St. Luke has taken from St. Mark are so steeped in his own peculiar style that the source is scarcely discernible, and that it is thus possible that a source may form the basis of chaps. i. and ii. The circumstances are here quite different. The characteristics of the Markan text are still discernible through the Lukan veil, but nothing of the sort appears through the veil of St. Luke i. and ii. The somewhat large proportion of ἅπαξ λεγόμενα in these chapters finds its explanation in the LXX., with the exception of περικρύπτειν (i. 27); but here we may note that such words as περιαιρεῖν, περιαστράπτειν, περίεργος, περιέρχεσθαι, περιέχειν, περιζώννυσθαι, περικρατής, περικυκλοῦν, περιλάμπειν, περιμένειν, περιοικεῖν, περίοικος, περιπίπτειν, περιποιεῖσθαι, περιρρηγνύναι, περισπᾶσθαι, περιτρέπειν, are found in St. Luke (gospel and Acts), while they are wanting in the other gospels. The first half of the hymn of Zacharias, in spite of its *parallelismus membrorum*, is, as I have shown (*loc. cit.*), a regularly formed, continuous Greek period, and by this amalgamation of two distinct styles, as well as by the repeated αὐτοῦ-ἡμῶν of the verse endings, it bears witness more clearly even than the prologue to the stylistic talent of the author.

[3] These sections therefore probably depend upon oral traditions which has been freely treated in regard to form. I may excuse myself from entering into detail upon the question whether St. Luke used for chaps. i. and ii. an Aramaic source (so, *e.g.*, Resch), or was dependent upon oral tradition, seeing that the solution of the problem

The situation is, in fact, the same as in the " we " sections: the style and vocabulary of the writer is everywhere so unmistakably recognisable, even in the minutest details, that a Greek source is excluded.[1]

And yet at the same time the situation is quite different from that of the " we " sections; for the narrative of St. Luke i.-ii., regarded from the linguistic standpoint, is the product of a combination of two elements—the Greek of the Septuagint and the Greek of the author. The former element is for the most part lacking in the " we " sections (and generally in the second part of the Acts). From the linguistic point of view—and there are not many writers whose works present

does not bear upon the criticism of the " we " sections. In this connection the question whether the narrative of St. Luke i. and ii. is based upon a Greek source is alone of importance. We may here mention that in St. Luke i. 5–ii. 52 there are no less than twenty-five words which occur neither in the remaining chapters of St. Luke nor in the other three gospels, though they are found in the Acts—namely, the verbs ἀνευρίσκειν, ἀντιλαμβάνεσθαι, διατηρεῖν, ἐπιδεῖν, ἐπιφαίνειν, περιλάμπειν, προπορεύεσθαι, and also ἀγαλλίασις, ἀπειθής, ἀπογραφή, βραχίων, δεσπότης, δόγμα, δούλη, δυνάστης, ἔναντι, εὐλαβής, κράτος, τὰ λαλούμενα, πατριά, σπλάγχνα, στρατιά, συγγένεια, ταπείνωσις, as well as ἐπέπεσε φόβος ἐπί. Since St. Luke and the Acts have in all about 203 words in common which are wanting in the other gospels, the number twenty-five is a larger proportion than one would expect for St. Luke i.-ii.—that is, these chapters are at least as closely allied to the Acts as is the rest of the gospel.

1 Wellhausen asserts that St. Luke ii. was composed without regard to chap. i. Hence one or two written sources must be postulated. But I cannot so interpret the repetitions in chap. ii. (verses 4, 5), which alone, so far as I can see, afford any support to this assertion. The repetition, it seems to me, is easily explained by the importance of the information given. And, moreover, the complete homogeneity of the narrative of i. 5–ii. 52 and its smooth and natural development are inconsistent with Wellhausen's hypothesis.

passages so clearly distinguishable from one another in style and language—St. Luke's gospel may be analysed into the following elements: (1) The linguistic type, represented by a large group (not all) of traditional sayings and discourses of our Lord, which has been corrected with a light hand and reads like a translation from the Aramaic—as, indeed, it is, though the translation is not from the hand of St. Luke; (2) narratives slightly tinged with the style of the LXX., and derived in the main from St. Mark,[1] which have, however, undergone a vigorous revision, both in form and sometimes in subject-matter, so that they read almost like the reviser's own text, though in very many places the characteristics of the source may be clearly discerned and though in some of his corrections the reviser has imitated the style of St. Mark's narrative; (3) the legendary narratives of chaps. i.–ii., and of some other passages, which in style and characteristics are modelled with admirable skill upon the Greek of the Septuagint, and yet verse by verse disclose a second element in the characteristic style and vocabulary of the author himself—the hypothesis of written Greek sources is here excluded; (4) the style of the prologue and those very elements which we find represented weakly under (1) and strongly under (2) and (3). These, by comparison with the style and vocabulary of the Acts (second half, but more especially the long speeches and letters therein), fall into their place in a consistent

---

[1] In addition to the Markan material, there is much besides that is similarly treated (even sayings of our Lord).

whole, and can be clearly distinguished as a constant element in this writer—*i.e., as his own style and vocabulary*.[1] Without the Acts all would be dubious and problematical.

But—and let this be our last word in this connection—are not written Greek sources (or one such source) employed in the first half of the Acts although these chapters are so completely Lukan in their linguistic attire? If this is so, then it is also possible that the " we " sections, in spite of their distinctly Lukan characteristics, depend upon a written Greek source.

Let us for the moment set aside the question whether, after all that has been disclosed in our previous investigations, the above conclusion can be validly drawn. Is there any evidence that a written Greek source, or sources, lies behind the first half of the Acts? I here pay no attention to those countless bubble theories which have exercised the ingenuity of so many critics, and will only deal with what seems to me the only noteworthy attempt to prove a source—that, namely, of Bernhard Weiss. This scholar, with great ingenuity, seeks to show that a single and, as it seems, continuous written source can be traced at the background of chaps. i.–xv. He gives as his authority numerous

---

1 The Greek is excellent—*vide* Hieron., "Epist.," 19 : " Inter omnes evangelistas Lucas Græci sermonis eruditissimus fuit." It occupies a middle position between the Κοινή and Attic Greek (the language of literature) ; it is closely allied to the Greek of the books of the Maccabees, especially of the second book, and also shows strong points of likeness with Josephus. There is an intermixture of Semitic idioms, which are not due solely to the influence of the LXX. ; but these are not numerous, and are scarcely unintentional.

instances of discord and discrepancy found in every passage of considerable extent, which declare that St. Luke is only an editor, standing here in the same relation to his subject-matter as in the gospel he stands to St. Mark.

The first objection to be brought against this theory is that from a linguistic point of view the parallel is not exact. The style and linguistic character of St. Mark and the sayings of our Lord—Semitic in a Greek dress—can be distinctly and clearly discerned in St. Luke's gospel, while nothing so distinct in style and language can be discerned underlying Acts i.–xv. It is true that in general the style of the first half of the Acts is more nearly allied to the style of the LXX., and is accordingly more Hebraic than that of the second half, and therefore stands midway between the latter and the style of the gospel.[1] But in each of the three parts of the great historical work (gospel, Acts I., Acts II.), so distinct from one another in linguistic character, passages are found in which the styles of the other parts make their appearance. Thus the gospel contains the prologue, carefully composed in the classical style, which is nearly allied to that of the best sections of Acts II.; it contains, also, chaps. i.–ii., xxiv., which partly remind us of Acts I. The situation is much the same in Acts I. Neither does the vocabulary of Acts I. afford us any grounds for the hypothesis of written, Greek sources. In chaps. i.–xii. and xv. there are, indeed, found about 188 words (including 83 verbs)

---

[1] It shows the literary style of the Κοινή.

which occur neither in the four gospels nor in the second half of the Acts; but in chaps. xiii., xiv., xvi.–xxviii. about 353 words are found which are wanting in the four gospels and the first half of the Acts—thus nearly double.[1] We are led to the same negative result by a linguistic investigation of the positive relationship of Acts I. to St. Luke's gospel. The gospel has in common with Acts i.–xii., xv., about sixty-two words which are not found in the other gospels nor in Acts II.; but the same gospel has about seventy words, wanting in the other gospels and Acts I. in common with Acts II.[2] No difference, therefore, exists here (especially as Acts I. has 480 verses and Acts II. 527 verses)—rather the greatest possible likeness. Finally, the discovery that a series of important words only occurs either in the one or the other half of the Acts respectively cannot be decisive; for, in the first place, these words are also often found in the gospel of St. Luke; secondly, as has been already observed by others, St. Luke, after he has once used a word, is fond of holding on to it, only to let it drop again after some little time; and, thirdly, the semi-evangelic style of the first chapters of the Acts required a somewhat different vocabulary

---

[1] One hundred and seventeen words, which are wanting in the four gospels, occur both in the first and in the second half; they are thus exclusively common to the two halves. Using the lexicon only, one would be led rather to assume written sources for the second half if its subject-matter were not so much more extensive and varied than that of the first half.

[2] Both in the first and also in the second half about seventy-one words are found which are wanting in St. Matthew, St. Mark, and St. John.

from that of the second half. For example, the word
σημεῖα is not found in the second half, while it occurs
thirteen times in the first half and forty-five times in
the gospels ; neither is the word τέρατα found in Acts II.,
though it occurs nine times in Acts I. and three times
in the gospels (but not in St. Luke). Προσκαρτερεῖν
occurs six times in Acts I. ; it is wanting in Acts II.,
but it is found in St. Mark. Ἐξιστάναι is found eight
times in Acts I.; it is wanting in Acts II., but it is
found eight times in the gospels (three times in St.
Luke). Ἀρνεῖσθαι is found four times (three times ?) in
Acts I., not at all in Acts II., but fourteen times in the
gospels (four times in St. Luke). It seems at first very
remarkable that the word ὅσοι (ὅσα) occurs no less than
seventeen times in Acts i.–xv., while it is wanting from
Acts xvi. to the end ; but it is found in the gospels
fifty-four times (ten times in St. Luke), and therefore
belongs to the gospel style, which St. Luke has allowed
to colour the first half of the Acts.[1] On the other

---

[1] Compare also αἰνεῖν. It occurs a few times in the first half of
the Acts, never in the second, but in St. Luke's gospel three (four)
times. Also προσέθηκε (προσέθετο) with the infin., which occurs only
in St. Luke and in Acts xii. That there exists a distinct gospel
vocabulary may be seen from studying the occurrence of such words
as ἐκβάλλειν, καρπός, σκανδαλίζειν, and σῴζειν. Ἐκβάλλειν occurs
twenty-eight times in St. Matthew, sixteen times in St. Mark (twice
in the spurious conclusion), twenty times in St. Luke, but only five
times in the Acts (vii. 58, ix. 40, xiii. 50, xvi. 37, xxvii. 38—"we"
section !). Καρπός occurs nineteen times in St. Matthew, five times
in St. Mark, twelve times in St. Luke, ten times in St. John, but only
once in the Acts (ii. 30, καρπὸς τῆς ὀσφύος, parallel only to St. Luke
i. 42, καρπὸς τῆς κοιλίας). Καρπὸν ποιεῖν is therefore never found in
the Acts. Σκανδαλίζειν occurs fourteen times in St. Matthew, eight

hand, while σέβεσθαι τὸν θέον, ἐπίστασθαι, διατρίβειν, ἡμέτερος (ὑμετερος), ἀπολογεῖσθαι are found exclusively, or almost exclusively, in Acts II.,[1] one at once notices that these words are either foreign to the synoptic gospels or of very rare occurrence in those writings.[2]

But Weiss does not base his hypothesis concerning sources ultimately upon phenomena of vocabulary and style (see, however, " Einl. i. d. N. T.," s. 546), but upon phenomena of subject-matter, upon instances of discord and discrepancy, and upon certain passages, of frequent occurrence at the close of a group of stories, which present the appearance of remarks interpolated by the author into a text which was not his own. All

times in St. Mark, in St. Luke twice only, but it is absolutely wanting in the Acts. Ἰόζειν occurs about fifty times in the four gospels, eleven times in the Acts, up to chap. xvi. inclusive, afterwards only twice, and then in the "we" sections (xxvii.), *but in the profane sense.* That the use of διδόναι must be very widely spread in the Greek of the gospels might at once be concluded from the fact that after chap. xv. it occurs only five times in the Acts, while up to that point it occurs thirty times, and in St. Luke sixty times.

[1] Ἡμέτερος (ὑμέτερος) is found three times in the second half of the Acts (including once in the "we" sections, xxvii. 34 !), once in the first half, twice in the synoptic gospels (in St. Luke).

[2] Of course, we cannot say that this is always the case. Thus πονηρός is only found in the Acts from chapter xvii. onwards (eight times), while it occurs in St. Luke eleven times (the rare κακός is remarkably equally distributed ; it occurs in St. Matthew three times, in St. Luke and St. Mark twice each, in St. John once, in the first half of the Acts once, in the second half three times, including once in a "we" section). Δὲ καί, which is of such frequent occurrence in St. Luke's gospel (twenty-five times, including one occurrence in chapter ii.), and is as good as wanting in St. Matthew and St. Mark (one and two times), is also remarkably rare in the Acts (nine times if I have counted correctly, including occurrences in the "we" sections).

passages in the first half which point towards Antioch, or describe events which either happen in that city or originate from thence, certainly belong to the author himself, for while they stand out prominently from the rest of the narrative, and are distinguished by their superior historical worth, they are also most intimately connected with the second half of the book (*vide supra*, pp. 5, 21ff.). The question of sources, accordingly, is concerned with those sections referring to St. Peter and St. Philip, chaps. i. 15—v. 42, viii. 5–40, ix. 32—xi. 18, xii. 1–24, xv. 1–33.[1] Now it is true that in every chapter of this portion of the book are to be found several instances of startling discrepancy and anomaly, which seem to point to the conclusion that two hands have here been at work.[2] But the interpretation of these phenomena is not so simple, for (1) we possess

---

[1] I pass by the account of the conversion of St. Paul, ix. 1–31. I will only remark that I consider that Zimmer (" Ztschr. f. wiss. Theol.," Bd. 25, 1882, s. 465 ff.) has conclusively proved that this narrative is founded on the accounts in chaps. xxii., xxvi.—*i.e.*, that this impersonal narrative presupposes these accounts essentially in the form given in these chapters. Of course, it does not therefore conclusively follow that the second half of the Acts was written before the first half, nor that chaps. xxii., xxvi. formed a source for St. Luke; rather the latter conclusion is only a possibility. The phenomenon is at once intelligible if St. Luke edited the narrative of the conversion of St. Paul in accordance with an older sketch of his own which rested upon an account which St. Paul himself had given. This older sketch is the foundation of the accounts in chaps. xxii. and xxvi., and is freely employed in chap. ix. We have already shown in our discussion of the " we " sections that it is necessary to suppose that St. Luke possessed such sketches or notes.

[2] Yet Weiss, I think, sees sometimes with too critical eyes, and assumes a greater number of glaring discrepancies than are necessary.

the text neither of the Acts of the Apostles nor of St. Luke as they left the hand of the author. Just as the gospel has certainly suffered from interpolation in chaps. i., iii., and xxiv.,[1] so also the Acts has suffered at the hand of correctors from the very first ages. This follows not only from the phenomena presented by the ancient so-called β-text—which is really not a homogeneous text, but a compendium of corrections and glosses already belonging to the first half of the second century—rather the β-text itself shows that this form of corruption has also infected the so-called a-text. We must therefore take into account not the possibility only, but even the probability that there are passages in the Acts where neither the a-text nor the β-text are genuine, where, indeed, both have already suffered at the hand of an interpolator. Whether we can point with certainty to many such passages is another question;[2] yet we have in the hypothesis of very ancient corruption and interpolation a trusty weapon for removing difficulties in the text of the Acts which do not permit of being otherwise smoothed away. The recourse to the hypothesis of sources, ill or carelessly used, is accordingly not

[1] The verses i. 34, 35, iii. 23, which are responsible for the discrepancies with chap. ii., and the word Μαριάμ in i. 46 are certainly interpolated. There are also several interpolations and alterations in chap. xxiv. In reference to Μαριάμ in i. 46, see my paper in "Sitzungsber.," May 17, 1900. I there reckoned Irenæus among the authorities for Μαριάμ; but now Burkitt ("Journ. of Theol. Studies," 1906, pp. 220 ff.) has convinced me that Irenæus also read "Elizabeth."

[2] It seems to me quite certain that the text of i. 1–6 has been corrected; but it also seems necessary to suppose that something has fallen out between verses 5 and 6.

the only means, and certainly in many cases not the
most likely means, for removing serious stumbling-
blocks in the text.

(2) St. Luke is an author whose writings read smoothly
but one has only to look somewhat more closely to discover that there is scarcely another writer in the New
Testament who is so careless an historian as he.   Like
a true Greek, he has paid careful attention to style and
all the formalities of literature—he must, indeed, be
called an artist in language ; but in regard to his
subject-matter, in chapter after chapter, where he is
not an eye-witness, he affords gross instances of carelessness, and often of complete confusion in the
narrative.   This is true both of the gospel and the
Acts.   Overbeck, indeed, in his commentary on the
latter book, in a spirit of pedantic criticism and from
the standpoint of an inflexible logic, has grossly
exaggerated the number of such instances;[1] yet after
making allowance for cases of exaggeration there still
remains, both here and in the gospel, an astounding
number of instances of discrepancy.   These are, however, also found in the second half of the book.   In this
connection I would not only mention the discrepancy
between the three accounts of the conversion of St.
Paul—here the narrator alone is to blame, for he
possessed only one account—but also, *e.g.*, the story of
the imprisonment of St. Paul in Philippi, or the discourse at Miletus.   As regards the former of these two
passages, one is at first inclined to regard the verses

---

[1] His explanations also are, for the most part, false, in that he
suspects tendency where, in fact, carelessness is the sole cause.

24-34 simply as a later interpolation or as derived from another special source; for the decision of the strategi to set the Apostle at liberty is not in the least determined by the miraculous earthquake; it seems rather that they considered one day's imprisonment sufficient. Yet these verses betray such unimpeachable tokens of the style of St. Luke as to prevent us from even thinking of them as interpolated. The following instances of discrepancy in detail are also found in this passage. In verse 23 we read, "the strategi cast them into prison"; in verse 24, "the jailor cast them into the inner prison." According to verse 27, the jailor did not notice the great earthquake, but only its consequence—the opened doors! In verse 28 St. Paul is represented as perceiving or knowing the jailor's intention to kill himself, although he could not have seen him from his cell. According to the same verse, the Apostle cries out to the jailor that all the prisoners were present, although he certainly could not have known this. According to verse 32, St. Paul preaches to the jailor *and all that were in his house,* and baptises them, and yet it is not until verse 34 that we find him first brought into the jailor's house. According to verse 36, the jailor *reports* to St. Paul the message which the lictors have brought from the strategi; in 37 St. Paul directly addresses the lictors. According to the same verse, St. Paul appeals to his Roman citizenship; we ask in amazement why he did not do this before. *These cases of inaccuracy and discrepancy are very similar to those occurring in many narratives of the first half of the Acts,*[1] *and the*

---

1 In particular such *hystera-protera* as occur in verse 32 in its

H

majority of them have been noticed by Weiss him-self. Here, however, Weiss rightly neglects the hypo-thesis of a written source that has been badly edited, and explains everything from the carelessness of the author himself; it follows, therefore, that the similar instances of discrepancy in Acts I. by no means necessarily involve the adoption of the theory of a written source in order to explain them. Nor is it otherwise with the discourse at Miletus. At the be-ginning of this discourse St. Luke reports that St. Paul reminded the Ephesians " of the many tears and tempta-tions which befell him by the lying in wait of the Jews " during the long period of his sojourn with them (xx. 19), and yet nothing is said about these trials in the fore-going narrative.—We are at once reminded of a similar instance in St. Luke's gospel. Here the same writer, represents our Lord as speaking, at His first appearance in Nazareth, of His mighty works at Capernaum (iv. 23), and yet of these works absolutely nothing has been previously told us.—Again, in verse 23 St. Paul says that the Holy Spirit testifies to him in every city that bonds and afflictions await him in Jerusalem; and yet

relation to verse 34, or such duplications as verses 23 and 24, are often found in Acts I. It is, besides, to be noted that two *hystera-protera* are found even in the " we " sections. In chap. xx. verse 12 comes logically before verse 11, and in chap. xxviii., strictly speaking, verse 15 should precede verse 14. In these same sections we also meet with an instance of serious discrepancy. The author tells us with complete equanimity that St. Paul, urged by the Spirit, goes up to Jerusalem, and that the disciples at Tyre, *inspired by the very same Spirit*, seek to restrain him from his journey (xxi. 4). Lastly, the prophecy of Agabus in the " we " sections (xxi. 11) is not fulfilled exactly to the letter.

up to this point in the history nothing has been said about these prophecies—on the contrary, we hear of them for the first time in the following section (xxi. 4, 10 ff.). Lastly, St. Paul's reference to his own example, in his exhortation to self-denying works of love, can only be regarded as very loosely connected with the context of this farewell discourse.[1]

These parallel instances perhaps throw upon the anomalies of the first half of the book a different light from that in which Weiss regards them. If one first learns in i. 12 that the scene of i. 6 ff. is the Mount of Olives, and not Jerusalem, as one would expect (of course, we must assume that the scene of i. 6 ff. is the same as that of i. 4 f.); if in i. 17–20 we are left in doubt as to what is meant by the $\ddot{\epsilon}\pi\alpha\nu\lambda\iota\varsigma$ of Juda Iscariot, whether his plot of ground or his apostolic office; if impossible qualifications are required as a condition of apostleship (i. 21 f.); if the description of the speaking with tongues (ii. 4) is involved, not to say self-contradictory, and if the same must be said of the passages concerning the community of goods (ii. 44 f. and elsewhere); if in the double narrative of chaps. x. and xi. small points of difference are found; if in xii. 3 f. $\pi\rho o\sigma\acute{\epsilon}\theta\epsilon\tau o$ $\sigma\nu\lambda\lambda\alpha\beta\epsilon\hat{\iota}\nu$ anticipates $\pi\iota\acute{\alpha}\sigma\alpha\varsigma$ in an awkward way; then all these anomalies may, at a pinch, be explained, here as in the gospel and the second half of the Acts, by the carelessness of a writer who has

---

[1] Also the prophecy concerning false teachers (verses 29 f.)—who would arise partly from without, partly from within the community itself—is strange, and points, at all events, to the author's interest in this community and to his knowledge of its after-history.

not thought out and realised what he is about to narrate.

Yet, after making all due allowance for this *vera causa*, there still remain other phenomena—and these by no means few—which cannot be satisfactorily explained thereby: (1) Even the involved account of the Pentecostal miracle is most easily explained by postulating an earlier account that has been misunderstood, and similar instances are not altogether rare; (2) those short passages above mentioned, which form the conclusions of groups of narrative, demand an explanation, and the hypothesis that the author here adds something of his own to a source which he employs is the most likely explanation; (3) the stereotyped combination of St. John's name with that of St. Peter in several passages, although the former apostle plays no part in the narrative, points to a source in which even the name of St. John was not mentioned; (4) the merely casual notice of such an important event as the execution of St. James is not in the manner of our author, who likes to set his facts in a dramatic framework; (5) two passages are produced which, it is said, prove that an Aramaic source has been employed in the first half of the Acts.

Here, however, the following points must be taken into consideration: (1) The hypothesis of a *written Greek source* for Acts I. is compassed by the greatest difficulties. For its refutation I do not appeal to the vocabulary of these chapters, although its likeness to the Lukan vocabulary is of great weight in the balance (*vide supra*), but I fall back upon the phenomena of style.

Weiss, beyond all others, has shown in his commentary ("Text. u. Unters.," Bd. 9) that in these chapters the characteristics of the Lukan style reappear verse by verse. Indeed, it often happens that those verses, which Weiss assigns to the text of the source as distinguished from the additions of the editor, are often more Lukan in style than the additions themselves! We must thus assume that the editor has remodelled his source, or, rather, has absolutely transformed it. But St. Luke in his gospel has not treated his sources in this way; and, indeed, how improbable such treatment is! Weiss, therefore, rightly warns us against attempting to fix the wording of the source in any part of the Acts. (2) The strange introduction of St. John as a kind of lay figure in company with St. Peter—the most striking instance occurs in iv. 19 [1]—is certainly not original; but it admits of two explanations: either St. Luke himself has inserted St. John's name into an account which dealt only with St. Peter, or some later editor is responsible for this interpolation. Either alternative is in itself alike possible [2]; but it is, at all events, a point in the favour of the alternative that St. Luke was the

---

[1] Compare i. 13, iii. 1, 3, 4, 11, iv. 13, 19, viii. 14 (note the τε-καί in i. 13). St. John does not appear in the later part of the book except in xii. 2, where St. James is described as his brother, in distinction from St. James the Lord's brother.—Since all mention of St. John in the Acts is due to interpolation either by the author or some later editor, E. Schwartz's idea that the Acts once contained an account of St. John's violent death, which has been suppressed, is quite improbable.

[2] Compare an instance in chap. xxiv. of the gospel, where verse 12, concerning St. Peter, is interpolated.

interpolator,[1] and therefore in favour of the hypothesis
of a source, that the martyrdom of St. James should be
treated so strangely.   If St. Luke were not here dependent upon a source which concerned itself essentially
with St. Peter, if it had been possible for him to fashion
his text as he liked upon the basis of information he had
acquired, he could scarcely have so cursorily passed over
an event which must have seemed to him of quite special
importance in connection with the aim of his history.
This passage, therefore, and many other similar passages,
together with those short remarks which form the conclusion of groups of narrative, strongly incline the
balance of probability towards the hypothesis that for
the Petrine sections of the Acts our author used a
source ; *but this source must have been in Aramaic, and
must have been translated by the author himself.*   This
hypothesis remains an hypothesis, and the two pieces
of direct evidence which Nestle thinks that he has
discovered are by no means conclusive.   He shows us
that in iii. 14 Cod. D. and Irenæus read ἐβαρύνατε where
the rest of the authorities have ἠρνήσασθε ; here, however, the former reading must be correct, because it
is the more difficult, but it was early replaced by
ἠρνήσασθε, *which occurs in the preceding verse.*   We
need not, therefore, assume with Nestle the confusion of
כפרתם and כברתם.[2]   Again, in ii. 27 D. reads ἔχοντες

---

1 Note also that in St. Luke xxii. 8 St. Peter and St. John are
mentioned together. They are the only disciples named here,
and the other evangelists give no names at all in their parallel
passages.

2 βαρύνω is also found in St. Luke xxi. 34 (cf. also the use of this
word in the LXX.), and in Acts. xx. 19 we hear of λύκοι βαρεῖς.

χάριν πρὸς ὅλον τὸν κόσμον ; but this is a simple clerical error for ὅλον τὸν λαόν (the scribe mechanically wrote κόσμον after ὅλον τὸν) ;[1] it is therefore unnecessary to postulate a confusion of עלמא and עמא in order to explain it.

The result of our investigation is, accordingly, ambiguous ; there are, on the one hand, weighty reasons for the conclusion that St. Luke in the first half of the Acts has translated and used an Aramaic source,[2] and yet it is impossible to refute the theory that he was only dependent upon oral information. We have no certain means of judging the extent of this source, nor of deciding whether there existed only one or more than one of such sources. The hypothesis of a single source is exceedingly improbable, because in v. 19 ff. evidently the same story is told as in xii. 3 ff., though St. Luke himself does not notice this. Only one of these two passages could have stood in his source, and that the first (if the hypothesis of a written source is to be accepted at all). On the other hand, the narratives concerning St. Peter and St. Philip are, indeed, connected together by the episode of Simon-Magus, but the connection is perhaps only artificial. We can

---

[1] Ὅλος ὁ κόσμος occurs six times in the New Testament.

[2] In the gospel St. Luke, with a view to Greek readers, omits, as a rule, Aramaic and foreign words (even names of places) ; in a few instances only he translates them, and then correctly. In Acts i. 19 he writes : ὥστε κληθῆναι τὸ χωρίον ἐκεῖνο τῇ διαλέκτῳ αὐτῶν Ἀχελδαμάχ τοῦτ' ἔστιν χωρίον αἵματος, and in ix. 36 : ὀνόματι Ταβιθά, ἣ διερμηνευομένη λέγεται Δορκάς. Knowledge of Aramaic and the ability to translate an easy Aramaic text may well be assumed in a native of Antioch, and one who was for many years a companion of St. Paul.

only say that the Petrine stories, which in fact give us the author's description of the Church of Jerusalem, form a consistent whole.   However, from the investigation of the first half of the Acts we gain nothing which helps us in the discussions of " we " sections, for in the most favourable case this investigation only justifies us in accepting one or more *Aramaic* sources, a conclusion which is quite irrelevant to the problem of the " we " sections.   Seeing that no one could ever imagine that these sections presuppose an Aramaic source, all the observations which we have made in regard to their vocabulary, style, and subject-matter—observations which bring home to us the absolute impossibility of separating the " we " sections from the work as a whole —remain unaffected in their convincing force.

CHAPTER III

IS IT REALLY IMPOSSIBLE TO ASCRIBE THE THIRD
GOSPEL AND THE ACTS OF THE APOSTLES TO ST.
LUKE?

SINCE it has been shown that from the manner in which
the author of this great historical work treats his
authorities nothing can be deduced to contradict his
identity with the author of the "we" account, this
identity may therefore now be regarded as established.
But here another objection presents itself. It runs
somewhat as follows : Though this identity be ever so
probable, it cannot really exist, but must be pro-
nounced to be a delusion ; for considerations of historical criticism absolutely prevent us from assigning
the Acts of the Apostles to a companion and fellow-
worker of St. Paul.[1]

---

[1] This, it seems, is not asserted in the case of the gospel (*vide supra*,
the opinion of Joh. Weiss) ; in fact, he who attributes the second
gospel to St. Mark can find no difficulty in assigning the third
gospel to St. Luke. One is not easily convinced, especially after
Wellhausen's comments, that an original member of the community
at Jerusalem, a disciple and friend of St. Peter, a man in whose house
the apostles and saints came together, wrote the former book.
Nevertheless, there is no adequate reason to dispute the tradition
that he did so, and there is much to be urged in its favour. If,
however, this tradition is accepted, we may demand that critics

" Absolutely prevent us "—but why ?   From whence
have we such certain knowledge of the apostolic

should, in their criticism of the Acts of the Apostles, make more
allowances for its author. Seeing that St. Mark of Jerusalem chiefly
deals with our Lord's mission in Galilee, and that his work presupposes strata of tradition, which must have taken form within a
period of three, or at the most four, decades ; seeing, also, that he has
almost transformed our Lord into a spirit-being of Divine power, or
had found such a conception of Him already in existence ; seeing,
finally, that he and his authorities have modified the tradition concerning Jesus in accordance with the experience of the Christian
Church—if we then consider that St. Luke was a Greek physician
from Antioch who may have first joined the Church anywhere in the
Roman Empire about fifteen or twenty years after the Crucifixion,
and that he had heard nothing of Palestine and had but slight
acquaintance with Jerusalem ; if, moreover, we consider that he had
not seen any of the twelve apostles (he had come into contact only
with St. James, the Lord's brother), and that he may have first
written down his wonderful experiences about twenty years after
they had happened, how indulgent should we be in our judgment of
him as an evangelist and historian ! But no other book of the
New Testament has suffered so much from critics as the Acts of the
Apostles, although, in spite of its notorious faults, it is in more than
one respect the best and most important book of the New Testament.
All the mistakes which have been made in New Testament criticism
have been focussed into the criticism of the Acts of the Apostles.
This book has been forced to suffer above all because an incorrect
conception had been formed of the nature and relationship of Jewish
and Gentile Christendom. It has been forced to suffer because
critics were still influenced by a strange survival of the old veneration for an apostolic man, and without any justification have made the
highest demands of a companion of St. Paul—he must thoroughly
understand St. Paul, he must be of congenial disposition and free
from prejudice, he must be absolutely trustworthy and his memory
must never fail ! It has been forced to suffer because of a dozen
other demands equally senseless or exaggerated ; but above all because
the critics sometimes have posed as the sublime "psychologist," sometimes have wrapped themselves in the gown of the prosecuting
barrister, at one time patronising or censuring, at another time
accusing and tearing the author in pieces. With their dry logic and

and post-apostolic ages that we can set up our mere knowledge against a surely established fact? I regard the following investigation purely as a work of supererogation, but it shall be treated as though it were not so.

Yet—where shall we begin? How can we be expected to disprove everything which has been conjectured and advanced in this connection? I must confine myself to the main points.

(1) It was just as possible for St. Luke the disciple of St. Paul to make historical blunders, like the *hysteronproteron* in regard to Theudas (v. 36),[1] as for any one else. He certainly believes himself to be an historian (see the prologue); and so he is; but his powers are limited, for he adopts an attitude towards his authorities which is as distinctly uncritical as that which he adopts towards his own experiences, if these admit of a miraculous interpretation.

(2) The picture of the Church at Jerusalem in the first five chapters and the Petrine stories in point of clearness and credibility leaves much to be desired;[2] but the

with intolerable pedantry they have forced their way into the work, and by doing this have caused quite as much mischief as by the columns of ingenious but fanciful theories which they have directed against it. Even two critics of peculiar intelligence—Overbeck and Weizsäcker—who have both done good work on the Acts—have in their criticism fallen into the gravest errors. The results of all their toil cannot be compared with those reached by Weiss and Wendt, Ramsay and Renan.

[1] Besides, the *hysteron-proteron* is not proved beyond doubt. It is also possible that there is a mistake in Josephus.

[2] But the instances of alleged incredibility have been much exaggerated by critics.

chief traits of that picture—the thoroughly Jewish character of the Church (which was, in fact, not a distinct community, but a Jewish sect nearly allied to those Jews believing in a resurrection), its relationship to the Jewish population up to the appearance of Stephen, and the motive assigned for the first great persecution [1]—all these stand the test of historical criticism —so far as one can speak of such a thing when only *one* authority exists (*cf.*, however, the gospel of St. Matthew, which comes to our help for the description in Acts i.– v.). Moreover, the legendary element is certainly not more striking nor more strongly marked here than in the gospel, and could have been deposited just as rapidly as the strata of gospel tradition. Besides, St. Luke may not have acquainted himself with these stories at the time when he came with St. Paul to Jerusalem. We, indeed, have not the least idea how long he remained there at that time. He may easily have become acquainted with his subject-matter or his sources—if there is a question of one or more Aramaic sources—for the first time between his sixtieth and eightieth year. But even if we do not choose to accept this hypothesis, and if, with good grounds, we regard St. Mark (for the gospel) and the evangelist Philip (with his daughters who were prophetesses) as St. Luke's authorities,[2] there is no reason why these stories should

---

[1] In particular the record that it was a question concerning the Temple is highly trustworthy.

[2] He met the former in Rome, the latter in Cæsarea (*vide supra*, pp. 39 f.). The way he speaks of the latter in chap. xxi.—or, rather, does not speak of him, but only mentions him significantly—suggests that he valued him as an authority. St. Philip must have been an

not have been already current about the years 55–60 A.D. In his veneration for the Church of Jerusalem —which, indeed, for a long period was *the* Church *par excellence*—St. Luke agrees with St. Paul. Nor can any objection be raised against the representation, indirectly given in the Acts, that the believers of Jerusalem first collected round the Twelve and their immediate following, and that then, as soon as they really became a Church, they set the Lord's brother at their head. The very fact that St. Luke does not describe this revolution arouses our confidence. He has related nothing which had not been handed down to him, and he possessed no tradition on this point. He is perfectly trustworthy so long as his faith in the miraculous, and his interest in his own " spiritual " gift of healing, do not come into play.

(3) Much fault has been found, in general and in detail, with his description of the origin and development of the non-Jewish Churches, and thus of the

" ecstatic " *par excellence* if all his daughters became prophetesses. But this is just what is expressly testified by St. Luke in Acts viii. 6 f. : προσεῖχον οἱ ὄχλοι τοῖς λεγομένοις ὑπὸ τοῦ Φιλίππου ὁμοθυμαδὸν ἐν τῷ ἀκούειν αὐτοὺς καὶ βλέπειν τὰ σημεῖα ἃ ἐποίει· πολλῶν γὰρ τῶν ἐχόντων πνεύματα ἀκάθαρτα βοῶντα φωνῇ μεγάλῃ ἐξήρχοντο· πολλοὶ δὲ παραλελυμένοι καὶ χωλοὶ ἐθεραπεύθησαν. Philip, therefore, like St. Luke, was endowed with the miraculous gift of healing, and his miracles were such as to provoke the admiration of St. Luke himself. The ecstatic nature of such a man could not but colour his memory of the past. Indeed, the story of St. Philip in viii. 26 ff. is a crying witness that this was so. Here an angel speaks to St. Philip, and the Spirit speaks to him (ἄγγελος κυρίου and πνεῦμα are thus identical here !) ; indeed, " the Spirit of the Lord " catches away (ἁρπάζειν) Philip from the side of the Æthiopian.—As for St. Mark, Acts xii. is sufficient testimony that he, at least in part, was one of St. Luke's authorities.

Church Catholic; but we forget that only a few decades later ideas sprang up which completely replaced our author's conception of this historic process. In comparison with these, St. Luke's description is remarkably trustworthy. If he so conceives of the presbytery of Jerusalem under the leadership of St. James, even in the time of Nero, that he represents them as saying (xxi. 20), θεωρεῖς, πόσαι μυριάδες εἰσὶν ἐν τοῖς Ἰουδαίοις τῶν πεπιστευκότων, καὶ πάντες ζηλωταὶ τοῦ νόμου ὑπάρχουσιν, and if he then allows St. Paul, during his trial at Jerusalem and Cæsarea, to lay the greatest emphasis upon his unity with those Jews that believed in a Resurrection,[1] what better can one wish? And, again, the way he leads up to the council at Jerusalem in chap. xv. (the conversion of Samaritans, the baptism of the Æthiopian eunuch, and then the baptism of the centurion of Cæsarea by St. Peter)[2] is by no means so clumsily conceived as to prevent him from recognising that the chief merit of having carried the Gospel to the Gentiles belongs to Jewish Christians of Cyprus and Cyrene and to St. Paul and St. Barnabas.[3] If he has

---

[1] Chap. xxiii. 6 ff., &c. That St. Luke here explains to his readers who the Pharisees and Sadducees were is the strongest proof that he has in his eye only Gentile readers.

[2] It may be doubted whether the baptism of the Æthiopian eunuch should be taken in this connection, for it is not exploited in this sense by our author. It is true that the conversion of the Samaritans also (see especially viii. 25) is not so exploited, and yet it is certain (see also the gospel) that it is narrated in the interest of the Gentiles.

[3] St. Peter does not really begin the mission to the Gentiles, but in a particular case, and by his agency, the Holy Spirit leads up to and sanctions that mission. The story itself, which must have attracted great attention, is certainly not entirely legendary, but has an

here assigned less honour to St. Paul than from his epistles seems to be due to him, and if in chaps. xxi. ss. he makes him appear more Jewish in his behaviour than we, judging from the same epistles, should imagine possible, it is at least permissible to ask which is right— our imagination or the representation given in the Acts. But even supposing this representation is incorrect, why could not a companion of St. Paul—who honoured St. Peter above everything (as apparently did all Christendom, and St. Paul too, *nolens volens*, if he did not happen to be provoked)—accept a tale current in Jerusalem that already "a good while ago"[1] St. Peter had baptised a Gentile? And why could not a Christian historian—who, as a Gentile by birth, could not comprehend or describe the subtle line which bounded the path of St. Paul as a Jew and a Christian—represent that apostle in one place as more Jewish, in another place as freer in his behaviour than he really was? From everything that we know and can conjecture of St. Paul in this connection, he must more than once have appeared very incomprehensible to his Gentile Christian as well as to his Jewish Christian companions. And we must also remember that St. Luke as a "theologian," like all Gentile Christians, was more a man of the Old Testament than St. Paul, because he had never come to a real grip with the problem it presented.[2]

historical nucleus. St. Luke, of course, first decked it up into its present form and significance.

[1] This is the expression in xv. 7. In those days every year must have felt like a generation.

[2] See St. Luke xvi. 17.

In hostility to the Jews—so far as that people had rejected the Gospel—he certainly cannot be surpassed ; but just as certainly (see also the gospel, especially chaps. i. and ii.) he had a theoretical reverence for Old Testament ordinances and Old Testament piety—an attitude in which he was, indeed, strongly affected by the problem which moved St. Paul (see xiii. 38 f.),[1] though he had not thoroughly thought it out.[2]   Just as in the gospel he considers it quite in order that the same Jesus Who brings salvation to the Samaritans and to every sinner should in His own Person respect the law of the Old Testament (see xvii. 14 and elsewhere), so also Jews devoted to their law and at the same time believers in Christ are apparently the Christians who impress him most forcibly.   They are, in fact, not only Christians, but also *homines antiquæ religionis* ; while the Gentile Christians come only in the second place.   How could St. Paul, who himself acknowledged the permanence of the promises to the Jews (Rom. xi.), have shaken our author in this faith ?   And if he drew somewhat different conclusions from St. Paul, are we to regard the great apostle as the head of some theological school, to which he propounded a definite system of Divine Revelation ?   As regards, however, the grand crisis and the settlement recorded in Acts xv., even

---

[1] I have already referred to this passage above (p. 19, note). Exactly interpreted, the words ἀπὸ πάντων ὧν οὐκ ἠδυνήθητε ἐν νόμῳ Μωϋσέως δικαιωθῆναι, ἐν τούτῳ πᾶς ὁ πιστεύων δικαιοῦται proclaim a doctrine which is considerably different from the doctrine of St. Paul, but still only one which might very well be attributed to a disciple of that apostle.

[2] But had St. Paul himself quite thoroughly thought it out ?

Keim and Pfleiderer have acknowledged, after the exaggerations of the Tübingen school, that more agreement than contradiction prevails between this account and the impassioned description in Gal. ii. The mistakes which occur, above all the wrong date of the so-called Apostolic decree, can easily be attributed to an early writer who was not himself present at the council. When in chap. xvi. 4 he relates that St. Paul imposed this decree upon the Churches of Lycaonia, we notice that here too he was not present;[1] and if in chaps. xxi., xxv. he yet again refers to the decree, it is possible that in the meantime something of the kind had really been issued.[2] The speeches at the council as well as the letter (xv. 23–29) are composed by St. Luke; but we should notice in regard to these speeches, and, indeed, in regard to the great discourses throughout the Acts, that St. Luke was conscious that he must make St. Peter speak differently from St. Paul. In these speeches we, of course, miss all kinds of things that we might justly require; but the fact that the author does presuppose this difference, and, indeed, even distinguishes the standpoint of St. Peter from that of St. James, is of far more importance than these deficiencies of his. Finally, St. Luke has been blamed with

---

[1] This comes out strikingly in the very summary account (or, rather, in the silence) concerning St. Paul's important mission in Phrygia and Galatia (xvi. 6). Ramsay's theory that St. Luke was called in as a physician by St. Paul during his severe illness in Galatia is thus untenable. The two men first met at Troas.

[2] This passage, however, rouses a suspicion that it is a later interpolation. It pays no regard to chap. xv., and the verse is not in any close connection with the preceding one.

I

special severity because in his description of St. Paul's mission he does not enlarge upon his disputes with the Jewish Christians, but confines himself entirely to the malicious assaults of the Jews,[1] and because, according

[1] Critics have withdrawn nearly all their earlier objections to the accounts given in the Acts (a few blunders excepted) concerning the attitude of the Jews towards the apostles and their mission (and *vice versa*). But critics still and all the more positively assert the absolute incredibility of St. Paul's last conference with the Jews (in Rome), and hence conclude with absolute assurance that the authentic record breaks off at chap. xxviii. 16, and thus is undoubtedly a source but not the work of the author of the complete book. Even here I cannot admit their justification (concerning the close agreement in language and style between this concluding passage and the "we" section, see above, p. 65, note). In the first place, it is clear that the passage xxviii. 17-31 was intended to be the conclusion of the complete work ; the whole point of the passage lies in the quotation from Isaiah vi. 9 f., and in the inference drawn from this quotation : γνωστὸν οὖν ἔστω ὑμῖν ὅτι τοῖς ἔθνεσιν ἀπεστάλη τοῦτο τὸ σωτήριον τοῦ θεοῦ· αὐτοὶ καὶ ἀκούσονται. The Jews are hardened in heart and are rejected, the Gentiles are accepted—this was just the *thema probationis* of the whole work. As an artist, the author had a right to invent a scene which illustrated this *thema*, but this conference with the Roman Jews was certainly not invented by him, for it agrees very badly with the inference he draws from Isaiah's prophecy. At this conference St. Paul explains the Gospel to the Roman Jews who crowded into his dwelling, and the result is : οἱ μὲν ἐπείθοντο τοῖς λεγομένοις οἱ δὲ ἠπίστουν. This result is not at all in agreement with the terrible curse of the quotation from Isaiah, which comes abruptly from St. Paul's lips like a pistol shot. The preceding account, therefore, is not founded on pure invention, but on tradition. So much the worse, it may be said, and all the more impossible that St. Luke wrote this passage. But what is really contained in the account ? It relates that St. Paul invited the Jewish elders in Rome to his house and brought forward in his apology all those points which he had made against the Jews both in Jerusalem and Cæsarea. If we reject this passage, then we must also reject the previous passages ; but it is quite credible that St. Paul, wherever it appeared to him useful and called for, professed himself to be simply

to his representation, all discords within the Christian communities are brought to an end with the holding

a Jew believing in a Resurrection—with the addition only that he waited for the appearance of the Messiah Jesus ; and there is also no reason to doubt that his protestations (that he had committed no offence against his people, that he did not come to accuse them, and that he wore his chain because of the Hope of Israel) are historical. There is therefore nothing here to which any one could take exception. But what is most perplexing is the reply of the elders, that they had neither received any (official) written communication concerning St. Paul, nor had they even been informed or prejudiced by the report of some brother travelling to Rome ; for up to that time all they knew of this sect was that it was everywhere spoken against. The absence of official news is, of course, just possible, but that no report had been brought by some travelling brother is quite improbable, while the indirect assertion that there were no Christians in Rome or that the Jews on the spot knew nothing about them— for this is the inference we seem compelled to make—is an impossibility. Weiss seeks to escape this difficulty by pointing out that the dispute concerning the Messiahship of Jesus in the Jewish community at Rome lay far behind the time of the present elders, and that the Christian Church then in Rome, as an essentially Gentile Christian community, kept themselves quite apart from the synagogue. But this expedient is obviously quite unsatisfactory. The dispute concerning the Messiahship of Jesus having once begun among the Roman Jews, could never have ceased ; and even if it had ceased, it is incredible that the elders should not have remained well informed about it, and yet in the following narrative it almost seems as if St. Paul now preached to them the Gospel message as something quite unknown to them. There is therefore a serious blunder in the text. But is it made better by shifting the responsibility for it on to the shoulders of a third and later writer, at a time when the Epistle to the Romans had long been widely known ? How, then, is the difficulty to be explained ? As we saw above, the accounts cannot have been invented by St. Luke. What, then, had been reported to him, and what did he know about it ? Naturally not the speeches made at the conference by St. Paul and the elders—for he was not then present, nor does he even pretend that he was an eye-witness— but the fact that St. Paul had a conference with the elders, whom he had invited to his hired dwelling, and, further, a second scene, of the apostolic council of Jerusalem. In reply to this grave objection, we have no right to appeal to the fact that, with the exception of the first short meeting in Troas and Philippi (during the second missionary journey), St. Luke first joined St. Paul at the commencement of the apostle's last journey to Jerusalem, and that then the time of fierce internal discord was past. St. Paul, of course, must often have told St. Luke about his relations with the Jewish Christians. Three points, however, must be taken into consideration : (1) St. Luke has not kept silence concerning the attitude of the Church at Jerusalem and of St. James towards the Law even as late as the time of Nero, as we

likewise in St. Paul's house, on which occasion he had an opportunity of expounding the Gospel to a considerable number of Jews (we do not know whether the elders were present) and of winning a portion of them for Christ. Nothing can be alleged against the authenticity of either of these scenes. It is quite credible that the Apostle had invited the elders — whose attitude towards his trial before the emperor was of the highest importance—to his house (not, of course, for the purpose of at once converting them, but in order to dispose them favourably towards himself at his trial—so much, indeed, is said in plain words)—and that these had accepted the invitation of a Roman citizen. Absolutely no objection can be raised against the authenticity of the next scene. We may also well believe that the elders hesitated to mix themselves up in the matter, and took up a diplomatic attitude. The idea of being mixed up in an accusation against a Roman citizen, with the prospect of being prosecuted as a calumniator, was not an alluring one, especially as St. Paul could also turn the tables against them, as he himself hinted. St. Luke wished to reproduce in a written record this diplomatic attitude, with which he was acquainted. But he has come to sad grief in his attempt, because—writing carelessly and thoughtlessly as he often does, except when he had been an eye-witness—he so exaggerates the cautious attitude of the elders, expressed in the words " we knew nothing of *thee* until now," until it almost seems as if all the inforhave seen, but he was no more scandalised by it than St. Paul himself, for the members of this Church were also Jews by birth. (2) The plan which guided him in the Acts did not oblige him to enter at all closely into the discussion of internal discords among Christians—indeed, must rather have prevented him from doing so. He wished to show how the Gospel had spread from Jerusalem to Rome through the power of the Holy Ghost, working in the apostles and in chosen men, and how in its triumphant progress it had won over the Gentiles, while the Jewish people became more and more hostile, until at last their heart was definitely hardened against it. What place had the internal disputes of Christians in such a plan, especially when these affairs after 70 A.D. had so changed in aspect from what they were before? That grand optimism which inspires St. Luke

mation they had received concerning Christianity up to this time had come from abroad. Still, it is important that this is not stated in the text in so many words, even if it almost sounds like it. Putting the matter shortly, we may say *that the bare facts of xxviii. 17 f. are proved to be quite credible both in themselves and because they do not fit in at all well with the quotation from Isaiah which is applied to them; indeed a writer who has here divided his account into two scenes* (one with the elders, the other with ordinary Jewish visitors) *is worthy of all trust,* and does not lose his right to pass as a contemporary who was himself on the spot, though not present at the conference. We may also believe that both scenes ended with a definite result; that the elders treated the case diplomatically and that some of the Jews were won over to the Gospel. *One unfortunate sentence alone that is attributed to the elders is quite incredible.* Now, according to all the rules of criticism, no conclusion at all can be drawn from one such sentence, especially if it becomes neither more intelligible nor more reasonable, when it is ascribed to that familiar scapegoat who has to bear the responsibility of all the errors of *homines noti.*

as he writes, and which already proclaims him to be a forerunner of the apologists and of Eusebius, did not allow him to dwell upon disturbing trifles. Moreover, (3) even in his gospel he has done a good deal in the way of omission ; this is apparent at once as soon as he is compared with his authority, St. Mark.[1] But why might not a disciple of the apostles purposely suppress things, and why, because he has acted thus, must he be divested of this his qualification ? Had not history itself in its inexorable yet providential progress made

---

[1] See the notes on this point in Wellhausen's " Commentar " (*e.g.*, ss. 42, 45, 134). Just as he has suppressed in the gospel things concerning our Lord which might give offence (*e.g.*, the cry, " Eli, Eli ") or that showed St. Peter and the disciples in an unfavourable light, or inconvenient details, such as the command that the disciples should set out for Galilee, so also in the Acts of the apostles we may be sure that he has purposely omitted much which was not to St. Peter's or St. Paul's credit. Thus he can scarcely have been ignorant of the scene in Antioch between the two apostles (Gal. ii.). It is therefore all the more surprising that he should relate the quarrel between St. Paul and St. Barnabas concerning St. Mark, and should apparently take a side against the two last named. This is most remarkable, considering the limits he observes elsewhere in his narrative, and can only be explained by supporting a certain animosity against St. Mark on the part of the author ; for he certainly revered St. Barnabas. *Vide infra* for further details on this question. The prophecy in St. Mark x. 39, together with the whole section in which it occurs, is also one of the passages suppressed by St. Luke. He suppressed it because it had not been fulfilled in the case of St. John. I cannot convince myself that the passage is a *vaticinium post eventum*, and that St. John really suffered a martyr's death. The negative evidence of Irenæus and Eusebius is, it seems to me, much stronger than that which, according to others, is alleged to have stood in Papias. St. Mark x. 35 ff. is a prophecy of our Lord which was only partly fulfilled. Accordingly, in order to correct it and to take its place, the other prophecy was invented (St. John xxi. 23) that St. John would not die at all.

evident what a writer about the year 80 A.D. must relate and what he had to pass over? However, in regard to the author's representation of the attitude of the Roman magistrates, all objections of this kind that critics have felt obliged to urge against St. Luke have been proved to be worthless. He is certainly biased in this part of his narrative. He wished to show that the Roman authorities were much more friendly to the youthful Church than the Jewish authorities and the Jews, who unceasingly strove to stir them up against the Christians. *But this bias is in accordance with actual fact.* And even if St. Luke has gone too far with it in some places,[1] as, for instance, in the gospel, where he exonerates Pilate beyond all bounds, yet this is far from being a proof that he cannot have been a companion of St. Paul.[2]

In the section chaps. xvii.–xix. all kinds of inequalities and small deviations from the facts related

---

[1] I have not, however, been able to find instances of such exaggeration in the Acts, unless it be the case that the account of the progress of the trial in Cæsarea (see also xxviii. 17–19) is somewhat too favourable to the Romans—which is at all events probable.

[2] And, besides, he has also recounted some things which tell against the authorities (as at Philippi), and, on the other hand, he has not suppressed the counsel of Gamaliel and its good effect on the Sanhedrin. I do not know how to solve the great problem which is presented in the two concluding verses in the Acts (could the author have intended to write a third book?—laying stress upon the πρῶτον [instead of πρότερον] in Acts i. 1). But to imagine that he did not relate the martyrdom of the apostle lest he should efface the impression of the friendliness of the Roman authorities is indeed a poor solution of the difficulty. How can we imagine an early Christian suppressing the account of an apostle's martyrdom for a political reason!

in St. Paul's epistles have been pointed out—some with reason, others are only alleged. On the whole, it may be said that these three chapters form a brilliant passage in the Acts of the Apostles, although the author was not here an eye-witness.[1] The historical data in St. Paul's epistles confirm St. Luke's narrative in a really remarkable way, and show quite clearly that he had here one or more reliable sources of information. One or two of these have been with good reason found in chap. xix. 29—namely, Aristarchus and Gaius (see p. 10, note[1]); it is difficult to understand why they should be mentioned here if they were not St. Luke's authorities; we remember, also, that on a later occasion St. Luke took the long journey to Cæsarea and from thence to Rome in company with Aristarchus. If we are astonished to find that we learn more concerning St. Paul from those passages of the Acts where the author does not write as an eye-witness than from the rest of the book, we forget that in the opinion of St. Luke and of his contemporaries nothing greater or more wonderful could be related of the apostle than what is recorded in the " we " sections. The incidents in question have been summarised above on page 33 (the exorcism of the girl " possessed with the spirit of divination," an instance of raising from the dead, the healing of a gastric fever, but above all St. Paul's conduct during the storm, together with the apparition of the angel and his prophecy); these at least are inferior to nothing that St. Luke has imparted to us

---

[1] Therefore mistakes made here must not be pressed without qualification against St. Luke as an author.

from reports he received. But if the " we " account offers a problem both in regard to what it contains and what it omits, yet this problem is surely not rendered less difficult by regarding it as a separate document. No one has as yet been able to fix with any probability the boundaries of such an hypothetical document. Some critics go back as far as chap. xi., and even include chaps. xxi.-xxvi., while others diminish the number of the existing ninety-seven verses by a theory of interpolation. Perplexity also reigns in regard to the purpose of the supposed author of such a document—whether he wished to write a diary for himself or a biography of St. Paul. But this perplexity disappears—even if everything does not become clear—when we once realise that St. Luke, who accompanied the apostle as a physician and a fellow-worker, and wrote his history at a much later date, first joined the apostle as his companion and helper during his last two great missionary journeys (from Troas to Jerusalem and from Cæsarea to Rome), while before this he had only once been with him—from Troas to Philippi—and then only for a short time. If we keep the fact well in view that, according to the " we " sections, St. Luke was not in St. Paul's company at the climax of his ministry—that is, during the years between his sojourn in Philippi and his last journey to Jerusalem—then most of these small difficulties find their explanation. Moreover, the picture which he has given of St. Paul is not, according to the ideas of ancient days, such as an eulogist would draw, but is an *historical portrait*. All eulogistic touches are here wanting, while the picture of the

Church of Jerusalem, and of the activity of the apostles in its midst, abounds with them.[1] Of course, the Acts of the Apostles is not a mirror which allows us to gaze into the very soul of St. Paul; but are we obliged to assume that a disciple of an apostle[2] must have been capable of seeing into the heart of the author of the Epistle to the Galatians and the two epistles to the Corinthians, and of portraying what he saw there? Yet, on the other hand, all that St. Luke has performed in portraying St. Paul by means of the three great discourses (in Antioch, Athens, and Ephesus) deserves high praise. Judging simply from the epistles, we may well believe that the apostle would have spoken to *receptive* Jews, in substance at least, just as he speaks in the Acts at Antioch, and to Gentiles as he speaks at Athens, and that he would have exhorted his own converts just as he does at Miletus; but this last dis-course also contains—apart from the sentimental touches[3] peculiar to St. Luke—several distinct utter-ances whose authenticity (as regards their content) is confirmed by the epistles.[4] Think only of his boast-

[1] Dark shadows are, however, not wanting even here (the story of Ananias, the quarrel of the Hellenists and Hebrews, the division between those Christians who were Pharisees and the rest of the Church).

[2] Moreover, we do not know whether St. Luke was a disciple of St. Paul in the exact sense of the word. The way in which he, in chap. xvi. 18, places himself side by side with St. Paul is not in keeping with this view, although he gives him all due honour in xvi. 14.

[3] St. Paul could also yield to the same feelings at times, but the emotional always speedily gave place to the heroic.

[4] It is well to notice that St. Luke was present at Miletus, but not at Antioch and Athens.

ing, his passionate assertion of his own personal dis-
interestedness and the remarkable expression (xx. 28),
τὴν ἐκκλησίαν τοῦ θεοῦ, ἣν περιποιήσατο διὰ τοῦ αἵματος
τοῦ ἰδίου.[1] If the words of xiii. 38, 39 remind us of
the epistles to the Galatians and Romans, so this expression reminds us of Ephesians and Colossians;
indeed, this whole discourse to the Ephesians calls to
mind the epistles to the Thessalonians. The author of
the Acts of the Apostles not a disciple of the apostle?
Who, I ask, except one who knew St. Paul personally
could portray him as he appears in this book? Was
it possible for an admirer of the apostle at the beginning of the second century to give so concrete a narrative
and to avoid eulogy to such a degree? Even if no " we "
appeared in the whole book, it would scarcely admit
of doubt that the author—so far as concerns the history
of St. Paul's missionary work from chap. xiii. to the
conclusion—wrote on the authority of an eye-witness
with whom he was a contemporary. In truth no one
has yet been able to draw a convincing portrait of
St. Paul from his epistles alone. All attempts in this
direction have led to productions which true historians
have ignored. For these the portrait given in the Acts
of the Apostles has always remained a concurring
factor, because the abundance of actual fact which is
therein afforded still makes it possible to pass behind
the external action to the inward motive. .

But the Paulinism of St. Luke—this has been just
as often asserted as disputed. Here one point has been

---

[1] The phrase is all the more remarkable in that *this* valuation of
the Church is found in St. Luke alone.

already noticed—namely, that in vocabulary (not only in words, but also in expressions) he resembles St. Paul much more closely than does St. Mark or even St. Matthew (*vide supra*, pp. 19 ff., note). But Acts xxvii. 35 and St. Luke xxii. 19 are already sufficient in themselves to prove St. Luke's Paulinism in the superficial sense. St. Luke is even more of a universalist than St. Paul, because with the Greeks universalism was never a matter of question; what insight, therefore, he shows in his story of the conversion of the centurion of Cæsarea, in that he here, though theoretically, yet so thoroughly appreciates the difficulty felt by the Jew ![1] Towards the unbelieving Jews St. Luke's attitude is almost more Pauline than that of St. Paul himself. He holds different views from St. Paul concerning the law and Old Testament ordinances,[2] and St. Paul's doctrine of sin and grace lies far outside his sphere of thought. He has a boundless—indeed, a paradoxical—love for sinners, together with the most confident hope of their forgiveness and amendment[3]—an attitude of mind which is only tolerable when taken in connection with his universal love for mankind.[4] This is quite un-Pauline. Nor is it here simply a question of difference in temperament only; in this point St. Luke is in no sense a disciple of St. Paul;[5] and just because he does not pierce into the

---

[1] Of course his respect for the *religio antiqua* helped him here.

[2] Wellhausen (" Luk," s. 134) very rightly points out that, according to St. Luke, blasphemy against the Temple was not the alleged reason for our Lord's condemnation.

[3] See Wellhausen, " Einleitung," s. 69.

[4] Herder has rightly named him the evangelist of philanthropy.

[5] How St. Paul regarded sin and sinners is well known. We may

depths of the problem of sin, he has no deep insight into the doctrine of Redemption. His "soteriology," in spite of all the deep and precious things he tells us of Christ, is his weakest point. In some passages we cannot repress the suspicion that with him everything is concentrated in the magical efficacy of the Name of Christ. Christ is for him the superhuman Physician and Exorcist; therefore miraculous healing is the essential function and forms the test of the new religion. Faith is not in the least a necessary condition. First the miracle and its effect, then faith; this is St. Luke's order. How deep and precious appears that cumbrous gnosis of the Cross of Christ which occupied the mental energies of St. Paul, how profound and worthy his difficult doctrine of Justification by Faith, of Spirit and New Life, when compared with these Greek superficialities! It is true that St. Paul also believes in the magical sacrament, that he also recognises the Spirit of Christ operating as a power of nature; *but he is not contented with these things*. Because his faith masters his inmost soul, because it pierces to the very depths of his moral consciousness, he ever struggles upwards out of the realm of magical rite. St. Luke, however, seems to rest contented in this lower sphere, and yet, at the same time, he can reproduce the deeper things which he had learnt

judge of St. Luke's standpoint, on the one hand, from his choice of parables concerning sinners, on the other hand from Acts x. 35 : οὐκ ἔστιν προσωπολήμπτης ὁ θεός, ἀλλ' ἐν παντὶ ἔθνει ὁ φοβούμενος αὐτὸν καὶ ἐργαζόμενος δικαιοσύνην [*cf.* Rom. ii. 10, iv. 4 f.; Gal. vi. 10 ; Eph. iv. 28] δεκτὸς αὐτῷ ἐστίν, and Acts xvii. 29 ff. (the Gentiles are now delivered from their state of ignorance—that is, from idolatry). Compare this with Rom. i. and ii.

from others, from our Lord and St. Paul. *He is no Paulinist*,[1] but he shows quite clearly that he is acquainted with Paulinism and draws from its resources. Could, then, one so mentally constituted have been and have remained a companion of St. Paul? We may answer with the counter question: What idea have we formed of those Greeks who were St. Paul's companions and friends? If all of them, or even only the majority of them, were Paulinists in the strict sense of the word, how was it that the Gentile Church in Asia, in Greece and in Rome, became so entirely un-Pauline? Where, indeed, did Paulinism remain, except with Marcion, and what did Marcion make of it? We must determine not only to accept a more elastic definition of Paulinism, but above all to form a different conception of what St. Paul tolerated in his nearest disciples. He who confessed Christ as the Lord, who shunned the riches and the wickedness of the world, who saw God revealed in the Old Testament, who waited for the Resurrection and proclaimed this faith to the Greeks, without imposing upon them the rite of circumcision and the ceremonial law—this man was a disciple of St. Paul. In this sense St. Luke also was a Paulinist.[2] He

---

[1] Neither are his ethics Pauline. His " Ebionitism " is Hellenistic in character ; it implies simply abnegation of the world and love for sinners. And yet the word ἀγάπη never occurs in the Acts and only once in the gospel (xi. 42, "love of God "); ἀγαπᾷν also is wanting in the Acts. His attitude of aversion from the rich coincides with the attitude of the poor in Palestine, but its motive is different.

[2] The problem which exists in regard to St. Luke's relation to the epistles of St. Paul (*vide supra*) is without significance for the question whether he was the author of the complete history. If, as

was a Paulinist too because of his respect and reverence for the Apostle, which taught him to recognise in St. Paul an authority almost as great as St. Peter,[1] and led him to mould himself on St. Paul's preaching, as far as was possible for a man of his nationality and personality. This personality, with all its large-heartedness, has its own distinct and unique traits. If we read the Acts of the Apostles guided by the ruling fashion of literary criticism, we may analyse it into some half-dozen separate strata of documents; but if we read with discernment we discover *one mind* and *one hand* even in that which has been appropriated by the author.[2]

The gulf which divides St. Luke as a Christian from St. Paul shows him at a disadvantage, but there is yet another and more favourable side presented in his works. Side by side with his predilection for the religious magic and exorcistic superstitions of Hellenism *he possesses the mind and sense of form of a Greek*; through both these qualities he has become in his

is believed, signs can be found of his having read these epistles, it would not be surprising; if these signs are considered fallacious, it is not of much importance. Yet the hypothesis that these epistles were not used by our author becomes the more unintelligible the later the date which it is thought necessary to assign to the book. In my opinion, it cannot be claimed in the case of any one of St. Paul's epistles that the author of the Acts must have read it (see, on the contrary, Weizsäcker and Jacobsen)—1 Thess., Coloss., and Ephes. are the first to suggest themselves. But, on the other hand, there is enough found in the Acts to show that the author had knowledge both of the system of thought and of the language of the author of those epistles.

[1] Concerning St. Luke and St. Peter, see Wellhausen, "Luk," s. 124.

[2] Apart, of course, from arbitrary changes and interpolations of later date.

writings an architect of that Gentile Church which has conquered the world and has spiritualised and individualised religion. This same man, like Philip a seer of spirits and an exorcist, was the first to cast the Gospel into Hellenistic form and to bring the clarifying influence of the spirit of Hellenism to bear upon the evangelic message. This would be evident even if he had written nothing else than St. Paul's discourse at Athens; but in his gospel he has Hellenised the message of Christ, both in substance and form, by simple and yet effective means, and in the Acts he has become the first historian of the Church. In this work of art—for the Acts of the Apostles is nothing less; it is, indeed, a literary performance of the first rank, in construction[1] no less than in style—he has produced something quite unique and lasting. We do not know the effect which the book produced, but we know that it was canonised, and that means a great deal. St. Luke is the first member and the archetype of a series of writers which is distinguished by the names of St. Clement of Rome (representing the Roman Church[2]), the Apologists, St. Clement of

[1] Much might be urged against the construction technically, because of the way in which it narrows down, first to the history of St. Paul and at last to the account of the shipwreck; but from a psychological point of view it is unsurpassable. The book begins with the solemn tones of the organ and the peal of the bells and with the vision of a new and heavenly world; we are led gradually into the world of real things, and at last, in the company of the great apostle, we are caught in the storm, we look in his face and hear his words.

[2] The significance of the Roman Church in this respect has not been sufficiently noticed. It may be gathered from the first epistle of St. Clement, which cannot be rated at its right value so long as this element in it is not appreciated.

Alexandria, Origen, and Eusebius. The great process
of transformation under the influence of the sober
Hellenic spirit was begun by the very man who at the
same time remained rooted in the twofold miracle-
world of Palestine and Greece, and who yielded to
no Jewish Christian in his ardent and passionate
longing for the last great day of wrath.[1] This in
itself is another proof that we really have here a
man of the first Greek generation in the history of
Christianity.[2] He stood in personal intercourse with
Christians of the first generation and with St. Paul.
In order to realise how absolutely differently those felt
who were Hellenists and nothing else, and who had not
breathed the air of the first ages, we need only study
the works of St. Clement of Rome, whose date is so
little later, and of St. Ignatius. St. Paul and St. Luke
stand as contrasting figures. Just as the one is only
comprehensible as a Jew who yet personally came into
the closest contact with Hellenism, so the other is only
comprehensible as a Greek who had nevertheless personal
sympathy with primitive Jewish Christendom. Such a
gift of sympathy could alone inspire a Greek with the
tremendous courage that enabled him to write a gospel
and to become the first historian of primitive Christendom. The other evangelists are all Jews by birth, the
author of the gospel of the Hebrews included.

[1] The fact that the Parousia was delayed can no longer be dis-
guised, but as yet no doubts have arisen that it would still come.

[2] Wellhausen lays great stress on this, and rightly so ("Luk," s. 97
and elsewhere).

K

CHAPTER IV

RESULTS

A name counts for nothing—in the case of history this aphorism is only partly true. No names, of course, can make an incredible story authentic or probable, but the name of a contemporary and eye-witness guarantees the truth of a probable story, provided that there is no other reason for raising objections. And, further, the name tells us, as a rule, where, under what circumstances, and with what motives a tradition took its final and definite form. But we must first of all picture to ourselves the personality which stands behind the name "Luke."

If the Luke whom St. Paul has mentioned three times in his letters is identical with the author of the great historical work, then for us he remains no longer in obscurity, *and the criticism of his narratives is confined within definite bounds.* During the so-called second missionary journey, at Troas (or shortly before) Luke the Greek physician of Antioch encountered St. Paul. We have no knowledge when and by whose influence he became a Christian, nor whether he had previously come into sympathetic touch with the

Judaism of the Dispersion; only one thing is certain—
that he had never been in Jerusalem or Palestine. He
had at his command an average education, and possessed
a more than ordinary literary talent. His medical profession seems to have led him to Christianity, for he
embraced that religion in the conviction that by its
means and by quite new methods he would be enabled
to heal diseases and to drive out evil spirits, and above
all to become an effectual physician of the soul.
Directed by his very calling to the weak and wretched,
his philanthropic sympathy with the miserable was
deepened in that he accepted the religion of Christ, and
as a physician and evangelist proved and proclaimed the
power and efficacy of the Name of Jesus and of the
Gospel. He joined St. Paul at once in the capacity of
a *fellow-worker*, crossing over with him and with Silas
to Philippi and preaching the Gospel there (xvi. 13).
But the companionship was only of short duration. He
parted from the Apostle—the reason is unknown—
while yet at Philippi,[1] to join him again after some
years had passed—this time also at Troas. Then he
accompanied St. Paul from Troas by Miletus and
Cæsarea to Jerusalem, together with a number of companions, including the Jewish Christian Aristarchus of
Thessalonica. In Jerusalem, where he saw James and
the presbyters, but none of the apostles (not even St.
Peter), he seems to have stayed only a short time, for

---

1 It is therefore not probable that Origen and Pseudo-Ignatius are
right in their assertion that he is the unnamed brother (2 Cor. viii. 18),
οὗ ἔπαινος ἐν τῷ εὐαγγελίῳ διὰ πασῶν τῶν ἐκκλησιῶν, or the other who
(2 Cor. viii. 22) is also introduced without a name.

he does not represent himself as having been an eye-witness of what befel the Apostle here and in Cæsarea.[1] But when St. Paul set out as a prisoner on the long voyage to Rome, we find St. Luke again in his company. With this exception, Aristarchus alone of the Apostle's friends voyaged with him. St. Paul was an invalid when he began the voyage (this was probably the reason why a physician went with him). Only one day after the Apostle had begun his voyage he was obliged to land at Sidon to take advantage of the special care of his friends, having obtained the permission of his humane commanding officer. In Malta, where they were compelled to make a considerable stay, St. Luke (together with the Apostle) had the opportunity of practising his medical art (Acts xxviii. 2 f.), with the aid of Christian science. In Rome he tarried a considerable time with St. Paul as his physician (see Coloss. and Philipp.), and took part in the work of evangelisation (Philemon 24). Yet he did not, like Aristarchus, share the Apostle's imprisonment (Coloss. iv. 10). Besides Jesus Justus, Epaphras, Demas, and others, he there made the acquaintance of St. Mark, the nephew of Barnabas (Coloss. iv. 10).[2] "Only Luke is with me" (2 Tim. iv. 11)—that is the last we hear of him. But we know from his works that he survived the destruction of Jerusalem, and was still at work a

---

[1] At least the fact of his being an eye-witness is uncertain.

[2] St. Luke also came into personal acquaintance with four among the number of prominent men in the primitive community at Jerusalem—Silas, Mark, Philip, and James. He was, however, more with the two former than the others.

good time afterwards. We cannot discover with certainty where he went after leaving Rome—not, at all events, to Jerusalem and Palestine, nor even to Antioch or Macedonia (both these provinces are excluded because of the way in which he writes of them in the Acts). He could hardly have remained in Rome (though indeed this is not excluded by the Acts, it is nevertheless not probable). We are therefore left to seek him either in Achaia (according to the earliest tradition) or in Asia. Asia, and more especially Ephesus, are suggested by the way in which he has distinguished this city and has made of St. Paul's parting discourse to the Church of Ephesus a farewell of the Apostle to his converts in general (see especially xx. 25: ὑμεῖς πάντες ἐν οἷς διῆλθον κηρύσσων τὴν βασιλείαν). That he has special interest in this city appears still more clearly to me from the heartfelt tones in which he speaks and the great anxiety which he expresses, but above all because he knows and refers to the later history of the Church in that city.[1] Similar traits are not found in the author's reference to any other Church.[2] From the prominence given to Ephesus it does not necessarily follow that

1 See the detailed warning, xx. 29 f.: 'Εγὼ οἶδα ὅτι εἰσελεύσονται μετὰ τὴν ἄφιξίν [does this mean death or departure ?] μου λύκοι βαρεῖς εἰς ὑμᾶς μὴ φειδόμενοι τοῦ ποιμνίου, καὶ ἐξ ὑμῶν αὐτῶν ἀναστήσονται ἄνδρες λαλοῦντες διεστραμμένα τοῦ ἀποσπᾶν τοὺς μαθητὰς ὀπίσω ἑαυτῶν. Cf. Rev. ii. 2.

2 St. Luke leaves his reader in no doubt that the foundation of the Church in Corinth was the grandest achievement of St. Paul's so-called second missionary journey; but the author himself has no relations with that Church.

the author wrote his book in that city itself, but it surely follows that it was written in some region for which Ephesus was an important centre (Achaia therefore remains open). It appears from the gospel, and also from the Acts, that the community of the disciples of St. John the Baptist was for ever irritating the Christian community, and the author's interest in this controversy is shown in close connection with Ephesus (xix. 1 ff.).[1] *Here we have the first and very clear instance of relationship between St. Luke and the gospel of St. John.* But St. Luke also shows that he is interested in St. Philip and his prophesying daughters (xxi. 9); *these people we know lived at a later time in Hierapolis, in Phrygia*[2]—another point in favour of the theory that St. Luke himself took up his abode at a later time in Asia. In this connection it must be further noticed that he has seven times smuggled St.

[1] According to Weiss and others, the men spoken of in this passage were not disciples of St. John, and even Apollos could not have been one (xviii. 25). I cannot go into this intricate question here. In my opinion, we must regard them as disciples of St. John, because they had received their sacrament of baptism from him ; but, on the other hand, they believed in Jesus. We can reconcile these two articles of their faith by supposing that they believed in Jesus as the *future* Messiah—*i.e.*, that they looked upon His first appearance as in every sense only preparatory. It is a most astonishing fact—but unfortunately this is not the only instance of the kind—that the critics actually presume to correct the essential characteristics of the information which St. Luke has given concerning the standpoint of Apollos and of the other disciples, advancing hypotheses of two sources and the like, as if they had complete information concerning these disciples. They thus destroy for us one of the most precious relics of early Christendom, which, short as it is, represents a complete department in the primitive Christian movement.

[2] Papias, in Eusebius, "H. E.," iii. 39.

John into the source which contains the Petrine stories, and this without any apparent reason (*vide supra*, p. 117). This circumstance, of course, need not necessarily be connected with the author's interest in Ephesus; indeed, it is not at all likely that it is so, since when speaking of Ephesus he is never reminded of St. John. Therefore his interest in St. John may very well have had another incentive. *Yet in relation to the problem concerning the later history of St. John the son of Zebedee it is of high significance that he alone among the apostles, with the exception of St. Peter, is the one in whom St. Luke shows interest.*[1] This interest is not easily accounted for otherwise than by assuming that the author had knowledge of some mission undertaken by St. John at a later time. Here let us remember that this apostle is introduced in a very artificial way into the account of the mission in Samaria. According to our author, St. John comes next in honour to St. Peter, and in the primitive community he is represented as inseparable from the chief apostle. As this idea concerning St. John can scarcely have arisen from the fact that he was one of our Lord's nearest disciples—for in that case our author must have placed St. James the son of Zebedee (whose martyrdom only is mentioned quite cursorily) as near to St. Peter as he does St. John —and as our author possessed absolutely no source of information concerning any specially prominent achievement of St. John in the early community at Jerusalem, it is difficult to avoid the conclusion that

---

[1] Strange that he has passed him over in Acts xv. ! This fact alone shows that he had not read the Epistle to the Galatians,

he has thus smuggled him as an important person into the history of the early Church because of some later achievements of that apostle which were known to him.

Let us now return to St. Luke. At Ephesus, or some place in Asia or Achaia, and about the year 80 A.D., he wrote his history for the "excellent" Theophilus. His chief authority for the gospel was the work of St. Mark, his late companion in Rome; besides this, he employed for the Lord's life a second source, which he shared with St. Matthew; [1] and, thirdly, he is dependent upon special traditions which had their origin in Jerusalem or Judæa, whose authenticity is almost entirely dubious, and which must, indeed, be described as for the most part legendary. It is most unlikely that he collected these during his probably only very short stay in Jerusalem during the first years of Nero's reign, for then they must also have been incorporated in St. Mark; but, so far from this being the case, they go beyond and even correct the conceptions and accounts of the latter gospel. This material, therefore, must have reached St. Luke at a later period. That it is connected with, or, rather, leads up to, what underlies the fourth gospel [2] has been emphasised by many writers, and lately by Wellhausen. [3] In all probability it did not reach either St. Luke or St. John in written form, [4]

[1] Concerning this source, see my book "Die Sprüche und Reden Jesu," 1907, an English translation of which will appear shortly.

[2] Concerning the relation between St. Luke and St. John, see Appendix IV.

[3] Wellhausen, "Luk," ss. 8, 11, 20, 45, 53, 123 ; "Einleit.," s. 65.

[4] If in writing, then in Aramaic,

but depended upon the oral tradition of Christians of Jerusalem or Judæa who had wandered from Palestine or Jerusalem at or after the time of the Great War. These we must think of as "ecstatics" altogether wanting in sober-mindedness and credibility, like Philip and his four prophesying daughters who came to Asia. Were not the latter, indeed, of just such a character? It is known that St. Luke made their acquaintance in Cæsarea, and it is very probable that on a later occasion he encountered them yet again in Asia. *Papias, who himself saw the daughters, expressly states that they transmitted stories of the old days.*[1] Doubtless we must picture to ourselves the people who were the authorities for the separate source allied to the fourth gospel, which St. Luke has so wonderfully and beautifully edited, as being something like the Philip of Acts viii., and like what we may imagine his daughters to have been, both from the fact that they were prophetesses and from Papias' notice concerning them. It is now most remarkable that very distinct prominence is given in this special source of St. Luke not only to prophecy (inspired by the Holy Ghost), but *still more to the feminine element*, as Plummer (" Comm. on St. Luke,"

---

[1] Papias, in Eusebius, "H. E.," iii. 39, 9: τὸ μὲν οὖν κατὰ τὴν Ἱεράπολιν Φίλιππον τὸν ἀπόστολον ἅμα ταῖς θυγατράσιν διατρῖψαι διὰ τῶν πρόσθεν δεδήλωται. ὡς δὲ κατὰ τοὺς αὐτοὺς ὁ Παπίας γενόμενος, διήγησιν παρειληφέναι θαυμασίαν ὑπὸ τῶν τοῦ Φιλίππου θυγατέρων μνημονεύει, τὰ νῦν σημειωτέον· νεκροῦ γὰρ ἀνάστασιν κατ' αὐτὸν γεγονυῖαν ἱστορεῖ καὶ αὖ πάλιν ἕτερον παράδοξον περὶ Ἰοῦστον τὸν ἐπικληθέντα Βαρσαβᾶν γεγονός, ὡς δηλητήριον φάρμακον ἐμπιόντος καὶ μηδὲν ἀηδὲς διὰ τὴν τοῦ κυρίου χάριν ὑπομείναντος. . . . καὶ ἄλλα δὲ ὁ αὐτὸς ὡς ἐκ παραδόσεως ἀγράφου εἰς αὐτὸν ἥκοντα παρατίθειται ξένας τέ τινας παραβολὰς τοῦ σωτῆρος κ. διδασκαλίας αὐτοῦ καί τινα ἄλλα μυθικώτερα.

p. xlii. s.) and others have already pointed out.[1] St. Mark, and also St. Matthew, still leave women very much in the background in the Gospel story. *St. Luke is the first to give them such a prominent place therein.* We find mentioned in his gospel (besides St. Mary, the Mother of our Lord):

1. The prophetess Elizabeth.
2. The prophetess Hanna.
3. The widow of Nain.
4. The woman who was a sinner.
5. The notice in chap. viii. 1 ff: οἱ δώδεκα σὺν αὐτῷ καὶ γυναῖκές τινες αἳ ἦσαν τεθεραπευμέναι ἀπὸ πνευμάτων πονηρῶν καὶ ἀσθενειῶν, Μαρία ἡ καλουμένη Μαγδαληνή, ἀφ' ἧς δαιμόνια ἑπτὰ ἐξεληλύθει, καὶ Ἰωάννα γυνὴ Χουζᾶ ἐπιτρόπου Ἡρῴδου[2] καὶ Σουσάννα καὶ ἕτεραι πολλαί, αἵτινες διηκόνουν αὐτοῖς ἐκ τῶν ὑπαρχόντων αὐταῖς. According to St. Luke (who knows more about them than he tells us—see Wellhausen on this passage), these women ministered to the necessity, not only of Jesus, but also of the whole inner circle of disciples[3] (the gist of the passage was, moreover, already given in St. Mark xv. 40 f.).

[1] In St. John also the feminine element is more prominent than in St. Mark and St. Matthew, but not nearly so much so as in St. Luke (*vide* the Mother in chap. ii., the woman of Samaria, Mary and Martha, St. Mary beside the cross, the words to St. Mary from the cross, *the Magdalene as the first* who saw the Risen One).

[2] Compare, moreover, Μαναὴν Ἡρῴδου τοῦ τετράρχου σύντροφος (Acts xiii. 1).

[3] Ἀὐτοῖς is to be read. Wellhausen follows the insufficiently attested reading αὐτῷ.

6. Mary and Martha.

7. The woman who called the Mother of our Lord blessed (xi. 27).

8. The woman who had a spirit of infirmity for eighteen years (xiii. 10 ff.).

9. The widow and the unjust judge (xviii. 1 ff.)

10. The woman and the lost piece of silver (xv. 8 ff.).

11. The widow's mite (xxi. 1 f.).

12. The daughters of Jerusalem weeping over our Lord's sufferings (xxiii. 27 ff.).

13. The women of Galilee beside the cross (xxiii. 49).

14. Women as the first evangelists of our Lord's Resurrection (xxiv. 10)—contrary to St. Mark.

And we may perhaps add (though on very slender grounds),

15. The story of the woman taken in adultery.

A very considerable portion of the matter peculiar to St. Luke is thus feminine in interest. It is therefore, perhaps, not too presumptuous to assign these traditions to Philip and his four prophesying daughters.[1] We may also remember that another collection of stories in St. Luke is distinguished by the interest shown for the Samaritans—a trait which is wanting in St. Mark

[1] Also in the Acts St. Luke is greatly interested in converted women—a trait which is purposely attenuated in the text of D. See my essay on Priscilla and Aquila in the "Sitzungsber. der Preuss. Akad.," 1900, January 11. But this interest is here determined by the facts themselves, and does not seem to be anywhere exaggerated.

and St. Matthew [1]—and that, according to the Acts, St. Philip's own grand achievement was the evangelisation of Samaria (viii. 14: ἀκούσαντες οἱ ἐν Ἱεροσολύμοις ἀπόστολοι ὅτι δέδεκται ἡ Σαμαρία [scil. through the preaching of Philip] τὸν λόγον τοῦ θεοῦ). Villages of Samaria in which the gospel was preached are only mentioned in the gospel of St. Luke (ix. 52–56) and in the Acts (viii. 25).[2] This coincidence of interest in the feminine element, in prophecy (the Holy Spirit), and in the Samaritans, taken together with the general stand-point—*that of Jerusalem*—of this source peculiar to St. Luke, makes it probable that we have here a body of tradition which rests upon the authority of St. Philip and his daughters.[3]

But this impression is confirmed by the Acts of the Apostles. We have already shown that (apart from the source common to St. Matthew and St. Luke) St. Mark certainly, and tradition originating with St. Philip most probably, formed the two chief authorities of St. Luke in the gospel; now our confidence in this conclusion is strengthened by the fact that it simply and easily fits in with the phenomena presented in the Acts of the Apostles. It is true that for the second

---

[1] This interest is also shared by the fourth evangelist.

[2] But in the fourth gospel compare with the words of the Acts (viii. 25: πολλάς τε κώμας τῶν Σαμαρειτῶν εὐαγγελίζοντο) the information of St. John iv. 39: ἐκ τῆς πόλεως ἐκείνης πολλοὶ ἐπίστευσαν εἰς αὐτὸν τῶν Σαμαρειτῶν.

[3] Amongst the number of later accounts concerning St. Philip (and his daughters) we must reckon that of St. Clement, "Strom.," iii. 4, 25. There it is asserted, as if it stood in the gospel, that St. Luke ix. 60 was spoken to him. Has St. Clement confused matters here?

half of the book the author's own recollections and the records of other companions of St. Paul were at his disposal (*e.g.*, for the tumult in Ephesus, judging from xix. 29, probably the record of Aristarchus—*vide supra*, p. 136); *but for the first half*—we see it at a glance—*he relies entirely* (apart from his account of St. Paul's conversion and all that concerns Antioch) *on tradition concerning St. Peter and St. Philip*. It is probable that the stories concerning St. Peter reached him through St. Mark, because St. Mark alone was closely connected both with St. Peter and, by kinship, with St. Barnabas (Coloss. iv. 10 : ὁ ἀνεψιὸς Βαρνάβα), two very prominent persons in the Acts of the Apostles ; and also because St. Luke shows (Acts xii.) that he is well informed concerning the house of St. Mark's mother in Jerusalem—indeed, he even knows the name of one of her maid-servants (Rhoda). In regard to St. Philip, however, there is no need of many words to show that St. Luke possessed traditions about him, and resting on his authority. It is possible that St. Luke received them only during his stay with Philip in Cæsarea (ix. 30 and xxi. 9—*vide supra*, p. 39), though it is more probable that he also at a later date conversed with St. Philip's prophesying daughters in Asia. However this may be, even if he received the tradition at an early date, from Philip and his daughters in Cæsarea and from St. Mark in Rome, we should never forget that St. Luke first composed his history at a considerably later date, and, moreover, has elaborated in his own way their somewhat questionable records.[1]

1 It does not seem to me difficult to distinguish broadly between

But his connection with St. Mark requires some further comment. St. Luke has incorporated three-fourths of the gospel into his book, yet he does not show great respect for its wording. He has neither mentioned this gospel by name in his prologue, nor has he there expressed an altogether favourable opinion concerning his predecessors,[1] amongst whom he must have -reckoned St. Mark in the first rank. But more than this—we may even say that St. Luke wrote his gospel in order to supplant the gospel of St. Mark, in the sense, at least, in which every author writing after another author on the same subject intends to supersede the work of his predecessor. He regarded it as containing in the main authentic tradition, but, apart from numerous corrections in style and other small points, on the ground of what he considered better information he has in important details condemned it as wrong in its order of events, too unspiritual, and imperfect and incorrect.[2] This is shown most clearly in the accounts

that which St. Luke obtained from St. Mark and that which he obtained from St. Philip or his daughters. In the mission to the Samaritans both streams of tradition flow together. Here doubt exists as to the share to be assigned to each, and, moreover, to the editor, St. Luke.

[1] Rather he indirectly criticises them. Eusebius ("H. E.," iii. 22, 15) who could certainly appreciate Greek style and the intention of an author, paraphrases the prologue of St. Luke as follows: ὁ δὲ Λουκᾶς ἀρχόμενος καὶ αὐτὸς τοῦ κατ' αὐτὸν συγγράμματος τὴν αἰτίαν προύθηκεν δι' ἣν πεποίηται τὴν σύνταξιν, δηλῶν ὡς ἄρα πολλῶν καὶ ἄλλων προπετέστερον ἐπιτετηδευκότων διήγησιν ποιήσασθαι ὧν αὐτὸς πεπληροφόρητο λόγων, ἀναγκαίως ἀπαλλάττων ἡμᾶς τῆς περὶ τοὺς ἄλλους ἀμφηρίστου ὑπολήψεως, τὸν ἀσφαλῆ λόγον ὧν αὐτὸς ἱκανῶς τὴν ἀλήθειαν κατειλήφει . . διὰ τοῦ ἰδίου παρέδωκεν εὐαγγελίου.

[2] Numerous examples may be adduced from the comparison of

of the Passion and the Resurrection. With regard to
the latter, St. Luke, following his special source, has
replaced St. Mark's account by later legends which had
arisen in Jerusalem, and, in direct opposition to St.
Mark, has ascribed the first announcement of the
Resurrection to women. Moreover, a special light is
thrown upon his connection with St. Mark by the Acts
of the Apostles. The only apostolic man about whom
something unpleasant is therein recorded is St. Mark—
a point which has been noticed above (p. 134, note).
He is accused of breach of faith (xiii. 13, *cf.* xv. 37 ff.),
and he is made answerable for the separation of St.
Barnabas and St. Paul. That is a bitter reproach
which St. Luke has not shrunk from perpetuating.[1]
But the Church—that is, the Church of Asia, followed
by the other Churches—did not reject the work of
the Jewish Christian of Jerusalem, when it came into
her hands ; though she, indeed, criticised it, she nevertheless acknowledged it as excellent, and set it quietly
side by side with the work of the Greek physician
of Antioch.

The traditions concerning Jesus which we find in St.

the two gospels to show that St. Luke criticised the gospel of St.
Mark from these points of view. Some of them agree remarkably
with those from which the presbyter John, as recorded by Papias,
has criticised the book. The presbyter admits (1) the incomplete-
ness of St. Mark, and, moreover, (2) its faulty order ; but he maintains its exactness, its veracity, and the conscientious effort of the
evangelist to give a full reproduction of the information which he
had received.

[1] It already struck Irenæus as strange that St. Luke in the Acts
parts St. Mark from the fellowship of St. Paul.

Mark and St. Luke are older than is generally supposed. This does not make them more credible, but it is a fact of no slight significance in relation to their criticism. In St. Mark we have the deposit of several strata of tradition originating entirely in Jerusalem. Wellhausen has brought forward good reasons for the view that they were first written in Aramaic. I do not profess to offer an independent opinion on this difficult question. The presbyter John maintains that the gospel was based upon the mission sermons of St. Peter ; only it is difficult to understand why a native of Jerusalem like St. Mark, whose maternal home had formed a centre for the primitive Church, and who knew the whole community, should have taken the *mission sermons* of St. Peter— and these, indeed, exclusively—as the basis of his work. This piece of information, therefore, does not seem reliable; it looks rather like a story that was invented for the purpose of excusing the deficiencies and omissions of this gospel. It is another point in its disfavour if it be true that St. Mark was still a boy and growing youth during the twelve years which St. Peter probably spent [1] with the primitive community ; and this supposition, judging from the nature of his connection with his uncle St. Barnabas and with St. Paul, is probably true, and fits in with the very emphatic statement of tradition (presb. John, Murat. fragment) that he had neither seen nor heard the Lord. We can also unreservedly accept the old tradition which tells of him that, after having accompanied St. Paul, first for a short time, then longer (in Rome), he also acted as interpreter to St. Peter, and

---

[1] It seems that later he only visited Jerusalem by the way.

thus heard something also from this apostle. But from this tradition little or nothing can be concluded in regard to the relation this gospel bears to St. Peter, if it be true that it was only after his death that St. Mark determined to give a written account of the gospel of Jesus Christ (see Irenæus). He then collected together all the material that he could lay hands upon,[1] and that would serve his purpose of proving Jesus to be the Christ from His mighty deeds and words. Though in this gospel we find different strata of tradition lying side by side or confused together, yet they serve but one and the same purpose, and this was all that St. Mark cared for. And yet everything that stands in this gospel was already in circulation before the year 70 A.D., or, as others think, soon afterwards. At that time contradictory and discrepant stories were mingled together in people's brains and minds, just as thoughts are nowadays. But it is probable that this same Mark also related—either by word of mouth or in an Aramaic writing—"classic" stories of the primitive community at the time when St. Peter was at the head of the brethren and St. James had not come to the helm of affairs. Thus the first attempt to crystallise the tradition concerning our Lord and the primitive " classic " days in a written account was made by one who was a

---

1 Wellhausen rightly says ("Einl.," s. 53) : " It seems that the tradition narrated by St. Mark does not rest mainly upon the authority of close acquaintances of Jesus. It has for the most part a somewhat rough, popular style, as if it had passed for a long time from mouth to mouth among the people, until it took the simple dramatic form in which it now lies before us."

disciple both of St. Peter and St. Paul;[1] and yet we must not expect to discover behind his work either St. Peter or St. Paul as his authorities. It may seem very strange to us that neither the intercourse of our Lord with his disciples nor St. Paul's theology is really reflected in this gospel, though it was written by a disciple of the apostles; but let us not forget that St. Mark was so possessed by his own conception of our Lord, and so convinced of its truth, that, paradoxical as it may sound, he was relieved of the duty of drawing His portrait in the closest possible accordance with historic fact, and was prevented from burdening the absolute simplicity of his doctrine concerning the Christ with the conceptions of systematic theology.[2] Neither the teaching of our Lord nor His mission as a Saviour and Healer, as such, specially interested him. His concern lay with words and deeds of Divine power; and the later tradition doubtless presented more striking instances of these than the earlier. It cannot be said with certainty for what readers St. Mark wrote. Not for Jewish Christians; very probably for Roman Christians; at all events, for those who knew Alexander and Rufus, the sons of Simon of Cyrene—and in Rome we hear that there dwelt one Rufus, a Christian, and his mother, who was a believer (Rom. xvi. 13).[3]

[1] There is no certain proof that St. Mark was dependent upon written sources which were already in existence.

[2] Even the argument from prophecy is almost entirely wanting, and this was the beginning of all theology. In other respects St. Mark among the synoptists is the nearest to St. Paul.

[3] The old "Argumentum," dating from about 220 A.D. (Corssen, "Texte und Unters.," Bd. 15, H. 1, s. 9), expressly states that St. Mark

After him comes St. Luke, a second disciple of St.
Paul. It is, indeed, a fact not without significance that
it was companions of St. Paul—even if they were not
the only ones—who undertook this task of literary
crystallisation. The great mental gulf between St. Luke
and St. Mark must not be measured by years ; for we
cannot place St. Luke as an author much later than the
year 80 A.D. He was a Greek and a native of Antioch,
while St. Mark was a Jew and a native of Jerusalem.
Under his hands the universalistic and humane, the social
and individualistic tendencies of Hellenism, the ecstatic
and magical elements of Greek religion, yet also Greek
thought and sense of form, gain the mastery over the
subject-matter of the traditional narratives. And yet,
at the same time, great respect is shown for the *religio
antiqua* of the Old Testament, as St. Luke depicts it,
for instance, in Zacharias and Elizabeth. He lays the
foundation of the second stage in the crystallisation of
the Gospel tradition, and at once proceeds to record the
history of the extension and triumph of the youthful
religion.[1] For both parts of his narrative he depends

wrote his gospel in Italy (this does not exclude, but includes Rome).
It also says that St. Mark was a Levite, and had cut off his thumb in
order to avoid becoming a priest. That this is a Roman tradition,
and that St. Mark bore the nickname ὁ κολοβοδάκτυλος in Rome,
follows from the fact that Hippolytus also bears witness to it
("Phil.," vii. 30). For further details see my essay "Pseudopapia-
nisches," in the "Ztschr. f. N. Tliche. Wissensch.," 1902, iii. s. 159 ff.

[1] What a trumpet-note of joy, courage, and triumph sounds
through the whole Lukan history, from the first to the last pages !
Vexilla regis prodeunt ! We listen in vain for this note in the other
evangelists. They are all burdened with a far heavier load of cares,
of thoughts, and of doctrines than this Greek enthusiast for Christ,

upon St. Mark. In the gospel, however, he has at least two other sources (Q=that which St. Luke has in common with St. Matthew, P=that originating in Jerusalem and related to St. John), the latter of which, distorted by many different tendencies, seems to be connected with those traditions in the Acts which have been referred to St. Philip. There is very much to be said in favour of the view that St. Philip and his prophetic daughters have contributed the truly ample material for both parts of this source. The chief point, however, is that the whole, in its main features at least, had its origin in Jerusalem (or in Judæa), that in St. Mark and St. Luke there are to be found only a few traditions and legends which sprang up as a secondary growth in Gentile-Christian soil,[1] and that the whole of St. Luke's material was already in existence about the year 80 A.D. If we consider the gulf that yawns between the latest accounts in St. Luke and the earliest in St. Mark we are astounded that such a tremendous development should have been accomplished in so short a time and exclusively on the soil of Judæa and Jerusalem. Both in St. Mark and St. Luke it is almost always only the history of the primitive community of

who courageously marches forward, surmounting every difficulty. He amply compensates us for his faith in magic, his enormous credulity and theological superficiality, by his own peculiar quality of confident, happy hopefulness and his genuine Greek delight in telling stories. As a story-teller, "all is grist that comes to his mill."

[1] But it is, of course, not without significance that the literary crystallisation of this material (except that of Q) took place *outside* Palestine (in Rome and Asia). St. Luke refers to the circumstances of the Diaspora in his accounts of the disciples of St. John, and perhaps in some parables.

Jerusalem or of the communities of Judæa which is reflected in the tradition these evangelists record.[1]   The history of Gentile Christianity is scarcely touched upon in the gospel and the first half of the Acts, except in so far as Gentile communities are expressly mentioned. But in what is told us of this subject in the second half of the Acts, St. Luke—writing partly as an eye-witness and partly from accounts given by eye-witnesses—has produced a splendid piece of work, and has given an historical account which, though it indeed leaves much to be desired, needs nevertheless only a few corrections, and excellently supplements the Pauline epistles.   What a wealth of matter of all kinds is found in peaceful juxtaposition in these two books !   The subject-matter, indeed, is even more varied than the forms of expression !   From this significant fact we may estimate and realise what a multitude of various conceptions could be accepted and reconciled with one another *in one and the same* mind.   St. Luke writes absolutely without bias; or, rather, he is biased in *one* direction only— his one object is to prove that our Lord is the Divine Saviour, and to show forth His saving ˙power in His history and in the working of His Spirit (in the mission of the apostles among the Gentiles, in contrast to the stubborn Jews).   In his gospel he, like St. Mark, almost entirely disregards theology, more particularly the

---

[1] Hence it is the picture of the primitive Church of Jerusalem (or of the Judaic Churches), shining forth in the gospels side by side with the portrait of our Lord, which has edified the Gentile Churches up to this very day.   In this sense Jewish Christianity still survives : ὑμεῖς μιμηταὶ ἐγενήθητε τῶν ἐκκλησιῶν τοῦ θεοῦ τῶν οὐσῶν ἐν τῇ Ἰουδαίᾳ ἐν Χριστῷ Ἰησοῦ (1 Thess. ii. 14).

argument from prophecy; in the Acts (first half) he makes copious use of it. This historical work, originating in Asia or Achaia, is even less Paulinistic in teaching than the gospel of St. Mark. In both these works St. Paul lives on in only the most general and universal aspects of his teaching; but with him the most general and universal was also the greatest and noblest.

No proof is required to show that Q and "St. Matthew" are based exclusively on traditions originating in Palestine or Jerusalem; for the horizon of "St. Matthew" is bounded by Palestine, and this gospel is the work of the Church of Palestine,[1] which therein shows itself to be free from the yoke of the Law and kindly disposed towards the Gentiles. The fact that St. Mark also forms the groundwork of this gospel is in itself a proof of liberal views in regard to the Law, and, moreover, affords strong evidence that the second gospel was written by St. Mark, a native of Jerusalem; for how could the Church of Palestine have so readily accepted a gospel which did not rest upon the authority of a native of Jerusalem? Our position is therefore unassailable when we assert that the whole synoptic tradition belongs to Palestine and Jerusalem, and has had no connection with Gentile Christian circles except in the redaction of St. Luke. The limits of the play of Hellenic in-

---

[1] Most probably the work is to be assigned to the Hellenistic portion of the primitive community of Jerusalem—to those circles, indeed, which had developed, both within and side by side with the primitive community, out of those Jews of the dispersion, described in Acts vi., who lived at Jerusalem (*e.g.*, Stephen).

fluence in the gospels, in so far as that influence had not already infected the very blood of Judaism, are thus sharply defined.[1]

It is a recognised fact that the gospel of St. Matthew speedily forced the two other gospels into the background in the Gentile Churches. If they had not been canonised, certainly St. Mark and probably St. Luke would have succumbed. What is the fault in St. Luke and St. Mark? and wherein lies the strength of St. Matthew? *The gospel of St. Matthew was written as an apology against the objections and calumnies of the Jews, which were soon also adopted by the Gentiles. This evangelist alone has a distinct interest in our Lord's teaching as such; he instructs, he proves, and all the while he keeps the Church well in the foreground.*[2] Already in the period which immediately followed the composition of this gospel these characteristics were found to outweigh all other advantages. Here, indeed, as we draw our investigation to a conclusion, we are brought face to face with a paradox. The gospel which in contents and bias is farthest removed from the Hellenic spirit—the gospel which is throughout occupied with sharp and detailed controversy with the unbelieving Jews of Palestine—was soon seized upon by Greeks themselves as the

[1] For example, it at once follows that the legend of the Virgin birth, first vouched for by St. Matthew, arose on Jewish Christian soil, more particularly among the Christians of Jerusalem.

[2] Wellhausen rightly lays special stress on this point. Note how St. Matthew restricts or deletes all novelistic traits, while he introduces an element of ceremonious solemnity into the style of his narrative.

gospel most to their mind,[1] because it answered the requirements of apologetics and of the controversy with Judaism—in short, because of its theological and doctrinal character and its solemn, ceremonious style. Hence it followed that this gospel replaced Paulinism in the Gentile Church—that is, in so far as this Church went beyond universalism in the direction of distinctly Pauline doctrine, she interpreted St. Paul in accordance with St. Matthew. And yet this result is not so wonderful after all. Of course, if we grant the truth of the old theory that Paulinism is equivalent to Gentile Christianity, then it is all most perplexing. But as soon as we realise what Paulinism really was—namely, the universalistic doctrine and dialectic of a Jewish Christian—it becomes easily comprehensible that Paulinism should have been replaced by St. Matthew, the gospel which both in positive and negative qualities, both in aim and in method, is much more nearly akin to it than are St. Mark and St. Luke

[1] Next to St. John, which in this respect is most like St. Matthew—in fact, is St. Matthew glorified. "St. John" also is a Jew, and, indeed, like "St. Matthew," a Jew of Palestine, but he also pays regard to the circumstances of the Diaspora in which he lived. If we have called St. John a glorified St. Matthew, because his aim also is didactic and apologetic, we may with equal justice call him a glorified St. Mark and St. Luke, for he shares in the aims which dominate both these evangelists. By means of the historic narrative he strives, like St. Mark, to show that Jesus is the Son of God, and, like St. Luke, to prove that He is the Saviour of the world, in opposition to the unbelieving Jews and the disciples of St. John the Baptist. Thus the leading ideas of the synoptists are found in combination in St. John. This cannot be accidental. From this conclusion light is thrown upon *one* of the great problems which this book presents.

(in the gospel). St. Paul was overshadowed by St. Matthew because of the Pauline dialectic, which very soon proved to be perilous, furthermore because with St. Paul the fulfilment of the Old Testament seemed to be overshadowed by his doctrine of the abrogation of the Law, and lastly because of the diffi- culty of reconciling the doctrine of the Freedom of the Will with his theology. And so the gospel which in every characteristic trait bears witness to its origin from Jerusalem, and which is absorbed in the con- troversy between the Jews and Jewish Christians, has become the chief gospel of the Gentile Church. How- ever, in regard to their subject-matter, all the gospels, that of St. Luke just as much as the others, are only varieties of the same species, because they are all of them built up upon traditions and legends which have one and the same native home, and are separated from one another in time by only a few decades of years. Two of the authors stand out in the light of history— St. Mark and St. Luke, the companions of St. Paul. It is not to be wondered at that we do not know the real name of the third writer; for the gospel of St. Matthew is not in the least a book which reflects the views of one man or of a small circle. It was compiled for the use of the Church, and has been edited probably several times.[1] It may be called the first liturgical book of the Christian Church, in the first place of the Church of Palestine, in so far as the latter,

---

[1] In its original form it was older than St. Luke ; in its present form it is probably the latest of the synoptic gospels. A whole series of passages are palpably later additions.

having outgrown its initial stage of legal Judaic Christianity, was no longer a Jewish sect, and thus was also
able to contribute something of its own to the Gentile
Church.[1] This Gentile Church, indeed, so soon as it

[1] This sketch of the peculiar character and of the circumstances of
the origin of the synoptic gospels receives weighty confirmation if
we institute a linguistic comparison of these works with the LXX.
and at the same time note the unclassical words which occur in
them (by unclassical words I mean those for which we have no evidence
of occurrence previous to the time of the gospels ; this is, of course,
an unsafe criterion, especially as we now have the papyri). The
best books of reference on this point are Moulton and Geden's
" Concordance " and Hawkins, *loc cit.* pp. 162–71. These show us
that in point of language St. Luke stands by far the nearest of
all to the LXX., and has relatively the fewest unclassical words (of the
319 words which are peculiar to him in the New Testament—here we
omit the Acts—239 are found in the LXX., *i.e.* three-quarters, and
only 40 of the 319 words, thus one-eighth part, are unclassical).
St. Matthew stands in the mean position—nearer, that is, to St. Luke
(of the 112 words which are peculiar to him in the New Testament
76 are found in the LXX., *i.e.* less than two-thirds, and 18 of the 112
words, thus about one-seventh, are unclassical).   St. Mark is furthest
removed from the LXX. (of the 71 words which are peculiar to him
in the New Testament only 40 are found in the LXX., *i.e.* little more
than half, and 20 of the 71 words, thus more than a quarter, are unclassical).   The relationship of St. Mark to the LXX. becomes yet
more distant if we take into consideration the words not occurring
in the LXX., which are common to him and St. Matthew, to him and
St. Luke, and to all three, *for they must all be set down to his account.*
This result is also confirmed in matter of detail.   For instance, the
plural οὐρανοί is not frequent in the LXX. (for twelve places with οὐρανός
there is one with οὐρανοί).   Accordingly the plural is also infrequent
in St. Luke (for nine places with οὐρανός there is one with οὐρανοί).
But in St. Mark, for two passages with οὐρανός we already find one
with οὐρανοί, and in St. Matthew—he is accordingly here the most
distant from the LXX.—the proportion is just the reverse.   What is
the explanation of these facts ? They coincide with our results
which are essentially the same as those of Wellhausen.   There lies
behind St. Mark not the Greek of the LXX., but Aramaic, which has

became a teaching Church—and that soon came to pass—preferred St. Matthew, and let St. Luke fall into the background. Yet the influence of this gospel of the Saviour of Sinners still continued to work, and still carried on its own special mission in the Christian community, while in the portrait of St. Paul drawn in the Acts, far more than in his own epistles, the great apostle still lives in the Catholic Church.

been translated into a rude Greek of its own. The author was thus not a Jewish Christian of the Diaspora, who lived in the atmosphere of the Greek Bible, even though he was acquainted with it, but a Jew of Palestine (this coincides with what we know of the person of St. Mark). In contrast with him, the author of the third gospel—subtracting all that he has borrowed from St. Mark—lives in the atmosphere of the LXX.; he is accordingly by descent a Jew of the Diaspora or a Gentile by birth. The latter alternative suits St. Luke, The intermediate position occupied by St. Matthew (except in the case of οὐρανοί)—here also we subtract what is borrowed from St. Mark—is explained excellently on the supposition that he was a Jew of the Diaspora living in Jerusalem or Palestine.

APPENDICES

APPENDIX 1 (to p. 15)

THE AUTHOR OF THE THIRD GOSPEL AND THE ACTS OF THE APOSTLES A PHYSICIAN[1]

St. Luke, according to St. Paul, was a physician. When a physician writes an historical work it does not necessarily follow that his profession shows itself in his writing; yet it is only natural for one to look for traces of the author's medical profession in such a work. These traces may be of different kinds: (1) The *whole* character of the narrative may be determined by points of view, aims, and ideals which are more or less medical (disease and its treatment); (2) marked preference may be shown for stories concerning the healing of diseases, which stories may be given in great number and detail; (3) the language may be coloured by the language of physicians (medical technical terms, metaphors of medical character, &c.). *All these three groups of characteristic signs are found, as we shall see, in the historical work which bears the name of St. Luke.*

---

[1] The quotations from the Greek medical authors are taken from Hobart's "The Medical Language of St. Luke," 1882. He has proved only too much. A good summary, after Hobart, is given by Zahn, "Einl. i. d. N. T." ii. ss. 435 ff.

Here, however, it may be objected that the subject-matter itself is responsible for these traits, so that their evidence is not decisive for the medical calling of the author. Jesus appeared as a great physician and healer. All the evangelists say this of Him; hence it is not surprising that one of them has set this phase of His ministry in the foreground, and has regarded it as the most important. Our evangelist need not, therefore, have been a physician, especially if he were a Greek, seeing that in those days Greeks with religious interests were disposed to regard religion mainly under the category of Healing and Salvation. This is true; yet such a combination of characteristic signs will compel us to believe that the author was a physician if (4) the description of the particular cases of disease shows distinct traces of medical diagnosis and scientific knowledge; (5) if the language, even where questions of medicine or of healing are not touched upon, is coloured by medical phraseology; and (6) if in those passages where the author speaks as an eye-witness medical traits are especially and prominently apparent. *These three kinds of tokens are also found in the historical work of our author.* It is accordingly proved that it proceeds from the pen of a physician.

The Evidence.

(1) I begin with the last point (traces of medical knowledge in the " we " sections). It has been already shown in the text (p. 15) that the terms of the diagnosis in xxviii. 8, πυρετοῖς καὶ δυσεντερίῳ συνεχόμενος

(attacks of gastric fever), are medically exact and can be vouched for from medical literature ; moreover, that it may be concluded with great probability from xxviii. 9 f. that the author himself practised in Malta as a physician. But this is not the only passage of the " we " sections which comes under consideration. It is immediately preceded by the narrative concerning St. Paul and the serpent. Here we read of the serpent— which is also termed θηρίον, and of which it is said that it came forth ἀπὸ τῆς θέρμης—as follows : καθῆψεν τὴν χεῖρα αὐτοῦ, and then : οἱ δὲ προσεδόκων αὐτὸν μέλλειν πίμπρασθαι ἢ καταπίπτειν ἄφνω νεκρόν, and, lastly: ἐπὶ πολὺ δὲ αὐτῶν προσδοκώντων καὶ θεωρούντων μηδὲν ἄτοπον εἰς αὐτὸν γινόμενον. The commentators almost universally translate καθῆψεν [1] by " seized," [2] most of them imagining that the idea " bite " must be understood ; but Hobart has shown (pp. 288 f.) that καθάπτειν was a technical term with physicians, and that Dioscorides uses the word of poisonous matter which invades the body. Vide " Animal. Ven. Prœm." : δι' ὕλης φθοροποιοῦ καθαπτομένης τῶν σωμάτων μόνων ἀπὸ μέρεος συνπίπτειν, cf. Galen, " Medicus," 13 (xiv. 754): οὐδὲ οὕτως χρηστέον τοῖς τροχίσκοις [certain pills]· οὐ γὰρ φθάνουσιν ἐπὶ τὰ πεπονθότα ἐξικνεῖσθαι· τῶν γὰρ ὑγιεινῶν καθαπτόμενοι ὄλεθρον ἐργάζονται, ἀνωτερικοῖς δὲ φαρμάκοις χρῆσθαι. Hence the serpent really bit the Apostle and the poison entered into his hand. Thus the passage only receives its right interpretation when brought into connection with the ordinary

---

[1] It occurs in the New Testament only in the Lukan writings.
[2] Blass rightly renders it momordit.

M

medical language of the times. Further, the fact that the viper (ἔχιδνα) is called θηρίον is not without significance; for this is just the medical term that is used for the reptile, and the antidote made from the flesh of a viper is accordingly called θηριακή. The same sort of remedy is signified in the passages, Aret., "Cur. Diuturn. Morb.," 138 : τὸ διὰ τῶν θηρίων [vipers] φάρμακον, 144 : ἡ διὰ τῶν θηρίων, 146 : ἡ διὰ τῶν ἐχιδνῶν, Aret., "Cur. Morb. Diuturn.," 147 : τὸ διὰ τῶν θηρίων, τῶν ἐχιδνῶν. Hobart further remarks (loc. cit. p. 51) that "Dioscorides uses θηριόδηκτος to signify 'bitten by a serpent.'" "Mat. Med.," iv. 24 : θηριοδήκτοις βοηθεῖν μάλιστα δὲ ἐχιοδήκτοις, Galen, "Natural. Facul.," i. 14 (ii. 53): ὅσα τοὺς ἰοὺς τῶν θηρίων ἀνέλκει—τῶν τοὺς ἰοὺς ἐλκόντων, τὰ μὲν τοῦ τῆς ἐχίδνης, Galen, "Meth. Med.," xiv. 12 (x. 986): τό τε διὰ τῶν ἐχιδνῶν ὅπερ ὀνομάζουσι θηριακὴν ἀντίδοτον, likewise in several other passages (διὰ τί ὁ Ἀνδρόμαχος τὴν ἔχιδναν μᾶλλον ἢ ἄλλον τινὰ ὄφιν τῇ θηριακῇ ἐπέμιξε, —διὰ τὸ ἔχειν αὐτὴν τῆς σαρκὸς τῶν ἐχιδνῶν ὠνόμασαν αὐτὴν θηριακήν). Nor is it without significance that the heat is described as θέρμη; for this word, rare, I believe, in ordinary use, and only found here in the New Testament, is among physicians the general term used for θερμότης, as Hobart (p. 287) shows by very numerous examples. When we proceed to read that the natives expected that St. Paul would have swollen or would have fallen down dead suddenly, here again the two possible results of snake-bite are described with extraordinary precision. If this were a layman's narrative, the latter result, the only one required to give a realistic effect, would alone have been mentioned. But the terminology also is medical; for πίμπρασθαι (here only in the New Testament) is the technical term for " to swell," and καταπίπτειν (κατά-πτωσις)—here only in the New Testament—can also be vouched for from medical language (Hobart, pp. 50 f.). Finally, μηδὲν ἄτοπον must also be noted—a phrase used by St. Luke alone among the evangelists. It is used by physicians not only to describe something unusual, but also to describe something fatal. Thus Galen says in " Antid.," ii. 15 (xiv. 195), that those who drink a certain antidote after having been bitten by a mad dog εἰς οὐδὲν ἄτοπον ἐμπεσοῦνται ῥαδίως, cf. a similar instance, ii. 5 (xiv. 134): μηδὲν ἄτοπον, μηδὲ δηλητήριον συνκατα-πεπτωκώς (both passages, of course, according to Damocrates); but see also Hippocr., " Aph.," 1251: ὁκόσοι ἐν τοῖσιν πυρετοῖσιν ἢ ἐν τῇσιν ἄλλῃσιν ἀρρωστίῃσι κατὰ προαίρεσιν δακρύουσιν οὐδὲν ἄτοπον · ὁκόσοι δὲ μὴ κατὰ προαίρεσιν ἀτοπώτερον, Galen, "Comm.," ii. 50, "Progn.," (xviii. B. 185): ἐν δὲ τῷ μακρῷ χρόνῳ πολλὰ μὲν καὶ τῶν ἄλλων ἀτόπων εἴωθε συμπίπτειν, ὅσα τε διὰ τὸν κάμνοντα καὶ τοὺς ὑπηρετοῦντας αὐτῷ. Hobart quotes numerous other passages. There is accordingly no doubt that the whole section xxviii. 3–6 is tinged with medical colouring; and seeing that in verses 7–10 both subject-matter and phraseology are medical, there-fore the whole story of the abode of the narrator in Malta is displayed in a medical light.

Elsewhere the "we" sections afford little opportunity for the appearance of medical traits; nevertheless the following instances are worthy of note. The whole work, as is well known, is much concerned with persons possessed by evil spirits (*vide infra*), but only one story of an exorcism is narrated by the author as an eye-witness (in the "we" section xvi. 16 ff.). Here he is not simply satisfied with speaking of the patient as one "possessed," but he particularly characterises her as ἔχουσαν πνεῦμα πύθωνα. This uncommon word, which accurately describes the case, only occurs here in the New Testament. Further, it is to be noticed that in the story given in the second "we" section of the raising of Eutychus the sleepy condition of the young man is twice described in xx. 9 by the same verb: καταφερόμενος ὕπνῳ βαθεῖ and κατενεχθεὶς ἀπὸ τοῦ ὕπνου. Hobart has (pp. 48 ff.) pointed out that this word, peculiar to St. Luke in the New Testament, is so usual in medical phraseology (and only in it) for "falling asleep" that the word "sleep" is often omitted, and that Galen speaks of two kinds of καταφορά ("De Comate Secund.," Hippocr., 2 [vii. 652]: μὴ γιγνώσκοντες ὅτι δύο εἰσὶν εἴθη καταφορᾶς, ὡς οἵ τε δοκιμώτατοι τῶν ἰατρῶν γεγράφασι καὶ αὐτὰ τὰ γιγνόμενα μαρτυρεῖ). Passow also only gives medical authorities for καταφέρεσθαι and καταφορά in the sense of sleep; cf. the multitude of instances quoted by Hobart (from Hippocrates to Galen), some of which closely coincide with the passage we are considering.[1] Lastly, in the description of the voyage, which has nothing to do with medical affairs *per se*, we find two remarkable passages. In the

---

[1] Hobart also makes an attempt to prove by examples that παρατείνειν, μέχρι μεσονυκτίου, ὕπνος βαθύς, and ἄχρι αὐγῆς are specific medical phrases; but I pass this by.

first place, there is the occurrence of the word ἐπιμέλεια (xxvii. 3—only here in the New Testament), and this reminds us of ἐπιμελεῖσθαι in the parable of the Good Samaritan (St. Luke x. 34, 35; only here in the gospels and the Acts). In both cases medical care for the sick is being spoken of, and for this, as Hobart shows (pp. 29, 269 f.), the words are technical terms; also ἐπιμελῶς (occurring only once in the New Testament—namely, in St. Luke xv. 8) is much used by physicians. Secondly, there is the strange expression occurring in xxvii. 17: "βοηθείαις ἐχρῶντο ὑποζωννύντες τὸ πλοῖον." The word ὑποζώννυναι is never used of the undergirding of ships;[1] but the phrase βοηθείας ἐχρῶντο ("they used helps") is also remarkable. Hobart (pp. 273 f.) now makes it probable that we have here a metaphor taken from medical phraseology. Ὑποζώννυμι is a word in constant use by medical writers for "undergirding," as is shown by very numerous examples. βοήθεια, however (a word that does not occur elsewhere in the gospels and the Acts), is a current medical term which is applied to all conceivable objects (ligaments, muscles, peritoneum, pancreas).[2]

---

[1] Polybius, it is true, in xxvii. 3, 3, uses ὑποζωννύναι of ships, but in another sense.

[2] Hobart also refers to the medical use of the words παραινεῖν, ἐμβιβάζειν, ἀνεύθετος (ἄθετος), χειμάζεσθαι, σάλος, &c., found in this chapter. These instances, however, have not much weight. There is perhaps more to be said for ἀσιτία and ἄσιτος, which are wanting in the LXX., and only found here (xxvii. 21, 33) in the New Testament, but, as may be well imagined, are of constant occurrence in medical language. Galen, in fact, writes ("Ven. Sect.," 9 xi. 242) "ἄσιτος διετέλεσεν," exactly like the "ἄσιτοι διατελεῖτε" of Acts xxvii. 33.

(2) I now proceed to deal with those stories of miraculous cures which the author of the third gospel has taken from St. Mark, and to investigate the manner in which he has reproduced them.

(a) In the story of the demoniac in the synagogue at Capernaum (St. Luke iv. 35 = St. Mark i. 26) "σπαράξαν" is replaced by "ῥίψαν" and the phrase "μηδὲν βλάψαν αὐτόν" is added.

(b) In the story of the cure of St. Peter's wife's mother (St. Luke iv. 38 = St. Mark i. 30) "ἦν συνεχομένη πυρετῷ μεγάλῳ" is put for "κατέκειτο πυρέσσουσα," and "καὶ ἐπίστας ἐπάνω αὐτῆς ἐπετίμησεν τῷ πυρετῷ" for "προσελθὼν ἤγειρεν αὐτὴν κρατήσας τῆς χειρός."

(c) In the story of the healing of the leper (St. Luke v. 12 = St. Mark i. 40) the afflicted one is described, not as λεπρός, but as "πλήρης λέπρας."

(d) The paralytic is called παραλελυμένος instead of παραλυτικός (St. Mark ii. 3 = St. Luke v. 18).

(e) In the story of the healing of the man with a withered hand (St. Luke vi. 6 = St. Mark iii. 1) St. Luke adds that it was his right hand.

(f) In the story of the demoniac at Gadara (St. Luke viii. 27 = St. Mark v. 2) it is added concerning the "possessed" that χρόνῳ ἱκανῷ οὐκ ἐνεδύσατο ἱμάτιον.

(g) In the story of the woman with the issue of blood we read (St. Luke viii. 43 = St. Mark v. 26): [ἰατροῖς προσαναλώσασα ὅλον τὸν βίον[1]] οὐκ ἴσχυσεν

---

[1] These five words are very probably a later interpolation, for they are wanting in some authorities (D., for instance).

ἀπ᾽ οὐθενὸς θεραπευθῆναι, while in St. Mark we read : πολλὰ παθοῦσα ὑπὸ πολλῶν ἰατρῶν καὶ δαπανήσασα τὰ παρ᾽ αὐτῆς πάντα, καὶ μηδὲν ὠφεληθεῖσα, ἀλλὰ μᾶλλον εἰς τὸ χεῖρον ἐλθοῦσα. Moreover, St. Luke (viii. 44) writes : ἔστη ἡ ῥύσις τοῦ αἵματος αὐτῆς, while we read in St. Mark (v. 29) : ἐξηράνθη ἡ πηγὴ τοῦ αἵματος αὐτῆς, καὶ ἔγνω τῷ σώματι ὅτι ἴαται ἀπὸ τῆς μάστιγος.

(h) In the story of the raising of Jairus's daughter (St. Luke viii. 55 = St. Mark v. 42) the words of St. Mark, καὶ εὐθὺς ἀνέστη τὸ κοράσιον καὶ περιεπάτει, are replaced by καὶ ἐπέστρεψεν τὸ πνεῦμα αὐτῆς, καὶ ἀνέστη παραχρῆμα, and εἶπεν δοθῆναι αὐτῇ φαγεῖν is transposed so as to come before the words telling of the wonder of the parents.

(i) In the story of the cure of the epileptic boy (St. Luke ix. 38 ff. = St. Mark ix. 17 ff.) St. Luke has interpolated into the address of the father the words, ἐπιβλέψαι ἐπὶ τὸν υἱόν μου, ὅτι μονογενής μοι ἐστίν, and in the description of the patient he adds : ἐξαίφνης κράζει [scil. the evil spirit] . . . καὶ μόγις ἀποχωρεῖ ἀπ᾽ αὐτοῦ συντρῖβον αὐτόν.

(k) In the story of Malchus (St. Luke xxii. 50, 51 = St. Mark xiv. 17) St. Luke says it was the right ear, and then further interpolates the words, ἀποκριθεὶς δὲ ὁ Ἰησοῦς εἶπεν· ἐᾶτε ἕως τούτου· καὶ ἀψάμενος τοῦ ὠτίου ἰάσατο αὐτόν.[1]

---

1 D. reads : καὶ ἐκτείνας τὴν χεῖρα ἥψατο αὐτοῦ καὶ ἀπεκατεστάθη τὸ οὖς αὐτοῦ. Wellhausen seems to prefer this reading, but it is especially characteristic of that crafty and wanton treatment of the text so frequent in D. It is quite clearly fashioned according to vi. 10,

Only a very small portion of these additions can be explained from the well-known anxiety of St. Luke to improve the language of the Markan text; *the great majority of them plainly reveal the pen of a man who was either a physician himself or at least had a special interest in medicine.*[1] As regards (*a*), ῥίπτειν is not only a verbal improvement, but it is also the technical term for the epileptic phenomenon in question, and the addition that the exorcised spirit did the man no harm both shows the interest of a physician and is also expressed in technical medical phraseology: ὠφέλησε μὲν ἱκανῶς, ἔβλαψε δ' οὐδέν (this phrase, or something similar, is of very frequent occurrence in medical writers).[2] In regard to (*b*), the medical writers distinguish between "slight" and "great" fevers;[3] therefore the epithet "great" in St. Luke is by no means insignificant. Moreover, while St. Mark contents himself with reporting that our Lord raised up the patient, taking her by the hand, St. Luke gives the method of healing that was employed: "He stood over her and rebuked the fever." He has therefore an interest in methods of healing. In regard to (*c*),

where the ἐκτείνειν τὴν χεῖρα has its appropriate place, while here it is quite superfluous.

[1] One can easily convince oneself by comparison that St. Luke and St. Matthew are here diametrically opposed to one another in their attitude towards the Markan text; for St. Matthew has deleted from the text of St. Mark all medical traits which are not absolutely necessary.

[2] See Hobart's quotations, pp. 2 f.

[3] Galen, "Different. Febr.," i. 1 (vii. 275) : καὶ σύνηθες ἤδη τοῖς ἰατροῖς ὀνομάζειν ἐν τούτῳ τῷ γένει τῆς διαφορᾶς τὸν μέγαν τε καὶ μικρὸν πυρετόν. Also συνέχεσθαι is a technical term,

"πλήρης λέπρας" is probably a by no means insignificant variant for λεπρός, for the more serious stages of diseases are distinguished in medical language by the word "πλήρης"; *vide* Hippocr., "De Arte," 5: πλήρεες τῆς νόσου.[1] In regard to (*d*), παραλελυμένος is linguistically an improvement, but it is also the technical word of the physicians who do not use παραλυτικός. In regard to (*e*) and (*k*), the addition in both these cases that it was the right hand and the right ear respectively is a token of an exactness which is specially intelligible in a physician. In regard to (*f*), the additional notice that the demoniac had for a long time refused to wear clothes answers to the precise diagnosis of a distinct form of mania, which was recognised by the ancients just as it is still recognised by us; *cf.* the statement of the physician Aretæus about the year 160 A.D. ("Sign. Morb. Diut.," 37): περὶ μανίης· ἐσθ᾽ ὅτε ἐσθῆτάς τε ἐρρήξατο.[2] In regard to (*g*), here the medical feeling of the author is especially obvious: *he simply erases St. Mark's somewhat malicious remark about physicians*[3]— how intelligible if he himself were a physician, and how unintelligible if he belonged to the general public! The layman's phraseology of St. Mark, ἐξηράνθη ἡ

---

[1] Hobart, pp. 5 f., quotes other passages.

[2] Hobart, pp. 13 f.

[3] It is also wanting in St. Matthew. But this means nothing, for that gospel here and in the other parallel sections has omitted all "unnecessary" detail. Zahn ("Einl.," ii. s. 437) speaks of this interpretation of St. Luke's action here as an unworthy insinuation; but his own explanation is forced, and does not take into consideration the main point at issue,

πηγὴ τοῦ αἵματος, is replaced by the technical expression, ἔστη ἡ ῥύσις τοῦ αἵματος (cf. Hippocr., " Prædic.," 80: οἷσιν ἐξ ἀρχῆς αἱμορραγίαι λάβραι, ῥῦγος ἵστησι ῥύσιν, Hippocr., "Morb. Sacr.," 306: ἵστησι τὸ αἶμα, Hippocr., " Morb. Mul.," 639 : ἐπειδὰν δὲ τὸ ῥεῦμα στῇ, Dioscor., "Mat. Med.," i. 132 : ἵστησι καὶ ῥοῦν γυναικεῖον προστιθέμενον, ib. 148 : ἵστησι δὲ καὶ αἱμορροίδας, and other passages quoted by Hobart, pp. 14 ff.), and he has discreetly suppressed the somewhat indelicate words which St. Mark has added. In regard to (h), in the story of the raising of Jairus's daughter St. Luke keeps the word ἀνέστη, but he has omitted the word περιεπάτει, which immediately follows, as offending against the natural order of things. The physician at once thinks that the maiden restored to life must have something to eat immediately, while St. Mark first tells us that our Lord forbade the bystanders to spread abroad the miracle, and only then proceeded to command that something should be given her to eat; so that this detail almost loses its significance in St. Mark. Again, in Acts ix. 18 St. Luke gives expression to the fact that with convalescents the first thing to be thought of is to bring them nourishment. Here, in his account of the healing of Saul, he writes : ἀναστὰς ἐβαπτίσθη καὶ λαβὼν τροφὴν ἐνίσχυσεν. Would a layman have made such an observation ? It is possible, too, that τὸ πνεῦμα in τὸ πνεῦμα αὐτῆς ἐπέστρεψεν is to be understood as signifying ἡ πνοή; yet this is not certain. In regard to (i), here the second and third interpolations elucidate the description of the disease by telling of symptoms that are characteristic of epilepsy.[1] Also, the word ἐπιβλέπειν in the first interpolation is not without significance ;[2] for Hobart teaches us[3] that this verb is used technically for a physician's examination of his patient. ῾Α δεῖ τὸν ἰατρὸν ἐπιβλέπειν, says Galen, and ἐπιβλέπειν δὲ χρῆναι καὶ εἰς τὰ νοσήματα καὶ τὴν δύναμιν τοῦ κάμνοντος, &c. In regard to (k), all four evangelists record the cutting off of the ear, but St. Luke alone allows it to be healed again by our Lord ; thus he alone was scandalised by the fact that the poor fellow had lost his ear. As he before defended the credit of the medical profession in general—see under (g)—so now he stands forth in championship of our Lord the Physician. It would have been inexcusable if He had not exerted His miraculous powers of healing on this occasion.[4]

It follows from these remarks that very nearly all of the alterations and additions which the third evangelist has made in the Markan text are most simply and surely explained from the professional interest of a physician. Indeed, I cannot see that any other explanation is even possible. We may also add that the third evangelist avoids popular medical expressions—*vide*

---

[1] *Vide* the examples given by Hobart, pp. 17 f.

[2] The "only" son is an addition which is characteristic of the somewhat sentimental pathos of the author.

[3] Pp. 18 f.

[4] This is a flagrant instance of the way in which a story of a miracle has arisen, and of what we may expect from St. Luke. He certainly is not following a separate source here ; but because he thinks it ought to have been so, he makes it happen so.

supra, p. 185 f., under (*g*). Here note that he does not use βάσανος as does St. Matthew of diseases, but only in a parable (chap. xvi.) of the pains of Hell. Also, βασανίζεσθαι occurs with him only once (viii. 28); μαλακία is altogether wanting.

(3) St. Luke in the gospel narrates three other miracles of healing peculiar to himself (the widow's son at Nain, the woman with a spirit of infirmity, and the man with the dropsy), and, moreover, two pertinent parables (the Good Samaritan and Dives and Lazarus), while in the Acts—excluding the " we " sections—he narrates the cure of the lame man at the Beautiful Gate, of Æneas, of Tabitha, of Saul's blindness, of the lame man in Lystra, and the story of Elymas. There are also pertinent notices in the story of Ananias and Sapphira and the vision of St. Peter. Everywhere in the stories (which are, moreover, remarkable for their fulness of detail) traits appear which declare the interest or the sharp eye or the language of the physician.

The stories of the raising of the young man at Nain and of Tabitha (St. Luke vii. 15, Acts ix. 40) agree in describing the first movement after the restoration to life by the word " ἀνεκάθισεν." This word [1] in the intransitive sense seems to be met with only in medical writers, [2] who use it to signify " to sit up again in bed "—see, for example, Hippocr., " Prænot.," 37: ἀνακαθίζειν βούλεσθαι τὸν νοσέοντα τῆς νόσου ἀκμαζούσης.

[1] Only here in the New Testament.
[2] See the instances given in Hobart, pp. 11 f.

In the story of the woman with the spirit of infirmity (St. Luke xiii. 11–13) we are at once struck by the exact description of the disease and the cure—an exactness which is not required in order to bring out the point of the narrative (healing on the Sabbath day): ἦν συνκύπτουσα καὶ μὴ δυναμένη ἀνακύψαι εἰς τὸ παντελές.[1] Also ἀπολύεσθαι and ἀνορθοῦσθαι sound quite professional—see the parallels given by Hobart (pp. 20 ff.). Both ἀνακύπτειν and ἀπολύειν (used here only in the New Testament of a disease) are corresponding *termini technici*, and ἀνορθοῦν likewise is the usual medical word for the restoring of the members or parts of the body to their natural position. Notice also how the loosening of the curvature is first described, and then the standing upright. What sort of person is interested in such exactness?

An "ὑδρωπτικός" (St. Luke xiv. 2) is not again met with in the New Testament, though the word is of frequent occurrence (and just as here, the adjective for the substantive) in Hippocrates, Dioscorides, and Galen.[2] The diseases dropsy, "great" fever, acute leprosy, dysentery with feverish symptoms, and the hysterical disease of the woman with a spirit of divination at Philippi are found in St. Luke alone of the writers of the New Testament.

The parable of the Good Samaritan (St. Luke x. 30 ff.) sounds like a typical medical instance to enforce the lesson never to deny help to the helpless. Hobart

1 *Cf.* the parallels in the description of Eutychus asleep (*vide supra*, p. 180): καταφερόμενος, κατανεχθείς.
2 See Hobart, p. 24.

(p. 27) quotes a very remarkable parallel from Galen, in which, indeed, the word "ἡμιθανής" (St. Luke x. 30, and here only in the New Testament) is also found. "De Morb. Different.," 5 (vi. 850): οἷα τοῖς ὁδοιπορήσασιν ἐν κρύει καρτερῷ γίγνεται· πολλοὶ γὰρ τούτων οἱ μὲν ἐν αὐταῖς ταῖς ὁδοῖς ἀπέθανον, οἱ δὲ εἰς πανδοχεῖον, πρὶν ἢ οἰκάδε παραγενέσθαι φθάσαντες ἡμιθνῆτές τε καὶ κατεψυγμένοι φαίνονται.[1] Medical expressions occur constantly in this story; and yet it cannot have been written by a physician if Wellhausen is right in saying: "Into a wound one pours oil, but not oil and wine. In the instance given by Land ('Anecd. Syr.,' 2, 46, 24) 'oil and wine' is most probably quoted from this passage." But he is mistaken; the physicians of antiquity used oil and wine not only internally, but also for external application (Hobart, pp. 28 f.); vide Hippocr., "Morb. Mul.," 656: ἢν δὲ αἱ μῆτραι ἐξίσχωσι, περινίψας αὐτὰς ὕδατι χλιερῷ καὶ ἀλείψας ἐλαίῳ καὶ οἴνῳ, and other passages.

In the parable of Dives and Lazarus (xvi. 21-26) the following words occur which are wanting elsewhere in the gospels: ἕλκος, ἑλκοῦσθαι, καταψύχειν, ὀδυνᾶσθαι, and χάσμα (ἐστήρικται). The first two words are technically used for sores. Likewise the relatively rare words ὀδυνᾶσθαι and καταψύχειν are used technically in the medical writers from Hippocrates onwards,[2] and

---

[1] One might almost imagine that Galen had read St. Luke. This is not impossible, for he had to do with Christians. Another passage, but not so much alike, occurs also in Galen, "De Rigore," 5 (vii. 602): ὡς ὅσοι γε χειμῶνος ὁδοιποροῦντες, εἶτα ἐν κρύει καρτερῷ καταληφθέντες, ἡμιθνῆτές τε καὶ τρομώδεις οἴκαδε παρεγένοντο.

[2] See Hobart, pp. 32 f.

we may perhaps say the same thing of χάσμα and
στηρίζειν.[1] The physician thinks of the absence of
medical help: the dogs licked his sores. Of course,
these things do not necessarily imply that the author
was a physician; but we have the same writer here as
he who relates the story of the Good Samaritan.

In the story of the lame man (Acts iii. 7 f.) the
exactness of detail is remarkable: ἤγειρεν αὐτὸν,
παραχρῆμα δὲ ἐστερεώθησαν οἱ βάσεις αὐτοῦ καὶ τὰ
σφυδρά, καὶ ἐξαλλόμενος ἔστη καὶ περιεπάτει. Could
one give a fuller and yet more concise description of a
process of healing? What kind of man is interested in
the stages of such a process? That which the physician
observes during the months of the ordinary *gradual*
cure of a lame man is here compressed into a moment.
Now notice also how we are reminded that the man
was χωλὸς ἐκ κοιλίας μητρός (iii. 2), and ἐτῶν ἦν πλειόνων
τεσσαράκοντα (iv. 22)—an age at which such cures no
longer occur. Σφυδρόν is a very rare word (*e.g.*, Passow
does not give it); it is the *term. tech.* for the con-
dyles of the leg-bones—*vide* Galen, "Medicus," 10 (xiv.
708): τὰ δὲ πέρατα τῶν τῆς κνήμης ὀστῶν εἴς τε τὸ
ἔνδον μέρος καὶ εἰς τὸ ἔξω ἐξέχοντα, σφυδρὰ προσαγο-
ρεύεται τὰ δὲ ἀπὸ τῶν σφυδρῶν κυρίως πόδες λέγονται.

In the story of Æneas (Acts ix. 33) we are again
struck by the exactness with which the time of the
duration of the disease is marked (eight years),[2] and

---

[1] See Hobart, pp. 33 f.

[2] St. Mark and St. Matthew mention the length of an illness only
in the case of the woman with an issue, but St. Luke not only here,
but in two other instances, mentions that the illness was congenital

one is also reminded how many different expressions the author of this great historical work has for "a sick-bed"; there are four of them: κράββατον, κλίνη, κλινίδιον, κλινάριον. The last two words are peculiar to him in the New Testament.[1] Can we not again see the physician?

The word ἀνεκάθισεν in the story of Tabitha has been already dealt with. The scene wherein St. Peter sets himself to perform the miracle is strikingly realistic: ἐπιστρέψας πρὸς τὸ σῶμα εἶπεν· Ταβιθά ἀνάστηθι. Σῶμα = a corpse.

In the story of the cure of Saul's blindness (Acts ix. 17 ff.) we read: ἀπέπεσαν αὐτοῦ ἀπὸ τῶν ὀφθαλμῶν ὡς λεπίδες. Here Hobart (p. 39) remarks: "'Αποπίπτειν[2] is used of the falling off of scales from the cuticle and particles from diseased parts of the body or bones, &c., and in one instance, by Hippocrates, of the scab, caused by burning in a medical operation, from the eyelid; and λεπίς[3] is the medical term for the particles or scaly substance thrown off from the body; it and ἀποπίπτειν are met with in conjunction"; vide Hippocr., "De Videndi Acie," 689: τὸ βλέφαρον ἐπικαῦσαι ἢ τῷ ἄνθει ὀπτῷ λεπτῷ προστεῖλαι, ὅταν δὲ ἀποπέσῃ ἡ ἐσχάρα, ἰητρεύειν τὰ λοιπά. Galen, "Comm.," ii. 23, "Offic." (xviii. B. 781): πολλάκις γὰρ ἀποσχίδες ὀστῶν

(Acts iii. 2, xiv. 8); the woman with a spirit of infirmity was ill for eighteen years, the lame man at the Beautiful Gate for forty years, Æneas for eight years.

[1] He also makes a distinction between them—vide Acts v. 15: τιθέναι ἐπὶ κλιναρίων καὶ κραβάττων.

[2] Only here in the New Testament.

[3] Only here in the New Testament.

καὶ λεπίδες ἀποπίπτουσιν. Galen, " Med. Defin.,"
295 (xix. 428): ἔσθ' ὅτε μὲν καὶ λεπίδας ἀποπίπτειν.
Galen, " De Atra Bile," 4 (v. 115): τὸ σῶμα πᾶν περιε-
ξήνθησε μέλασιν ἐξανθήμασιν ὁμοίοις, ἐνίοτε δὲ καὶ οἷον
λεπὶς ἀπέπιπτε ξηραινομένων τε καὶ διαφορουμένων
αὐτῶν. Galen, " Med. Temper. et Facult.," xi. 1
(xii. 319): καὶ τοῦ δέρματος ἀφίσταταί τε καὶ
ἀποπίπτει καθάπερ τε λέπος ἡ ἐπιδερμὶς ὀνομα-
ζομένη.

In the story of Elymas (Acts xiii. 11) the blinding
is thus described : παραχρῆμα ἔπεσεν [ἐπέπεσεν ?] ἐπ'
αὐτὸν ἀχλὺς καὶ σκότος, καὶ περιάγων ἐζήτει χειραγωγούς.
Hobart (pp. 44 f.) shows that ἀχλύς, according to Galen,
is a distinct disease of the eyes (" Medicus," 16, xiv.
774: ἀχλὺς δέ ἐστι περὶ ὅλον τὸ μέλαν ἀπ' ἑλκώσεως
ἐπιπολαίου, οὐλὴ λεπτοτάτη ἀέρι ἀχλυώδει παραπλησία.
See also numerous other passages—e.g., νεφέλιόν ἐστιν
ἀχλὺς ἡ ἕλκωσις ἐπιπόλαιος ἐπὶ τοῦ μέλανος) ; but his
remarks upon σκότος are also worthy of notice. The
additional statement—that he sought for people to
lead him—is natural in a physician, who at once realises
the sad consequences of the miracle.

The man of Lystra, lame from his mother's womb, is
described as an ἀνὴρ ἀδύνατος τοῖς ποσίν (Acts xiv. 8)·
See the medical examples for ἀδύνατος in Hobart,
p. 46.

In the story of Ananias and Sapphira (Acts v. 5, 8)
are found the words ἐκψύχειν and συστέλλειν. The
former seems to be entirely confined to medical literature. Before St. Luke (l.c., and Acts xii. 23) instances
of its use are found only in Hippocrates, and then in

Aretæus and Galen (see Hobart, p. 37).[1]   On συστέλλειν[2] Hobart remarks (l.c.): "This word is met with
in one other passage in the New Testament (1 Cor. vii.
29)—ὁ καιρὸς συνεσταλμένος—and is found only once
in classical Greek in the sense it bears in this passage,
'to shroud'—Eurip., 'Troad.,' 378: πέπλοις συνε-
στάλησαν. In medical language the word is very
frequent,[3] and its use varied ; one use was almost
identical with that here, viz., 'to bandage a limb,'
'to compress by bandaging.'"

In the story of the vision of St. Peter the word
ἔκστασις is used (Acts x. 10: ἐγένετο ἐπ' αὐτὸν ἔκστασις).
Although visions constantly occur in the New Testament, St. Luke alone uses for them this word (here and
Acts xi. 5, xxii. 17).   It is of constant use in a technical
sense in medical language (Hobart pp. 41 f.).

This review of the stories of diseases and subjects
of allied character peculiar to St. Luke confirms the
impression we receive from the character of his corrections of the narrative of St. Mark.[4]

---

[1] It occurs once in the LXX. (Ezek. xxi. 7), and also in Jam-
blichus.

[2] In the context in which it occurs the sense is not " they covered
him " (so Weiss), but " they enfolded him."

[3] Examples are quoted from Hippocrates, Galen, and Dioscorides.

[4] If the verses St. Luke xxii. 43 f. are genuine—and I think that
I have shown that this is very probable in the " Sitzungsber. d. Preuss.
Akad.," 1901, February 28—then St. Luke has used in them technical
terms which are wanting elsewhere in the New Testament—i.e.,
ἐνισχύειν, ἀγωνία, ὁ ἱδρὼς ὡσεὶ θρόμβοι αἵματος καταβαίνοντες (see the
striking instances quoted by Hobart, pp. 79 ff.).   It is the same
medical writer who writes ἔστη ἡ ῥύσις τοῦ αἵματος and θρόμβοι αἵματος
καταβαίνοντες, and who says ἐν ἀγωνίᾳ γενόμενος and ἔπεσεν ἐπ' αὐτὸν
ἔκστασις. In distinction from the ἀγωνία of our Lord, verse 45 speaks

(4) There is no need to prove that the representation of our Lord given in the third gospel is dominated by the conception of Him as the wondrous Healer and Saviour of the sick, as, indeed, the Healer above all healers. But it is significant that St. Luke, when he summarises our Lord's activity—and he often does so—only mentions His cures of diseases, and at the same time distinguishes sharply [1] between natural illnesses and cases of " possession " (because they required a completely different medical treatment). See iv. 40 f. : Πάντες ὅσοι εἶχον ἀσθενοῦντας νόσοις ποικίλαις ἤγαγον αὐτοὺς πρὸς αὐτόν· ὁ δὲ ἐνὶ ἑκάστῳ αὐτῶν τὰς χεῖρας ἐπιτιθεὶς ἐθεράπευεν αὐτούς. ἐξήρχετο δὲ καὶ δαιμόνια ἀπὸ πολλῶν, κράζοντα καὶ λέγοντα ὅτι σὺ εἶ ὁ υἱὸς τοῦ θεοῦ, καὶ ἐπιτιμῶν οὐκ εἴα αὐτὰ λαλεῖν, vi. 18 f. : ἦλθον ἀκοῦσαι αὐτοῦ καὶ ἰαθῆναι ἀπὸ τῶν νόσων αὐτῶν, καὶ οἱ ἐνοχλούμενοι ἀπὸ πνευμάτων ἀκαθάρτων ἐθεραπεύοντο· καὶ πᾶς ὁ ὄχλος ἐζήτουν ἅπτεσθαι αὐτοῦ, ὅτι δύναμις παρ' αὐτοῦ ἐξήρχετο καὶ ἰᾶτο πάντας, vii. 21 : ἐθεράπευσεν πολλοὺς ἀπὸ νόσων καὶ μαστίγων [2] καὶ πνευμάτων πονηρῶν, καὶ τυφλοῖς πολλοῖς ἐχαρίσατο βλέπειν, xiii. 32, ἰδοὺ

only of a λύπη of the disciples, and this word (ἀπὸ τῆς λύπης), wanting elsewhere in the synoptists, is expressly added to the Markan phrases "sleeping" and "their eyes were heavy." Hobart shows (p. 84) how closely λύπη is connected with medical phraseology. Lastly, notice that here again we have another example (vide supra) of St. Luke's practice of replacing ordinary lay expressions by accurate medical phrases. St. Mark had written of our Lord : ἤρξατο ἐκθαμβεῖσθαι [unclassical ; St. Matthew also has expunged the word] καὶ ἀδημονεῖν ; St. Luke substitutes the exacter phrase, γενόμενος ἐν ἀγωνίᾳ.

[1] Differently from the other gospels.

[2] These are serious and acute diseases, in distinction from νόσοι.

ἐκβάλλω δαιμόνια καὶ ἰάσεις ἀποτελῶ σήμερον καὶ αὔριον. Nor is it otherwise (in the case of the apostles) in the Acts—see v. 16: συνήρχετο δὲ καὶ τὸ πλῆθος τῶν πέριξ πόλεων Ἰερουσαλήμ, φέροντες ἀσθενεῖς καὶ ὀχλουμένους ὑπὸ πνευμάτων ἀκαθάρτων, οἵτινες ἐθεραπεύοντο ἅπαντες, Acts xix. 11: δυνάμεις τε οὐ τὰς τυχούσας ὁ θεὸς ἐποίει διὰ τῶν χειρῶν Παύλου, ὥστε καὶ ἐπὶ τοὺς ἀσθενοῦντας ἀποφέρεσθαι ἀπὸ τοῦ χρωτὸς αὐτοῦ σουδάρια ἢ σιμικίνθια καὶ ἀπαλλάσσεσθαι ἀπ' αὐτῶν τὰς νόσους, τά τε πνεύματα τὰ πονηρὰ ἐκπορεύεσθαι. This invariable disposition to see in the miracles of healing the chief function of the mighty forces of the new religion, and at the same time on each occasion to distinguish with anxious care between ordinary sick folk and the "possessed," points to a physician as the author.

(5) Hobart has only too amply shown, in two hundred pages of his book, that the language of St. Luke elsewhere is coloured by medical phraseology. It is difficult here to offer convincing proofs. It is certainly of no slight significance that it is only in St. Luke that our Lord inserts in His discourse at Nazareth the proverb, "Physician, heal thyself" (iv. 23; *vide supra*, p. 17). Let me select some other examples. Παραχρῆμα (seventeen times in St. Luke, only twice elsewhere in the New Testament—in St. Matthew) is in medical language a technical term for the prompt taking effect of a medicine *in utramque partem*. Hobart (pp. 97 f.) quotes sixteen occurrences of the word from *one* work of Hippocrates ("Intern. Affect."), and a superabundance from the writings of

Dioscorides and Galen. With Zahn I further quote προσδοκᾶν (Hobart, p. 162), ἀνάπειρος (Hobart, p. 148), ὁλοκληρία (p. 193), ἀποψύχειν, καταψύχειν, ἀνάψυξις together with ἐκψύχειν (pp. 166, 32, 37), πνοή, ἐνπνέειν, ἐκπνέειν (p. 236), ζωογονεῖν (p. 155), εἰς μανίαν περιτρέπειν (pp. 267 f.), κραιπάλη (p. 167), χρώς (p. 242). Even the phrase οὐκ ἄσημος πόλις of Acts xxi. 39 may be paralleled from Hippocrates (Hobart, p. 249). Lagarde ("Psalter. Hieron.," 1874, p. 165) was the first to assert that the style of the prologue, little as it might seem at first sight, is akin to that of the medical writers. To prove his point he brought forward instances from Dioscorides, and, indeed, from a prologue of that author. The point has been somewhat better established by Hobart (pp. 87 ff., 229, 250 f.) with special reference to numerous passages in Galen. One of these (a prologue !—" Theriac. ad Pis.," 1, xiv. 210) runs as follows : καὶ τοῦτόν σοι τὸν περὶ τῆς θηριακῆς λόγον, ἀκριβῶς ἐξετάσας ἅπαντα, ἄριστε Πίσων, σπουδαίως ἐποίησα (vide Acts i. 1, ἐποιησάμην). Finally, as Zahn rightly says (ii. 436) : "Seeing that the needle in surgical use is as a rule called βελόνη, and not ῥαφίς, and the eye of the needle is named τρῆμα, not τρύπημα or τρυμαλία, and seeing that we read in Galen τοῦ κατὰ τὴν βελόνην τρήματος or τοῦ διατρήματος τῆς βελόνης (Hobart, pp. 60 f.), then St. Luke xviii. 25, when compared with St. Matthew xix. 24 = St. Mark x. 25, shows distinct traits of medical authorship. And seeing that Galen expressly reflects upon his use of 'ἀρχαί' as the name for the ends (πέρατα) of the bandage (οἱ ἐπιδέσμιοι, often also ὀθόνια and ὀθόνη)—a use which was already frequent with Hippocrates—then it is clear that Acts x. 11 and xi. 5 were written by a physician."

The six conditions which were propounded at the beginning of this appendix are amply satisfied in the case of the third evangelist. The evidence is of overwhelming force ; so that it seems to me that no doubt can exist *that the third gospel and the Acts of the Apostles were composed by a physician.*

APPENDIX II (to p. 102)

(i. 39) Ἀναστᾶσα δὲ Μαριὰμ ἐν ταῖς ἡμέραις ταύταις ἐπορεύθη εἰς τὴν ὀρεινὴν μετὰ σπουδῆς εἰς πόλιν Ἰούδα,

THIS pleonastic ἀνιστάναι is found once or twice in St. Matthew, four times in St. Mark, never in St. John, a few dozen times in St. Luke (gospel and Acts). For ἀναστᾶσα ἐπορεύθη, vide St. Luke xv. 18: ἀναστὰς πορεύσομαι, xvii. 19: ἀναστὰς πορεύου, Acts viii. 26: ἀνάστηθι καὶ πορεύου, ix. 11: ἀναστὰς πορεύθητι, xxii. 10: ἀναστὰς πορεύου.— ἐν ταῖς ἡμέραις ταύταις (or similar words) wanting in St. Matthew, St. Mark, and St. John, but found again twelve times in St. Luke (six times as here, in vi. 12, xxiii. 7, xxiv. 18, Acts i. 15, vi. 1, xi. 27; also μετὰ δὲ ταύτας τὰς ἡμέρας, i. 24, Acts i. 5, xxi. 15—πρὸ τούτων τῶν ἡμέρων, Acts v. 36, xxi. 38—τὰς ἡμ. ταύτας, Acts iii. 24).—τὴν ὀρεινήν]. Vide i. 65. Wanting elsewhere in the New Testament, but occurring in the book of Judith.—μετὰ σπουδῆς]. Occurs elsewhere in the

New Testament only in St. Mark
vi. 25.—πόλιν Ἰούδα, like πόλις
Δαβείδ, St. Luke ii. 4, 11, is copied
from the style of the LXX. (γῆ,
οἶκος, φυλὴ Ἰούδα). Or is Ἰούδα the
corrupted form of the name of the
town, as in St. Luke πόλις Ναζαρέτ,
πόλις Ἰόππη, πόλις Θυάτειρα, πόλις
Λασαία?

(40) καὶ εἰσῆλ-
θεν εἰς τὸν οἶκον
Ζαχαρίου καὶ
ἠσπάσατο τὴν
Ἐλισάβετ.

For οἶκος see the note on Acts
xvi. 15; it is much more frequent in
St. Luke than in the other evangelists, who prefer οἰκία.—ἠσπάσατο].
Vide x. 4, Acts xviii. 22, xx. 1;
xxi. 7, 19 (εἰσῄει καὶ ἀσπασάμενος
ἐξηγεῖτο), xxv. 13.

(41) καὶ ἐγένε-
το ὡς ἤκουσεν τὸν
ἀσπασμὸν τῆς
Μαρίας ἡ Ἐλισ-
άβετ, ἐσκίρτησεν
τὸ βρέφος ἐν τῇ
κοιλίᾳ αὐτῆς, καὶ
ἐπλήσθη πνεύμα-
ματος ἁγίου ἡ
Ἐλισάβετ,

For the construction with ἐγένετο
see the note on i. 8 (above, p. 98).—
ὡς temp. wanting in St. Matthew
and St. Mark, but found in St. Luke
(gospel and Acts) about forty-
eight times—e.g., Acts xxi. 12: ὡς
ἠκούσαμεν. — ἐσκίρτησεν]. Found
elsewhere in the New Testament
only in St. Luke i. 44 and vi. 23!—
βρέφος]. Wanting in St. Matthew,
St. Mark, and St. John; occurring
in St. Luke not only in chaps. i.
and ii., but also in xviii. 15 (where
it replaces the τὰ παιδία of the
Markan text) and in Acts vii. 19.—
ἐπλ. πν. ἁγ.]. See the note on i. 15
(above, p. 101).

(42) καὶ ἀνε-
φώνησεν κραυγῇ
μεγάλῃ καὶ εἶπεν·
Εὐλογημένη σὺ
ἐν γυναιξίν, καὶ
εὐλογημένος ὁ
καρπὸς τῆς κοι-
λίας σου,

κραυγὴ μεγάλη is found elsewhere in the New Testament only in Acts xxiii. 9 and Rev. xiv. 18. With ἀνεφ. κρ. μεγ. compare the ἀνακραυγάσαν which St. Luke has inserted in the Markan text (St. Luke iv. 35 = St. Mark i. 26). In both works St. Luke shows a preference for strong expressions.—There is nothing in the gospel to compare with ὁ καρπὸς τῆς κοιλίας, but in Acts ii. 30 we find ὁ καρπὸς τῆς ὀσφύος αὐτοῦ.

(43) καὶ πόθεν
μοι τοῦτο ἵνα ἔλθῃ
ἡ μήτηρ τοῦ κυ-
ρίου μου πρὸς
ἐμέ;

πόθεν μοι τοῦτο, as in St. Matthew xiii. 54, 56, xv. 33, St. Mark vi. 2 (πόθεν τούτῳ ταῦτα). — ἵνα]. This use in the Κοινή in place of the infin. is not, I think, found elsewhere in St. Luke, though it, indeed, frequently occurs in the New Testament.—It is well known that St. Luke constantly uses ὁ κύριος for Christ.

(44) ἰδοὺ γὰρ
ὡς ἐγένετο ἡ φωνὴ
τοῦ ἀσπασμοῦ
σου εἰς τὰ ὦτά
μου, ἐσκίρτησεν
ἐν ἀγαλλιάσει τὸ
βρέφος ἐν τῇ κοι-
λίᾳ μου.

See note on verse 40.—ἰδοὺ γάρ wanting in St. Matthew, St. Mark, and St. John; occurring in St. Luke's gospel five times and in the Acts once.—ἐγένετο ἡ φωνή]. Wanting in St. Matthew, St. John, and St. Mark (in i. 11 it is interpolated from St. Luke); on the other hand, it occurs seven times elsewhere in St. Luke, viz., iii. 22, ix. 35, 36, Acts ii. 6, vii. 31, x. 13, xix. 34.—

εἰς τὰ ὦτά μου]. Wanting in St. Matthew, St. Mark, and St. John; but cf. St. Luke ix. 14 : θέσθε εἰς τὰ ὦτα ὑμῶν, and Acts xi. 22 : ἠκούσθη ὁ λόγος εἰς τὰ ὦτα τῆς ἐκκλησίας.— ἐν ἀγαλλιάσει]. See the note on i. 14 (above, p. 100). The word is wanting in St. Matthew, St. Mark, and St. John, but occurs again in St. Luke in i. 14 and Acts ii. 46.

(45) καὶ μακαρία ἡ πιστεύσασα ὅτι ἔσται τελείωσις τοῖς λελαλημένοις αὐτῇ παρὰ κυρίου.

μακάριος wanting in St. Mark, and occurring in St. Matthew, apart from the Beatitudes, only four times ; in St. Luke's gospel, however, eleven times.—τελείωσις found elsewhere in the New Testament only in Hebrews vii. 11.—τοῖς λελαλημ.]. This use of the perfect (or present) participle passive of λαλέω is only found in ii. 33, Acts xiii. 45 (xvii. 19). The passive λαλεῖσθαι is found twelve times in St. Luke (gospel and Acts), in St. John not at all, in St. Matthew and St. Mark once (in the same passage).—A noteworthy parallel is found in Judith x. 9 : ἐξελεύσομαι εἰς τελείωσιν τῶν λόγων ὧν ἐλαλήσατε μετ' ἐμοῦ.

(46) καὶ εἶπεν·

"Not a change of speaker, but of the mode of speech"; cf. St. John i. 50 f., St. Mark vii. 8, 9 (Burkitt).

In what follows I place the passages of the LXX.,

from which the "Magnificat" has been composed, side by side with the text. I call no special attention to the many stylistic improvements made by St. Luke.

(46, 47) Μεγαλύνει ἡ ψυχή μου τὸν κύριον, καὶ ἠγαλλίασεν τὸ πνεῦμά μου ἐπὶ τῷ θεῷ τῷ σωτῆρί μου.

(1) 1 Sam. ii. 1: ἐστερεώθη ἡ καρδία μου ἐν κυρίῳ, ὑψώθη κέρας μου ἐν θεῷ μου.

μεγαλύνειν is not found in St. Mark and St. John; found in St. Matthew once (xxiii. 5), and in a quite different sense; in St. Luke, on the other hand, five times (i. 58, Acts v. 13, x. 46, xix. 17).—ἀγαλλίασις wanting in the other gospels, occurring three times in St. Luke (i. 14, 44, Acts ii. 46); ἀγαλλιᾶν occurs four times in St. Luke, is wanting in St. Mark, occurs once in St. Matthew and twice in St. John. Σωτήρ for God (and Christ) is found elsewhere in the synoptists only in St. Luke ii. 11; in the Acts, however, twice (v. 31, xiii. 23).

(48) ὅτι ἔβλεψεν ἐπὶ τὴν ταπείνωσιν τῆς δούλης αὐτοῦ· ἰδοὺ γὰρ ἀπὸ τοῦ νῦν μακαριοῦσίν με πᾶσαι αἱ γεννεαί·

(2) 1 Sam. i. 11: ἐὰν ἐπιβλέπων ἐπιβλέψῃς τὴν ταπείνωσιν τῆς δούλης σου, Gen. xxx. 13: μακαρία ἐγώ, ὅτι μακαρίζουσίν με πᾶσαι αἱ γυναῖκες.

ἐπιβλέπειν ἐπί found elsewhere in the synoptists only in St. Luke ix. 38.—Concerning the exclusively Lukan phrase ἰδοὺ γάρ, vide supra, note on verse 44.—ἀπὸ τοῦ νῦν found elsewhere in the New Testament only in St. Luke (v. 10, xii. 52, xxii. 18, 69, Acts xviii. 6).

(49) ὅτι ἐποίησέν μοι μεγάλα [μεγαλεῖα] ὁ δυνατός, καὶ ἅγιον τὸ ὄνομα αὐτοῦ·

(3) Deut. x. 21 : ὅστις ἐποίησεν ἐν σοὶ τὰ μεγάλα, Ps. cxi. 9 : ἅγιον . . . τὸ ὄνομα αὐτοῦ.

μεγαλεῖα found elsewhere in the New Testament only in Acts ii. 11.—δυνατός (of a person) occurs in the gospels only in St. Luke (xiv. 31, xxiv.19—of our Lord ; also Acts vii. 22, xi. 17, xviii. 24).

(50) καὶ τὸ ἔλεος αὐτοῦ εἰς γενεὰς καὶ γενεὰς τοῖς φοβουμένοις αὐτόν.

(4) Ps. ciii. 17 : τὸ δὲ ἔλεος τοῦ κυρίου ἀπὸ τοῦ αἰῶνος καὶ ἕως τοῦ αἰῶνος ἐπὶ τοὺς φοβουμένους αὐτόν.

τὸ ἔλεος peculiar to St. Luke of the evangelists (i. 54, 58, 72, 78, x. 37.—οἱ φοβούμενοι τ. θεόν is probably intended by St. Luke to be understood in its technical sense (also of the Gentiles devoted to the worship of God), as so often in the Acts.

(51) ἐποίησεν κράτος ἐν βραχίονι αὐτοῦ, διεσκόρπισεν ὑπερηφάνους διανοίᾳ καρδίας αὐτῶν·

(5) Ps. lxxxix. 11 : σὺ ἐταπείνωσας ὡς τραυματίαν ὑπερήφανον, καὶ ἐν τῷ βραχίονι τῆς δυνάμεώς σου διεσκόρπισας τοὺς ἐχθρούς σου.

κράτος elsewhere throughout the gospels and the Acts found only in Acts xix. 20, and there used in the same sense as here.

(52) καθεῖλεν δυνάστας ἀπὸ θρόνων καὶ ὕψωσεν ταπεινούς,

(6) Job xii. 19 : δυνάστας γῆς κατέστρεψεν, v. 11 : τὸν ποιοῦντα ταπεινοὺς εἰς ὕψος.

καθαιρεῖν found again five times in St. Luke ; elsewhere in the gospels only in St. Mark xv. 36, 46 (but in the significance "to take down"). Here and in the next verse St. Luke's well-known Ebionitism is prominent.

(53) πεινῶντας ἐνέπλησεν ἀγαθῶν καὶ πλουτοῦντας ἐξαπέστειλεν κενούς.

(7) 1 Sam. ii. 7: κύριος πτωχίζει καὶ πλουτίζει, ταπεινοῖ καὶ ἀνυψοῖ, Ps. cvii. 9: ψυχὴν πεινῶσαν ἐνέπλησεν, ἀγαθῶν, Job xii. 19: ἐξαποστέλλων ἱερεῖς αἰχμαλώτους.

ἐντίμπλημι elsewhere in the gospels only in St. Luke vi. 25 and St. John vi. 25, but also in Acts xiv. 17.—The verb ἐξαποστέλλειν is found ten times in St. Luke; elsewhere in the New Testament only in Galatians. *The remarkably singular phrase ἐξαποστ. κενούς occurs twice again in St. Luke—viz., xx. 10, 11—but never elsewhere.*

(54) ἀντελάβετο Ἰσραὴλ παιδὸς αὐτοῦ, μνησθῆναι ἐλέους

(8) Is. xli. 8: σὺ δέ, Ἰσραηλ, παῖς μου, οὗ ἀντελαβόμην, Ps. xcviii. 3: ἐμνήσθη τοῦ ἐλέους αὐτοῦ τῷ Ἰακώβ.

ἀντιλαμβάνεσθαι is not found elsewhere in the gospels; yet it occurs in Acts xx. 35: ἀντιλαμβ. τ. ἀσθενούντων.

(55) —καθὼς ἐλάλησεν πρὸς τοὺς πατέρας ἡμῶν — τῷ Ἀβραὰμ καὶ τῷ σπέρματι αὐτοῦ εἰς τὸν αἰῶνα.

(9) Micah vii. 20: δώσει . . . ἔλεον τῷ Ἀβραάμ, καθότι ὤμοσας τοῖς πατράσιν ἡμῶν, 2 Sam. xxii. 51: καὶ ποιῶν ἔλεος . . . τῷ Δαυεὶδ καὶ τῷ σπέρματι αὐτοῦ ἕως αἰῶνος.

λαλεῖν πρός wanting in the other gospels (λαλεῖν εἰς also wanting); on the other hand, it is found again five times in St. Luke's gospel and nine times in the Acts— e.g., xxviii. 25: ἐλάλησεν πρὸς τοὺς πατέρας ὑμῶν.

(56) Ἔμεινεν δὲ Μαριὰμ σὺν αὐτῇ ὡς μῆνας τρεῖς, καὶ ὑπέστρεψεν εἰς τὸν οἶκον αὐτῆς.

μένειν σύν in the New Testament found again only in St. Luke xxiv. 29: εἰσῆλθεν τοῦ μεῖναι σὺν αὐτοῖς.— ὡς = circiter occurs again seven times in St. Luke (gospel and Acts), never in St. Matthew, twice in St. Mark. — ὑποστρέφειν occurs twenty-two times in St. Luke's gospel, eleven times in the Acts, and is wanting in the other gospels. ὑποστρέφειν εἰς τὸν οἶκον is also found in St. Luke vii. 10, viii. 39, xi. 24.

(68) Εὐλογητὸς (κύριος) ὁ θεὸς τοῦ Ἰσραήλ, ὅτι ἐπεσκέψατο καὶ ἐποίησεν λύτρωσιν τῷ λαῷ αὐτοῦ,

(1) Ps. xli. 14 (lxxii. 18, cvi. 48): εὐλογητὸς κύριος ὁ θεὸς Ἰσραήλ, Ps. cxi. 9: λύτρωσιν ἀπέστειλεν τῷ λαῷ αὐτοῦ.

The weakly supported κύριος should be deleted. St. Luke evidently felt that this word, without the article, coming before ὁ θεός, was a solecism.—τοῦ is a grammatical improvement. — ἐπεσκέψατο (used absolutely as in Acts xv. 14). St. Luke alone of the New Testament writers uses this word of God; vide i. 78, vii. 16, Acts xv. 14.— ἐποίησεν, a verbal improvement.

(69) καὶ ἤγειρεν κέρας σωτηρίας ἡμῖν ἐν οἴκῳ Δαυεὶδ παιδὸς αὐτοῦ

(2) Ps. cxxxii. 17: ἐξανατελῶ κέρας τῷ Δαυείδ, Ps. xviii. 3: κύριος . . . κέρας σωτηρίας, 1 Sam. ii. 10: ὑψώσει κέρας χριστοῦ αὐτοῦ, Ezek. xxix. 21: ἀνατελεῖ κέρας παντὶ τῷ οἴκῳ Ἰσραήλ.

ἤγειρεν with an implied reference to the Resurrection of Christ. With ἡμῖν cf. Acts ii. 39, xiii. 26: ἡμῖν ὁ λόγος τ. σωτηρίας ταύτης ἐξαπεστάλη.—For παιδὸς αὐτοῦ see verse 54. Σωτηρία is a favourite expression with St. Luke (wanting in St. Matthew and St. Mark, occurring only once in St. John); St. Luke xix. 9: σωτηρία τῷ οἴκῳ τούτῳ ἐγένετο.

(70) —καθὼς ἐλά-
λησεν διὰ στόματος τῶν
ἁγίων (τῶν) ἀπ' αἰῶνος
προφητῶν αὐτοῦ—

This parenthesis
(like verse 55) is just
in St. Luke's style.
Διὰ στόματος is only
found with him of
the New Testament
writers (Acts i. 16,
iii. 18, 21, iv. 25, xv.
7). The epithet ἅγιος
is also Lukan—vide
verse 72, and the
exactly verbal paral-
lel in Acts iii. 21:
ἐλάλησεν ὁ θεὸς διὰ
στόματος τ. ἁγίων ἀπ'
αἰῶνος αὐτοῦ προφητῶν.
Also ἀπ' αἰῶνος is only
found in St. Luke
(Acts xv. 18: γνωστὰ
ἀπ' αἰῶνος).

(71) σωτηρίαν ἐξ
ἐχθρῶν ἡμῶν καὶ ἐκ
χειρὸς πάντων τῶν
μισούντων ἡμᾶς,

(4) Ps. cvi. 10:
ἔσωσεν αὐτοὺς ἐκ χει-
ρῶν μισούντων καὶ
ἐλυτρώσατο αὐτοὺς ἐκ
χειρὸς ἐχθροῦ (cf. Ps.
xviii. 18).

σωτηρίαν]. In very
effective apposition to
κέρας σωτηρίας.

(72–75) ποιῆσαι ἔ-
λεος μετὰ τῶν πατέρων
ἡμῶν καὶ μνησθῆναι
διαθήκης ἁγίας αὐτοῦ,
ὅρκον ὃν ὤμοσεν πρὸς
Αβραὰμ τὸν πατέρα
ἡμῶν, τοῦ δοῦναι ἡμῖν
ἀφόβως ἐκ χειρὸς ἐχ-
θρῶν ῥυσθέντας λατρεύ-
ειν αὐτῷ ἐν ὁσιότητι
καὶ δικαιοσύνῃ ἐνώπιον
αὐτοῦ πάσας τὰς ἡμέρας
ἡμῶν.

(5–8) Numerous
passages in the Old
Testament — vide
Micah vii. 20: δώσει
ἔλεος τῷ 'Αβραάμ, κα-
θότι ὤμοσας τοῖς πατρά-
σιν ἡμῶν, Ps. cv. 8,
cvi. 45; Exod. ii. 24;
Lev. xxvi. 42; Jerem.
xi. 5; Ps. xviii. 18;
Jerem. xxxii. 39:
φοβηθῆναί με πάσας τ.
ἡμέρας. All the ele-
ments of the verse
are given here.

ποιῆσαι (ἔλεος) μετά
is in the New Testa-
ment exclusively Lu-
kan; cf. x. 37: ὁ ποιήσας
τὸ ἔλεος μετ' αὐτοῦ.—
ἁγίας is a distinc-
tively Lukan epithet;
see note on verse 70.
—This use of πρός is
Lukan; πρός with
acc. occurs in St.
Matthew 44 times, in
St. Luke's gospel 166
times, in the Acts 140
times; vide supra, note
on i. 13 (p. 99).—For
δοῦναι with infin. see
Acts iv. 29: δὸς τ.
δούλοις σου μετὰ παρ-

ρησίας λαλεῖν.—ῥυσ-
θέντας after ἡμῖν is not
un-Hellenic.—λατρεύ-
ειν wanting in St.
Mark and St. John,
and found in St.
Matthew only in a
quotation; see, on the
other hand, St. Luke
ii. 37, iv. 8, Acts vii.
7, 42, xxiv. 14, xxvi.
7, xxvii. 23.—ἐν ὁσ. κ.
δικ.]. Cf. Wisd. of Sol.
ix. 3 and Ephes. iv.
24.—ἐνώπιον wanting
in St. Matthew and
St. Mark, occurring
once in St. John, but
in St. Luke (gospel
and Acts) about
thirty-six times.

(76, 77) καὶ σὺ δέ,
παιδίον, προφήτης ὑψί-
στου κληθήσῃ· προπο-
ρεύσῃ γὰρ ἐνώπιον κυ-
ρίου ἑτοιμάσαι ὁδοὺς
αὐτοῦ, τοῦ δοῦναι γνῶ-
σιν σωτηρίας τῷ λαῷ
αὐτοῦ ἐν ἀφέσει ἁμαρ-
τιῶν αὐτῶν.

(9, 10) Mal. iii. 1:
ὁδὸς πρὸ προσώπου
μου, Is. xl. 3: ἑτοι-
μάσατε τὸν ὁδὸν κυρίου,
Deut. xxxi. 3 : κύριος
... προπορευόμενος πρὸ
προσώπου σου, Jerem.
xxxi. 34.

ὑψίστου]. See note
on Acts xvi.17 (above,
p. 51); it is Lukan.
—προπορεύεσθαι is
found again in the
New Testament only
in Acts vii. 40.—ἐνώ-
πιον]. Vide verse 75.
—δοῦναι]. Vide verse
74.—γνῶσιν]. Occurs
in the gospels only
here and in St. Luke
xi. 52 (τ. κλεῖδα τ.
γνώσεως).—σωτηρίας].
Vide verse 69, Acts
xvi. 17: ὁδὸν σωτη-
ρίας.—ἄφεσις ἁμαρτ.
eight times in St.
Luke, wanting in St.
John, once each in
St. Matthew and St.
Mark.

(78, 79) διὰ σπλάγ-
χνα ἐλέους θεοῦ ἡμῶν,
ἐν οἷς ἐπισκέψεται ἡμᾶς

(11, 12) Test. Levi :
ἕως ἐπισκέψηται κύριος
πάντα τὰ ἔθνη ἐν σπλάγ-

σπλάγχα]. Wanting
in the gospels ; vide
Coloss.iii.12:σπλάγχα

ἀνατολὴ ἐξ ὕψους, ἐπιφᾶναι τοῖς ἐν σκότει καὶ σκιᾷ θανάτου καθημένοις, τοῦ κατευθῦναι τοὺς πόδας ἡμῶν εἰς ὁδὸν εἰρήνης.

χνοις υἱοῦ αὐτοῦ, Ps. cvii. 10 : καθημένους ἐν σκότει καὶ σκιᾷ θανάτου, Ps. xl. 3 : ἔστησεν ... τοὺς πόδας μου καὶ κατηύθυνεν τὰ διαβήματά μου.

οἰκτιρμοῦ. — For ἐπισκεψ. vide verse 68.— For ἐξ ὕψους vide St. Luke xxiv. 49 : ἐνδύσησθε ἐξ ὕψους δύναμιν. It does not occur elsewhere in the gospels and the Acts.— ἐπιφᾶναι]. Wanting elsewhere in the gospels ; but cf. Acts xxvii. 20 : ἄστρων ἐπιφαινόντων. — Acts xvi. 17 : ὁδὸν σωτηρίας (this is the same as ὁδ. εἰρ.); ii. 28 : ὁδοὺς ζωῆς. The construction here is exactly the same as that of verse 72 (ποιῆσαι) in its relation to verse 74 (τοῦ δοῦναι) and of verse 76 and 77 (ἑτοιμάσαι and τοῦ δοῦναι). We thus see what a delicate sense of style St. Luke has. Three times he gives a final clause in the infin. without the article when this final clause is subordinate as a means to another final clause ; and he distinguishes the latter in each instance by a τοῦ before the infin.

(ii. 15) καὶ ἐγένετο ὡς ἀπῆλθον ἀπ᾽ αὐτῶν εἰς τὸν οὐρανὸν οἱ ἄγγελοι, οἱ ποιμένες ἐλάλουν πρὸς ἀλλήλους· διέλθωμεν δὴ ἕως

Concerning the Lukan construction with ἐγένετο, see note on Acts xvi. 16 (above, p. 49).—ἀπῆλθον οἱ ἀγγ.]. The only parallel is Acts x. 7 : ὡς δὲ ἀπῆλθεν ὁ ἄγγελος (differently in St. Luke vii. 24 : ἀπελθόντων τ. ἀγγ.).—λαλεῖν πρός is exclusively Lukan. See note on

o

Βηθλεὲμ καὶ ἴδω-
μεν τὸ ῥῆμα τοῦτο
τὸ γεγονὸς ὃ ὁ
κύριος ἐγνώρισεν
ἡμῖν.

i. 55 (above, p. 205).—διέρχεσθαι occurs thirty times in St. Luke, elsewhere in the gospels six times (but the occurrences are not all well attested); in the weaker meaning it occurs only in St. Luke.—δή with the imperat. is found again in Acts xiii. 2 and xv. 36; elsewhere in the New Testament only in 1 Cor. vi. 20, where it is not quite certain.—διελθ. ἕως Βηθλ.]. *Vide* Acts ix. 38: διελθεῖν ἕως αὐτῶν; Acts xi. 9: διῆλθον ἕως Φοινίκης; Acts xi. 22: διελθεῖν ἕως Ἀντιοχείας (only in St. Luke).— ῥῆμα, in the sense of *res quædam*, is found again in i. 37 and Acts v. 32, x. 37, and never elsewhere in the New Testament.—τ. ῥῆμα τοῦτο]. St. Luke loves this pleonastic use of the demonstrative pronoun (see also verses 17 and 19).—τὸ γεγονός]. Occurs once in St. Mark, never in St. Matthew and St. John, again in St. Luke viii. 34 (ἰδόντες οἱ βόσκοντες τὸ γεγονός), 35 (ἰδεῖν τὸ γεγονός), 56, [xxiv. 12], Acts iv. 21, v. 7 (μὴ εἰδυῖα τὸ γεγ.), xiii. 12 (ἰδὼν τὸ γεγ.).

(16) *καὶ ἦλθαν*
σπεύσαντες καὶ
ἀνεῦραν τήν τε
Μαριὰμ καὶ τὸν
Ἰωσὴφ καὶ τὸ
βρέφος κείμενον
ἐν τῇ φάτνῃ·

σπεύδειν, intrans., is found in the New Testament only with St. Luke (xix. 5, 6, Acts xx. 16, xxii. 18); as a transitive verb it occurs only once in the New Testament (2 Peter iii. 12).—ἀνευρίσκειν occurs only once again in the New Testament, viz.,

in the " we " section Acts xxi. 4.—
Concerning the Lukan word βρέφος,
see above on i. 41.—φάτνη]. Except
in i. 2 this word is only found again
in the New Testament in St. Luke
xiii. 15.

(17, 18) ἰδόν-
τες δὲ ἐγνώρισαν
περὶ τοῦ ῥήματος
τοῦ λαληθέντες
αὐτοῖς περὶ τοῦ
παιδίου τούτου.
καὶ πάντες οἱ
ἀκούσαντες ἐθαύ-
μασαν περὶ τῶν
λαληθέντων ὑπὸ
τῶν ποιμένων
πρὸς αὐτούς.

For the passive λαλεῖσθαι and τὰ
λαληθέντα see the notes on Acts
xvi. 14 (above, p. 47) and on St.
Luke i. 45.—τούτου]. See note on
verse 15.—πάντες οἱ ἀκούσαντες].
Only in i. 66, ii. 47, and Acts ix. 21
(πάντες οἱ ἀκούοντες).—ἐθαύμασαν
περί is singular.—For λαλεῖν πρός
see note on i. 55.

(19) ἡ δὲ Μα-
ρία πάντα συνε-
τήρει τὰ ῥήματα
ταῦτα συνβάλ-
λουσα ἐν τῇ καρ-
δίᾳ αὐτῆς.

συνβάλλειν is confined to St.
Luke in the New Testament; vide
xiv. 31 and Acts iv. 15, xvii. 18,
xviii. 27, xx. 14 (" we " section).

(20) καὶ ὑπέ-
στρεψαν οἱ ποι-
μένες δοξάζοντες
καὶ αἰνοῦντες τὸν
θεὸν ἐπὶ πᾶσιν
οἷς ἤκουσαν καὶ
εἶδον καθὼς ἐλα-
λήθη πρὸς αὐ-
τούς.

Concerning the Lukan ὑποστρέφειν, see note on i. 56.—αἰνοῦντες].
This word is found seven times in
St. Luke (ii. 13, xix. 37, xxiv. 53
[doubtful], Acts ii. 47, iii. 8, 9); elsewhere only in Rom. xv. 11 (LXX.)
and Rev. xix. 5.—οἷς]. This attraction is frequent in St. Luke (not in
the other gospels); vide iii. 19, v. 9,

ix. 43, xii. 46, xv. 16, xix. 37, xxiv.
25, Acts iii. 21, x. 39, xiii. 39,
xxii. 10, xxvi. 2.—For ἐλαλήθη πρός
see verse 18.

(ii. 41) καὶ ἐπο-
ρεύοντο οἱ γονεῖς
αὐτοῦ κατ᾽ ἔτος
εἰς Ἰερουσαλὴμ
τῇ ἑορτῇ τοῦ
πάσχα.

πορεύεσθαι]. A favourite word with
St. Luke.—ἔτος]. Once in St. Matthew, twice in St. Mark, three times
in St. John, twenty-seven times in
St. Luke ; κατ᾽ ἔτος occurs here
only.—τῇ ἑορτῇ τ. π.]. Vide xxii. 1 :
ἑορτὴ τ. ἀζύμων. The expression is
not found in St. Matthew and St.
Mark. The dative of time is frequent
in St. Luke.

(42, 43) καὶ
ὅτε ἐγένετο ἐτῶν
ιβ´, ἀναβαινόν-
των αὐτῶν κατὰ
τὸ ἔθος τῆς ἑορτῆς
καὶ τελειωσάντων
τὰς ἡμέρας, ἐν τῷ
ὑποστρέφειν αὐ-
τοὺς ὑπέμεινεν
Ἰησοῦς ὁ παῖς ἐν
Ἰερουσαλήμ, καὶ
οὐκ ἔγνωσαν οἱ
γονεῖς αὐτοῦ.

ἐγένετο ἐτ. ιβ´]. So also in iii. 23,
viii. 42, Acts. iv. 22.—κατὰ τὸ ἔθος].
Again only in i. 9 and xxii. 39 ; nowhere else in the New Testament. See
note on i. 8 (above, p. 98).—ὑποστρέ-
φειν]. Lukan ; see note on i. 56.—
ὑπέμεινεν]. In the sense of " to stay
behind," only again in Acts xvii.
14.—The whole sentence is genuinely
Lukan, also in the variation of tense
in ἀναβαινόντων and τελειωσάντων.

(44, 45) νομί-
σαντες δὲ αὐτὸν
εἶναι ἐν τῇ συνο-
δίᾳ ἦλθον ἡμέρας
ὁδὸν καὶ ἀνε-
ζήτουν αὐτὸν ἐν

νομίσαντες]. Nine times in St.
Luke, wanting in St. Mark and St.
John, three times in St. Matthew.—
συνοδία is ἀπ. λεγ. in the New Testament, but συνοδεύειν is found in
ix. 7.—ἀναζητεῖν is found elsewhere

τοῖς συγγενέσιν καὶ τοῖς γνωστοῖς, καὶ μὴ εὑρόντες ὑπέστρεψαν εἰς Ἰερουσαλὴμ ἀναζητοῦντες αὐτόν.

in the New Testament only in St. Luke ii. 45 and Acts xi. 25.— συγγενεῖς is found six times in St. Luke, once each in St. Mark and St. John; wanting in St. Matthew.— μή]. A delicate Lukan touch (causal)—*vide* iii. 9. Note also the use of the participle imperf. as a Lukan trait.—γνωστός is found eleven times in St. Luke, in all the rest of the New Testament only three times; οἱ γνωστοι occurs again only in St. Luke xxiii. 49.—ὑπέστρεψαν]. Lukan; see note on i. 56.

(46, 47) καὶ ἐγένετο μετὰ ἡμέρας γ′ εὗρον αὐτὸν ἐν τῷ ἱερῷ καθεζόμενον ἐν μέσῳ τῶν διδασκάλων καὶ ἀκούοντα αὐτῶν καὶ ἐπερωτῶντα αὐτούς· ἐξίσταντο δὲ πάντες οἱ ἀκούοντες αὐτοῦ ἐπὶ τῇ συνέσει καὶ ταῖς ἀποκρίσεσιν αὐτοῦ.

ἐγένετο Lukan. — καθεζόμ.]. See Acts xx. 9.—ἐξίσταντο]. Eleven times in St. Luke, elsewhere in the New Testament only six times; with ἐπί (like θαυμάζειν) here only.—πάντες οἱ ἀκ.]. See note on ii. 18, and Acts ix. 21: ἐξίσταντο δὲ πάντες οἱ ἀκούοντες.

(48, 49) καὶ ἰδόντες αὐτὸν ἐξεπλάγησαν, καὶ εἶπεν πρὸς αὐτὸν ἡ μήτηρ αὐτοῦ· τέκνον, τί ἐποί-

ἐξεπλάγησαν]. *Vide* ix. 43, Acts xiii. 12.—ὀδυνώμενοι]. Occurs again in the New Testament only in St. Luke xvi. 24, 25 and Acts xx. 38.— τί ὅτι]. Again in the New Testament only in Acts v. 4, 9.—τὰ τοῦ πατρός].

ησας ἡμῖν οὕτως; ἰδοὺ ὁ πατήρ σου κἀγὼ ὀδυνώμενοι ἐζητοῦμέν σε. καὶ εἶπεν πρὸς αὐτούς· τί ὅτι ἐζητεῖτέ με; οὐκ ἤδειτε ὅτι ἐν τοῖς τοῦ πατρός μου δεῖ εἶναί με;

St. Luke is fond of such constructions; see note on Acts xxviii. 15 (above, pp. 63 f. and elsewhere).

(50, 51) καὶ αὐτοὶ οὐ συνῆκαν τὸ ῥῆμα ὃ ἐλάλησεν αὐτοῖς. καὶ κατέβη μετ' αὐτῶν καὶ ἦλθεν εἰς Ναζαρέθ, καὶ ἦν ὑποτασσόμενος αὐτοῖς. καὶ ἡ μήτηρ αὐτοῦ διετήρει πάντα τὰ ῥήματα ἐν τῇ καρδίᾳ αὐτῆς.

ὑποτάσσεσθαι is wanting in St. Matthew, St. Mark, St. John, and in the Acts; is found, however, in St. Luke x. 17, 20.—ἦν with participle is especially frequent in St. Luke, and is characteristic of his style.— διατηρεῖν occurs again in the New Testament only in Acts xv. 29.

(52) καὶ Ἰησοῦς προέκοπτεν τῇ σοφίᾳ καὶ ἡλικίᾳ καὶ χάριτι παρὰ θεῷ καὶ ἀνθρώποις.

προέκοπτεν]. Here only in the gospels; but cf. St. Paul.—χάριτι]. Wanting in St. Matthew and St. Mark, occurring in St. John only in the prologue, but found twenty-five times in St. Luke.—For St. Luke's exemplar in this verse see 1 Sam. ii. 26: καὶ τὸ παιδάριον Σαμουὴλ ἐπορεύετο ... καὶ ἀγαθὸν καὶ μετὰ κυρίου καὶ μετὰ ἀνθρώπων.

From the above investigation (together with that

given on pages 97–101) it is perfectly clear that a Greek source cannot lie at the foundation of the first two chapters of St. Luke's gospel. The agreement of the style with that of St. Luke is too close. The source, indeed, must have been revised sentence by sentence.[1] It is possible that for the narrative an Aramaic source has been used, but this hypothesis is not probable. In any case, the " Magnificat " and " Benedictus " are works of St. Luke himself.

The " Magnificat " falls into nine verses of two clauses each. The nine verses are, however, so composed that they form four divisions, 1, 2–4, 5–7, 8–9, each with its own characteristic thought.[2] Of the eighteen clauses, six end with αὐτοῦ (αὐτόν, αὐτῶν), which also occurs twice in other positions. Notice also the μου which occurs three times in the first verse, then the αὐτοῦ which follows in 2ª and 3ᵇ; further, the αὐτοῦ in the middle of 4ª which refers back to 3ᵇ, and the αὐτοῦ—αὐτῶν in 5 which answers to the αὐτοῦ—αὐτόν in 4. Thus the first verse is still more closely held together by the μου, and verses 2–5 by αὐτοῦ (note also how ἐποίησεν in verse 5 answers to the same word in verse 3).

[1] But the verses i. 34, 35 are a later interpolation. See my essay in the " Ztschr. f. N. Tliche. Wissenschaft," 1901, ss. 53 ff.

[2] So, at least, the arrangement appears to the thoughtful reader of to-day. I will not discuss the mysteries of ancient versification. A number of scholars divide the canticle into four strophes of three verses each, making the first verse end in the middle of verse 48, the second after verse 50, the third after verse 53. This method of division is more artificial than that into four strophes of four verses each (46–48, 49–50, 51–53, 54–55), in which the verses 52 and 53 are counted each as one (not each as two). I think that St. Luke himself intended the latter system of division.

Moreover, just as the μου which is characteristic of verse 1 is echoed in verse 2 (με) and verse 3 (μοι), although these verses are dominated by the αὐτοῦ, so also the latter word is continued in verse 5, although this verse both in thought and form belongs to verses 6–7, and thus occupies a double position. The three verses 5–7 are most closely bound together by the parallelism of their construction, verses 6–7 still more so by the rhyme (6ᵃ θρόνων, 7ᵃ ἀγαθῶν, 6ᵇ ταπεινούς, 7ᵇ κενούς). In verses 8 and 9 αὐτοῦ (of God) appears again; moreover, the μου of the introductory verse is also taken up and amplified in the ἡμῶν of the concluding verse; while the whole poem comes to a solemn conclusion in the words εἰς τὸν αἰῶνα.—The excelling art of St. Luke first clearly appears when we realise that a poem so noble in form and so consistent in thought is purely a collection of reminiscences from the Old Testament (LXX.). A close examination of the poem verse by verse brings out with convincing clearness the author's method. We then see how he edits his material in regard to vocabulary, style, and poetic form, and recasts the whole in better Greek without obliterating its Hebraic (LXX.) character. Such an examination has been already carried out by me in the number of the "Sitzungsberichte" quoted above. It is, moreover, evident from the comparison already made in this appendix that nearly all the words in the "Magnificat" which vary from the words of the parallel verses of the Old Testament are the special property of St. Luke—i.e., belong to his vocabulary (the words are: μεγαλύνειν, ἀγαλλιᾶν, ὁ σωτήρ, ἐπιβλέπειν ἐπί, ἰδού γάρ, ἀπὸ τοῦ νῦν, γενεαί, μεγαλεῖα, ὁ δυνατός, κράτος, διάνοια καρδίας, καθαιρεῖν, ἐξαποστέλλειν κενούς, λαλεῖν πρός).

Exactly the same may be said of the "Benedictus," though here the material from the Greek Bible has been more severely edited than in the case of the "Magnificat," and hence a finer poem has been produced. That both these canticles were composed by the same author is shown not only by several important cases of coincidence and by the same discreet manner of referring to the Messiah, but in detail also—in the αὐτός and ἡμεῖς, which are as characteristic of the "Benedictus" as the αὐτός and μου are of the "Magnificat"; above all, it is shown by the fact that in the "Benedictus" also the peculiar vocabulary of St. Luke is unmistakably present. Lastly, the first three strophes of the "Benedictus" (verses 68–75; the whole canticle contains five strophes of four verses each) are only superficially fashioned according to the style of the Hebrew psalm. On closer view *they present the form of a single, complicated, correctly constructed Greek period* that does all honour to the author of the prologue (St. Luke i. 1 ff.) and of numerous other excellent Greek periods. This period is simply forced into its Hebrew dress. The hands are Esau's hands, but the voice is that of Jacob. But if this is so, then it is plain that St. Luke in composing these canticles has *purposely* kept to the language of the Psalms and prophets (LXX.). The Hebraisms, whether adopted or inserted from the Old Testament, are *intentional*; the whole style is artificial, and is intended to produce an impression of antiquity—a purpose which has been really fulfilled. A continuation of the examination into the style of St. Luke undertaken by Vogel and Norden ("Antike Kunstprosa," s. 483) leads to the conclusion that he was a master in the imitation of style (in the gospel, chaps. 3–23, how excellently he imitates the typical gospel narrative style even where he corrects it!), and that at the same time, by sober avoidance of all exaggeration, as well as by the introduction of his own peculiar vocabulary and style, he has understood how to give to his work a by no means indistinct individuality of its own and a tone and colouring which is truly Hellenic.

APPENDIX III (to p. 129)

IF the epistle from Jerusalem were genuine, it would be the most ancient Christian document that we possess. Its genuineness is strenuously upheld by Zahn ("Einl.," ii. ss. 344 f., 353 f., 397, 413, 431 f., 438), who says: "The style does not bear the stamp of St. Luke, and the secular tone of the introductory and concluding formulæ does not favour the hypothesis that the author has fabricated the document out of his own head or from some indefinite tradition." But is the secular tone of the introductory formula—which, moreover, is also found in St. James i. 1—more suitable in the case of the apostles and elders of Jerusalem than in the case of the Greek physician? Zahn also produces a list of ἀπ. λεγ. occurring in the epistle and wanting in St. Luke (those which are wanting elsewhere in the New Testament are marked with an asterisk)— viz.: ἀνασκευάζειν,* βάρος, διαστέλλεσθαι, ἐπάναγκες,* εὖ πράττειν,* οἱ ἀγαπητοὶ ἡμῶν (without ἀδελφοί), the appositional use of ἀδελφοί* (after πρεσβύτεροι).

We may not dismiss the question with the hasty

sentence that in ancient historical narratives of this
kind the epistles are always fabricated. Here the
circumstances are different. We may not without
hesitation assume that St. Luke dared to fabricate such
an important historical document. And we have just
as little justification for concluding, from the fact that
the text which precedes the epistle presents many
striking points of connection with it, that the epistle is
therefore a forgery; for the narrator could easily have
used the document lying before him for his narrative,
before he copied the letter itself into his work. We
must therefore examine into the matter without prejudice.
Such an investigation has been most thoroughly carried
out by Weiss, among others. In his commentary this
scholar has examined the epistle both in regard to
subject-matter and language, and has arrived at the
conclusion that the epistle was put together by St. Luke.
I do not wish to repeat the evidence derived from the
subject-matter, although this is perhaps the more important, but I wish to investigate the linguistic phenomena yet more closely than Weiss, paying the while
special attention to the arguments of Zahn.

Verse 23. Here the reading οἱ ἀπόστολοι καὶ οἱ
πρεσβύτεροι [καὶ οἱ] ἀδελφοί is doubtful. "καὶ οἱ" is,
at all events, the more difficult reading, as we are not
told in what comes before of any participation of the
whole community in the decision. The remarkable
expression οἱ πρεσβύτεροι–ἀδελφοί is thus of at least
doubtful authority.—οἱ ἀδελφοὶ οἱ ἐξ ἐθνῶν is a phrase
that one would expect St. Luke to use to describe the
Gentile Christians.—With οἱ κατὰ τ. Ἀντοχ. κ. Συρίαν

compare xi. 1: οἱ ὄντες κατὰ τὴν Ἰουδαίαν, also viii. 1: διεσπάρησαν κατὰ τὰς χώρας τ. Ἰουδαίας, and ii. 10: Λιβύης τῆς κατὰ Κυρήνην.

Verse 24. Ἐπειδὴ . . . ἔδοξεν ἡμῖν, as in St. Luke i. 1 ff. ἐπειδή is not found in St. Mark, St. Matthew, and St. John; it occurs, however, in St. Luke vii. 1, xi. 6, Acts xiii. 46, xiv. 12.—τινὲς ἐξ ἡμῶν, thus only in xi. 20: ἦσαν δέ τινες ἐξ αὐτῶν (τίς and τινές play an important rôle in St. Luke's style).—ἐξελθόντες, as in xii. 17, xvi. 36, 40.—The following words, ἐτάραξαν ὑμᾶς, λόγοις ἀνασκευάζοντες τὰς ψυχὰς ὑμῶν, of which Zahn has described ἀνασκευάζοντες as un-Lukan, are coloured by medical phraseology. St. Luke uses in his writings the words τάραχος, ταράσσειν, διαταράσσειν, ἐκταράσσειν (the last two are confined to St. Luke in the New Testament). These words, together with ταρακτικός, ταραχώδης, ἐκτάραξις, ἐπιταράσσειν, συνταράσσειν, ὑποταράσσειν, are shown by Hobart (pp. 93 f.) to be frequently used in medical language "to express disturbance of body and mind." The same is true of ἀνασκευάζειν. This word, it is true, only occurs here in St. Luke's writings; yet in Acts xxi. 15 ἀποσκευασάμενοι is found (and nowhere else in the New Testament). Hobart (p. 232) shows how often ἀνασκευάζειν occurs in Galen, and, moreover, in Dioscorides in the sense of subvertere; it is a technical term for the dispersion (as a rule) of some pathological symptom.—With the pleonastic use of "your souls" for "you" compare xiv. 22: τὰς ψυχὰς τῶν μαθητῶν, also xx. 24, xxvii. 10, 22.—διαστέλλεσθαι occurs, indeed, only here in St. Luke; but cases of attraction such as οἷς διεστειλ. are in great favour with our author (*vide, e.g.*, Acts i. 1, and elsewhere).

Verse 25. For ἔδοξεν see verse 22.—The participle γενόμενος occurs in St. Mark and St. Matthew almost always in temporal clauses (it is only once used in St. Mark of a person); on the other hand, *cf.* St. Luke xxii. 40, 44, Acts i. 16, 18, (iv. 11), vii. 32, 38, x. 4, xii. 11, 23, xiii. 5, xvi. 27, 29, xix. 26, 28, xxi. 17, xxiv. 25, xxv. 15, xxvii. 7, 36.—ὁμοθυμαδόν *occurs in the Acts eleven times*, and only once elsewhere in the New Testament (Romans xv. 6); *cf.* especially Acts v. 12: ἦσαν ὁμοθυμαδὸν ἅπαντες, also xii. 20.—ἐκλέξασθαι is wanting in St. Mark and St. Matthew, is found eleven times in St. Luke's writings.—ἄνδρας as in Acts vi. 3: ἐπισκέψασθε ἄνδρας ἐξ ὑμῶν, vi. 11: ὑπέβαλον ἄνδρας, x. 5: πέμψον ἄνδρας εἰς Ἰόππην.—πέμψαι: See the passage just quoted.—οἱ ἀγαπητοὶ ἡμῶν is wanting elsewhere in St. Luke.

Verse 26. Ἀνθρώποις: This use of ἀνθρ. is Lukan (numerous examples).—τὰς ψυχάς, meaning " the life," as in St. Luke vi. 9, xii. 20.—ὑπὲρ τοῦ ὀνόματος κτλ— *vide* Acts xxi. 13: ἐτοίμως ἔχω ἀποθανεῖν ὑπὲρ τ. ὀνόματος τοῦ κυρίου Ἰησοῦ (v. 41, ix. 16), Acts xx. 21: πίστις εἰς τὸν κυρίον Ἰησοῦν Χριστόν (never again in the Acts).

Verse 27. Ἀπεστάλκαμεν: " ἀπεσταλ. alternates with πέμψ. of verse 25 just as in Acts x. 5, 8 " (Weiss). The perfect of ἀποστέλλω is not found in St. Matthew and St. Mark; in St. Luke's writings it occurs five times.—καὶ αὐτούς is specially distinctive of the Lukan style; it is unnecessary to give examples.—ἀπαγγέλλειν is found twice both in St. Mark and St. John, but

twenty-five (twenty-six) times in the Lukan writings.—
Unless I am mistaken, τὰ αὐτά is found again in the
gospels and the Acts only in St. Luke vi. 23, 26.

Verse 28.   Τῷ πνεύματι τῷ ἁγίῳ : We have here the
Lukan conception of the Holy Spirit ; cf., e.g., Acts v. 3.
—μηδὲν πλέον is only found again in St. Luke iii. 13.—
βάρος : Only here in St. Luke, but occurring elsewhere
in the New Testament.—πλὴν, with the genitive, is not
found in St. Matthew and St. John ; it occurs once in
St. Mark, and again in the Acts viii. 1 and xxvii. 22.—
τούτων τῶν ἐπάναγκες : This use of οὗτος is Lukan ;
ἐπάναγκες is only found here in the New Testament.

Verse 29.   Διατηρεῖν occurs again in the New Testament only in St. Luke ii. 51.   Hobart (pp. 153 ff.),
moreover, makes it very probable that the Lukan words
παρατήρησις (also found in the New Testament only in
the Lukan writings), παρατηρεῖν, διατηρεῖν, τήρησις
are technical medical terms.—The concluding formulæ
(the reading is doubtful) are irrelevant, because the
New Testament affords no material for comparison.

The result of our investigation is that the epistle is
Lukan in style and vocabulary (in opposition to Zahn).
The few ἀπ. λεγ.—whose occurrence, however, may in
part be explained from medical phraseology—are not
sufficient to disturb this impression.   St. Luke, therefore, has manufactured this document.

APPENDIX IV (to p. 152)

ST. LUKE AND ST. JOHN

THE sections of Holtzmann's article "Das Schriftstellerische Verhältnis des Johannes zu den Synoptikern" ("Ztschr. f. Wissensch. Theol.," 1869, Bd. 12, ss. 62 ff.) which deal with the relation of St. John to St. Luke form the foundation of all investigations into this question. Since the publication of that article additional observations have been contributed from many quarters, but the last word has not yet been said. Neither is completeness aimed at in the following remarks.

(1) St. Luke and St. John have added narratives to the Gospel history, and have made corrections therein, in accordance with tradition originating in Jerusalem or Southern Palestine. The most important of these are the Resurrection narratives, wherein we are told that the first appearances of our Lord took place in Jerusalem, that they were such as proved His corporal Resurrection, that He was first seen by women (a woman),[1] and that there were two angels at the

---

[1] St. Matthew xxviii. 9, 10 is, I believe, a later interpolation. Compare also the *rôle* which St. Mary, the Mother of our Lord, plays

sepulchre. Almost as important are the new accounts, which correct the more ancient tradition concerning our Lord's behaviour during His Crucifixion, and also supply other details in the history of the Passion (Wellhausen, on St. Luke xxii. 26 f., points out the correspondence between our Lord's διακονία towards His disciples and the "washing of the feet" in St. John). Also, the high priest Annas is only mentioned in St. Luke and St. John (St. Luke iii. 2, Acts iv. 6, St. John xviii. 13, 24), and the conduct and character of Pilate is similarly conceived in both gospels. In this connection we may further adduce the stories of Mary and Martha,[1] the journey through Samaria and the interest shown in the Samaritans, in St. Luke the local Judaic colouring of the narrative of the first two chapters of the gospel,[2] and much else of the same kind in St. John.

(2) St. Luke and St. John first introduce the words Ἑβραῖοι (Ἑβραϊστί), Ἕλληνες, Ἑλληνιστί, Ῥωμαῖοι, Ἰσραηλῖται [Λευῖται], Στόα Σολομῶντος into the sacred history, and in certain passages speak of the Jewish people as τὸ ἔθνος. In critical situations in their narrative they both use the same quotation from

both in St. Luke and St. John, while the other evangelists say almost nothing of her.

1 "St. John" professes to know that they lived at Bethany.

2 It is only an accidental coincidence that both speak of things which happened at Siloam.—The apostle Judas "of James" is mentioned only in St. Luke and St. John. St. Peter and St. John appear together in St. Luke xxii. 8 and in the Acts; cf. St. John xx. 3 ff. Some scholars have held that the Philip of the fourth gospel and of the Acts are one and the same person.

P

the Old Testament to describe the hardening of the heart of the Jewish people and their rejection by God.

(3) In respect to St. John the Baptist, both evangelists (*vide* St. Luke iii. 15) regard the disciples of St. John as a phenomenon irritating to the Christian community, and they adopt a polemical attitude towards the question whether the Baptist was " He that should come " (see St. Luke iii. 15 and the other sections in the gospel and the Acts concerning the disciples of St. John).

(4) In Christology St. Luke approaches to the Johannine type. (*a*) Jesus is ὁ σωτήρ (St. Luke ii. 11, Acts v. 31, xiii. 23, St. John iv. 42, 1 John iv. 14; the word is wanting in St. Mark and St. Matthew); He brings τὴν σωτηρίαν (St. Luke i. 69, 71, 77, Acts iv. 12, [vii. 25], xiii. 26, xvi. 17, St. John iv. 22, wanting in St. Mark and St. Matthew);[1] (*b*) for St. Luke also the goal of the earthly history of our Lord is His ascension into Heaven (ix. 51); (*c*) also in St. Luke Jesus is brought into contrast with the devil as the being into whose power the world is delivered, who is accordingly ὁ ἄρχων τοῦ κόσμου (iv. 6 f.)—compare also the use of ὁ κόσμος in both gospels; (*d*) also in St. Luke our Lord knows thoughts before they are uttered (vi. 8); (*e*) in this gospel also Jesus passes through the midst of His foes without their being able to lay hands upon Him (iv. 29 f.); (*f*) in both gospels our Lord affords a miraculous draught of

---

[1] Γνῶσις σωτηρίας (St. Luke i. 77) suits St. John even better than St. Luke.

fishes to St. Peter and appoints him to be "the Fisher of Men," or (in St. John) the Shepherd of the Faithful; [1]

[1] The view that St. John xxi. depends upon St. Luke v. 1 ff. (according to Wellhausen and others) is one that I cannot bring myself to accept (the argument drawn from the comparison of St. Luke v. 6 with St. John xxi. 11 is by no means convincing, for though, indeed, in St. John the net signifies the Church, yet this trait is secondary). The narrative of St. John xxi., even in its present form, shows that this legend, before it was adopted and edited by the fourth evangelist, was described as the *first* appearance of the Risen Christ, and this impression is confirmed by the conclusion of the fragment of the gospel of Peter, lately discovered, which breaks off just as it is about to give an account of the appearance (and that the first appearance) of the Risen Christ by the lake of Gennesareth. The fourth evangelist emphatically asserts that this was the *third* appearance, and accordingly adopts a distinctly antagonistic attitude towards the view that it was the first appearance (xxi. 14: τοῦτο ἤδη τρίτον ἐφανερώθη Ἰησοῦς τοῖς μαθηταῖς ἐγερθεὶς ἐκ νεκρῶν). St. Luke, or his authority before him, has boldly transformed and transplanted this story of the Risen Christ into the earthly history of our Lord; but, in my opinion, even as it stands in St. Luke it presupposes St. Peter's denial, as we see from the words of St. Peter in verse 8: ἔξελθε ἀπ' ἐμοῦ, ὅτι ἀνὴρ ἁμαρτωλός εἰμι κύριε, and, moreover, the promise that he should be a "fisher of men," to which the "Feed my sheep" is parallel, is more appropriate in the mouth of the Risen Christ than as spoken at a very early period of the earthly ministry. I therefore cannot but regard it as extremely probable that this narrative formed the genuine conclusion of St. Mark, especially as the author of the gospel of Peter reproduces St. Mark xvi. 1-8, and then, without any joint or hiatus in the narrative, proceeds to describe the flight of the disciples to Galilee and the lake of Gennesareth, mentioning, moreover, in this connection, Levi, the son of that Alphæus whose name is given by St. Mark alone (ii. 14). This first appearance of the Risen Lord to St. Peter—an appearance which is historical, and is vouched for by St. Paul and St. Luke (by the latter abruptly in xxiv. 34), and which the later tradition of the Church of Jerusalem endeavoured to depose from its premier position or to suppress altogether—really took place at the lake of Gennesareth after St. Peter had again returned to his ordinary occupation (as is expressly stated in the gospel of Peter,

(g) in both gospels Jesus speaks of βαστάζειν τὸν σταυρόν; in both (h) of ὁ φίλοι μου (St. Luke xii. 4 and St. John xv. 14); (i) the use of ὁ κυρίος for Jesus in both gospels is important; (k) in St. Luke as a rule God is called "Father" in relation to the Son just as in St. John; (l) the passage St. Luke xxii. 29 (κἀγὼ διατίθεμαι ὑμῖν καθὼς διέθετό μοι ὁ πατήρ μου βασιλείαν) sounds quite Johannine.

(5) The words μαρτυρεῖν and μαρτυρία are very prominent in St. John and in the Acts.

(6) Both evangelists speak of the "love of God" (*vide* St. Luke xi. 42); the phrase does not occur in St. Matthew and St. Mark.

(7) With the conception "life," so prominent in the Johannine writings, compare Acts iii. 15, v. 20, xiii. 48.

(8) With St. John iii. 21, ἔργα ἐν θεῷ εἰργασμένα, compare St. Luke xii. 21, εἰς θεὸν πλουτῶν.

(9) The Holy Spirit (the Paraclete) plays an impor-

---

verses 59 ff. It could not but happen that this inconvenient narrative of St. Mark should be suppressed). By this appearance of the Risen Christ St. Peter was again established in his calling as a disciple. and became the "Fisher of Men" and the chief of the apostles. St. Luke, of course, does not depend upon St. John as his source, but goes back to the authority upon which St. John depends —that is, probably, to the original conclusion of St. Mark.

The word μονογενής does not belong to the cases of coincidence between St. John and St. Luke; for St. Luke never uses it of Christ. It is, however, worthy of note that τὸ εὐαγγέλιον is not found in St. Luke (gospel) and St. John, while it appears in St. Mark and St. Matthew (it, however, occurs twice in the Acts); also that both evangelists use ἰδεῖν in the metaphorical sense (to see death, life, &c.), and that both speak of a "choosing" of the apostles from the rest of the disciples (these two traits also are foreign to St. Mark and St. Matthew).

tant part in both gospels (this is not yet the case in St. Mark and St. Matthew).

(10) Both evangelists assign great importance to the σημεῖα—first the miraculous sign, then comes faith.

(11) Both evangelists either translate (ἑρμηνεύειν, μεθερμηνεύειν) Aramaic words or leave them out altogether.

(12) The critical attitude which St. Luke in his gospel practically adopts towards St. Mark is similar in character to the judgment which John the presbyter (in Papias) passes upon the gospel of St. Mark. John the presbyter, however, is probably the author of the fourth gospel.

There is something to be said for the view that " St. John " had knowledge of the Lukan writings, but no real evidence can be adduced in its favour. It is possible that they both are only dependent upon a common source. An examination of the linguistic relations of the two gospels speaks rather against the hypothesis of direct dependence, for the results of such an examination are exceedingly scanty. I proceed to give a list of all the words which St. John has in common with St. Luke *while they are wanting in St. Mark and St. Matthew*. Words which are also found in the ten Pauline epistles are included in brackets. The important proper names, already given above, are omitted.[1]

(1) St. John's gospel has in common with St. Luke's gospel the following words which do not occur in St. Mark and St. Matthew : (ἀγωνίζεσθαι), (ἀληθινός), (ἀποβαίνειν), ἀπόκρισις, ἀριστᾶν, βάπτειν, (βοῦς),

[1] Also ὁ σωτήρ and ἡ σωτηρία.

γείτων, (εἶδος), ἐκμάσσειν, ἐντεῦθεν, κῆπος, (λύπη), μονογενής, (νικᾶν), ὀθόνιον, (ποτέ), προτρέχειν, πώποτε, (στάδιον), στῆθος, (ταχέως), ὑπομιμνήσκειν, φρέαρ, (φωτίζειν).

(2) The gospel of St. John has in common with the Acts of the Apostles the following words which do not occur in St. Mark and St. Matthew: ἅλλεσθαι, ἀμνός, (ἀπειθεῖν), ἀρεστός, βασιλικός, διατρίβειν, (δωρεά), ἑλκύειν, ἐπιλέγειν, ἐχθές, (ζῆλος), ζήτησις, ζωννύναι, καίτοι, (λιθάζειν), (λοιδορεῖν), λούειν, (μαίνεσθαι), μάχεσθαι, νεύειν, περιστάναι, (περιτομή), (πιάζειν), πλευρά, σημαίνειν, στοά, σύρειν, σχοινίον, (τύπος), ψῦχος.

(3) The gospel of St. John has in common with St. Luke's gospel and the Acts the following words which do not occur in St. Matthew and St. Mark: (ἀντιλέγειν), (ἀπορεῖν), (ἀριθμός), (ἀτιμάζειν), βαθύς, (βουλεύεσθαι), βραχίων, βραχύς, (γνωρίζειν), (γνωστός), (γράμμα), διαδιδόναι, ἔθος, εἰσάγειν, (ἐνπίμπλασθαι), ἐνθάδε, (ἐνιαυτός), (ἐνώπιον), ἐξηγεῖσθαι, (ἐπικεῖσθαι), ἰᾶσθαι (with active significance), κόλπος, κυκλοῦν, λαγχάνειν, (μηνύειν), (περιτέμνειν), (πράσσειν), σουδάριον, συντιθέναι, (τελειοῦν), (ὑμέτερος), οἱ φίλοι, (χάρις).

These eighty-eight words,[1] of which thirty-eight are also found in St. Paul's epistles,[2] would prove abso-

---

[1] Cf. also ὁδοιπορεῖσθαι (St. Luke) and ὁδοπορία (St. John).

[2] Of the fifty remaining words, twenty-four are also found in other writings of the New Testament (principally Hebrews and Revelation), viz.: βάπτειν, βραχύς, ἐντεῦθεν, μονογενής, στῆθος, ὑπομιμνήσκειν, φρέαρ, ἀμνός, βασιλικός, ἐχθές, καίτοι, λούειν, μάχεσθαι, περιστάναι, σημαίνειν, σύρειν, ψῦχος, βαθύς, διαδιδόναι, ἔθος, εἰσάγειν, κυκλοῦν, λαγχάνειν, ὁ φίλος, so that altogether only twenty-six words in the New Testament are exclusively common to St. Luke and St. John.

lutely nothing if it were not that the vocabulary of St. John is so very scanty; but even taking account of this fact, we can scarcely give another verdict than that *no traces of the dependence of St. John upon the Lukan writings can be discovered by means of the lexicon.* There is no connection between them in vocabulary—scarcely a single word characteristic of St. Luke can be found in St. John. Nor does it appear that the style of St. John shows any trace of the influence of the Lukan style. Nevertheless—on other grounds—the possibility that the fourth evangelist read the Lukan writings must be left open.

Printed by BALLANTYNE & Co. LIMITED
Tavistock Street, London

A Catalogue

of

Williams & Norgate's

Publications

Divisions of the Catalogue

FULL INDEX OVER PAGE

London

Williams & Norgate

14 Henrietta Street, Covent Garden, W.C.

INDEX.

I. Theology and Religion.

THEOLOGICAL TRANSLATION LIBRARY.
New Series.

A Series of Translations by which the best results of recent Theological Investigations on the Continent, conducted without reference to doctrinal considerations, and with the sole purpose of arriving at the truth, are placed within reach of English readers.

Vols. I.–XII. were edited by the Rev. T. K. Cheyne, M.A., D.D., Oriel Professor of Interpretation in the University of Oxford, Canon of Rochester; and the late Rev. A. B. Bruce, D.D., Professor of Apologetics, Free Church College, Glasgow.

Vol. XIII. was edited by Rev. Allan Menzies, D.D., Professor of Divinity and Biblical Criticism in the University, St Andrews.

Vols. XV., XVII., XVIII., and XXI. are edited by Rev. W. D. Morrison, M.A., LL.D.

Vols. XIX. and XX. are edited by Rev. James Moffatt, B.D., D.D., St Andrews.

The Price of Vols. I.–XXI. is 10s. 6d.;
Vol. XXII. and after, 10s. 6d. net.

Subscribers to the Series obtain three volumes for 22s. 6d. carriage free, payable before publication of the volumes.

New Subscription.—Vols. XXII.–XXIV., of which Vol. XXII. is ready.

PRIMITIVE CHRISTIANITY: Its Writings and Teachings in their Historical Connections. By Otto Pfleiderer, Professor of Practical Theology in the University of Berlin.

Vol. XXIII. in active preparation.

THE INTRODUCTION TO THE CANONICAL BOOKS OF THE OLD TESTAMENT. By Carl Cornill, Professor of Old Testament Theology at the University of Breslau.

Vol. XXIV. in active preparation.

HISTORY OF THE CHURCH. By Hans von Schubert, Professor of Church History at Kiel. Translated from the Second German Edition. By arrangement with the author, an Additional Chapter will be added on "Religious Movements in England in the Nineteenth Century," by Miss Alice Gardner, Lecturer and Associate of Newnham College.

Vol. XXI.

ST. PAUL: The Man and his Work. By Prof. H. Weinel of the University of Jena. Translated by Rev. G. A. Bienemann, M.A. Edited by Rev. W. D. Morrison, M.A., LL.D.

14 Henrietta Street, Covent Garden, London, W.C.

THEOLOGICAL TRANSLATION LIBRARY—Continued.

Vols. XIX. and XX.

THE EXPANSION OF CHRISTIANITY IN THE FIRST THREE CENTURIES. By Adolf Harnack, Ordinary Professor of Church History in the University, and Fellow of the Royal Academy of the Sciences, Berlin. Translated and edited by James Moffatt, B.D., D.D., St Andrews.

Vol. XVIII.

CHRISTIAN LIFE IN THE PRIMITIVE CHURCH. By Ernst von Dobschütz, D.D., Professor of New Testament Theology in the University of Strassburg. Translated by Rev. G. Bremner, and edited by the Rev. W. D. Morrison, LL.D.

"It is only in the very best English work that we meet with the scientific thoroughness and all-round competency of which this volume is a good specimen; while such splendid historical veracity and outspokenness would hardly be possible in the present or would-be holder of an English theological chair." —Dr RASHDALL in *The Speaker.*

"Some may think that the author's finding is too favourable to the early churches; but, at any rate, there is no volume in which material for forming a judgment is so fully collected or so attractively presented."—*British Weekly.*

Vol. XVI.

THE RELIGIONS OF AUTHORITY AND THE RELIGION OF THE SPIRIT. By the late Auguste Sabatier, Professor of the University of Paris, Dean of the Protestant Theological Faculty. With a Memoir of the Author by Jean Réville, Professor in the Protestant Theological Faculty of the University of Paris, and a Note by Madame Sabatier.

"Without any exaggeration, this is to be described as a great book, the finest legacy of the author to the Protestant Church of France and to the theological thought of the age. Written in the logical and lucid style which is characteristic of the best French theology, and excellently translated, it is a work which any thoughtful person, whether a professional student or not, might read without difficulty."—*Glasgow Herald.*

Vols. XV. and XVII.

THE BEGINNINGS OF CHRISTIANITY. By Paul Wernle, Professor Extraordinary of Modern Church History at the University of Basel. Revised by the Author, and translated by the Rev. G. A. Bienemann, M.A., and edited, with an Introduction, by the Rev. W. D. Morrison, LL.D.

Vol. I. **The Rise of the Religion.**
Vol. II. **The Development of the Church.**

From some of the Reviews of the Work.

Dr. Marcus Dods in the *British Weekly*—"We cannot recall any work by a foreign theologian which is likely to have a more powerful influence on the thought of this country than Wernle's *Beginnings of Christianity.* It is well written and well translated; it is earnest, clear, and persuasive, and above all it is well adapted to catch the large class of thinking men who are at present seeking some non-miraculous explanation of Christianity."

14 Henrietta Street, Covent Garden, London, W.C.

THEOLOGICAL TRANSLATION LIBRARY—Continued.

"This translation of Prof. Wernle's lectures deserves a very hearty welcome in England. The style is alive and vigorous, the thought suggestive; the whole narrative is admirably clear and simple, popular in the best sense of the term. . . . It may be accepted as a companion volume to Harnack's *What is Christianity?* as an announcement of a liberal position of slightly differing tendency. It is quite easy and pleasant reading for the ordinary layman who may be desirous of knowing the present position of the more advanced schools, and how much of the traditional theology these are prepared to retain. One could wish that a few more English theologians would attempt a similar apologia for the edification of the perplexed lay mind."—*Daily News.*

"No English book covers the same ground, or is conceived with the same breadth and sanity; in few works in any language are learning and insight so happily combined."—*Edinburgh Review.*

"The translation is well done, and the book is full of interest."—*Athenæum.*

The Earlier Works included in the Library are :—

HISTORY OF DOGMA. By Adolf Harnack, Ordinary Professor of Church History in the University, and Fellow of the Royal Academy of the Sciences, Berlin. Translated from the Third German Edition. Edited by the Rev. Prof. A. B. Bruce, D.D. 7 vols. (New Series, Vols. II., VII., VIII., IX., X., XI., XII.) 8vo, cloth, each 10*s.* 6*d.* ; half-leather, suitable for presentation, 12*s.* 6*d.*

ABBREVIATED LIST OF CONTENTS :—Vol. I.: INTRODUCTORY DIVISION :—I. Prolegomena to the Study of the History of Dogma. II. The Presuppositions of the History of Dogma. DIVISION I.—The Genesis of Ecclesiastical Dogma, or the Genesis of the Catholic Apostolic Dogmatic Theology, and the first Scientific Ecclesiastical System of Doctrine. BOOK I. :— *The Preparation.* Vol. II. : DIVISION I. BOOK II. :—*The Laying of the Foundation.—*I. Historical Survey.—*I. Fixing and gradual Secularising of Christianity as a Church.—II. Fixing and gradual Hellenising of Christianity as a System of Doctrine.* Vol. III. : DIVISION I. BOOK II.:—*The Laying of the Foundation—* continued. DIVISION II.—The Development of Ecclesiastical Dogma. BOOK I. :—*The History of the Development of Dogma as the Doctrine of the God-man on the basis of Natural Theology. A. Presuppositions of Doctrine of Redemption or Natural Theology. B. The Doctrine of Redemption in the Person of the God-man in its historical development.* Vol. IV. : DIVISION II. BOOK I. :— *The History of the Development of Dogma as the Doctrine of the God-man on the basis of Natural Theology*—continued. Vol. V.: DIVISION II. BOOK II. :—*Expansion and Remodelling of Dogma into a Doctrine of Sin, Grace, and Means of Grace on the basis of the Church.* Vol. VI. : DIVISION II. BOOK II. :—*Expansion and Remodelling of Dogma into a Doctrine of Sin, Grace, and Means of Grace on the basis of the Church*—continued. Vol. VII.:

THEOLOGICAL TRANSLATION LIBRARY—Continued.

DIVISION II.   BOOK III. :—*The Threefold Issue of the History of Dogma.*—Full Index.

"No work on Church history in recent times has had the influence of Prof. Harnack's *History of Dogma.*"—*Times.*

"A book which is admitted to be one of the most important theological works of the time."—*Daily News.*

WHAT IS CHRISTIANITY? Sixteen Lectures delivered in the University of Berlin during the Winter Term, 1899-1900. By Adolf Harnack. Translated by Thomas Bailey Saunders. (New Series, Vol. XIV.) Demy 8vo, cloth, 10s. 6d. ; half-leather, suitable for presentation, 12s. 6d.

Prof. W. Sanday of Oxford, in the examination of the work, says :—"I may assume that Harnack's book, which has attracted a good deal of attention in this country as in Germany, is by this time well known, and that its merits are recognised—its fresh and vivid descriptions, its breadth of view and skilful selection of points, its frankness, its genuine enthusiasm, its persistent effort to get at the living realities of religion."

"Seldom has a treatise of the sort been at once so suggestive and so stimulating. Seldom have the results of so much learning been brought to bear on the religious problems which address themselves to the modern mind."—*Pilot.*

"In many respects this is the most notable work of Prof. Harnack. . . . These lectures are most remarkable, both for the historical insight they display and for their elevation of tone and purpose."—*Literature.*

THE COMMUNION OF THE CHRISTIAN WITH GOD : A Discussion in Agreement with the View of Luther. By W. Herrmann, Dr. Theol., Professor of Dogmatic Theology in the University of Marburg. Translated from the Second thoroughly revised Edition, with Special Annotations by the Author, by J. Sandys Stanyon, M.A. (New Series, Vol. IV.) 8vo, cloth. 10s. 6d.

"It will be seen from what has been said that this book is a very important one. . . . The translation is also exceedingly well done."—*Critical Review.*

"We trust the book will be widely read, and should advise those who read it to do so twice."—*Primitive Methodist Quarterly.*

"Instinct with genuine religious feeling ; . . . exceedingly interesting and suggestive."—*Glasgow Herald.*

A HISTORY OF THE HEBREWS. By R. Kittel, Ordinary Professor of Theology in the University of Breslau. In 2 vols. (New Series, Vols. III. and VI.) 8vo, cloth. Each volume, 10s. 6d.

Vol. I. **Sources of Information and History of the Period up to the Death of Joshua.** Translated by John Taylor, D.Lit., M.A.

Vol. II. **Sources of Information and History of the Period down to the Babylonian Exile.** Translated by Hope W. Hogg, B.D., and E. B. Speirs, D.D.

"It is a sober and earnest reconstruction, for which every earnest student of the Old Testament should be grateful."—*Christian World.*

"It will be a happy day for pulpit and pew when a well-thumbed copy of the *History of the Hebrews* is to be found in every manse and parsonage."—*Literary World.*

"It is a work which cannot fail to attract the attention of thoughtful people in this country."—*Pall Mall Gazette.*

AN INTRODUCTION TO THE TEXTUAL CRITICISM OF THE GREEK NEW TESTAMENT. By Professor Eberhard Nestle, of Maulbronn. Translated from the Second Edition, with Corrections and Additions by the Author, by William Edie, B.D., and edited, with a Preface, by Allan Menzies, D.D., Professor of Divinity and Biblical Criticism in the University of St. Andrews. (New Series, Vol. XIII.) With eleven reproductions of Texts. Demy 8vo, 10s. 6d.; half-leather, 12s. 6d.

"We have no living scholar more capable of accomplishing the fascinating task of preparing a complete introduction on the new and acknowledged principles than Prof. Nestle. This book will stand the most rigorous scrutiny; it will surpass the highest expectation."—*Expository Times.*

"Nothing could be better than Dr. Nestle's account of the materials which New Testament textual criticism has to deal with."—*Spectator.*

"We know of no book of its size which can be recommended more cordially to the student, alike for general interest and for the clearness of its arrangement. . . . In smoothness of rendering, the translation is one of the best we have come across for a considerable time."—*Manchester Guardian.*

THE APOSTOLIC AGE. By Prof. Carl von Weizsäcker. Translated by James Millar, B.D. 2 vols. (New Series, Vols. I. and V.) Demy 8vo, cloth. Each 10s. 6d.

"Weizsäcker is an authority of the very first rank. The present work marks an epoch in New Testament criticism. The English reader is fortunate in having a masterpiece of this kind rendered accessible to him."—*Expository Times.*

". . . No student of theology or of the early history of Christianity can afford to leave Weizsäcker's great book unread."—*Manchester Guardian.*

"In every direction in this work we find the mark of the independent thinker and investigator . . . this remarkable volume . . . this able and learned work. . . ."—*Christian World.*

"The book itself . . . is of great interest, and the work of the translation has been done in a most satisfactory way."—*Critical Review.*

THEOLOGICAL TRANSLATION FUND LIBRARY.
Old Series.

Uniform Price per Volume, 6s.

BAUR (F. C.). CHURCH HISTORY OF THE FIRST THREE CENTURIES. Translated from the Third German Edition. Edited by Rev. Allan Menzies. 2 vols. 8vo, cloth. 12s.

—— **PAUL, THE APOSTLE OF JESUS CHRIST, HIS LIFE AND WORK, HIS EPISTLES AND DOCTRINE.** A Contribution to a Critical History of Primitive Christianity. Edited by Rev. Allan Menzies. 2nd Edition. 2 vols. 8vo, cloth. 12s.

BLEEK (F.). LECTURES ON THE APOCALYPSE. Translated. Edited by the Rev. Dr. S. Davidson. 8vo, cloth. 6s.

EWALD'S (Dr. H.) COMMENTARY ON THE PROPHETS OF THE OLD TESTAMENT. Translated by the Rev. J. F. Smith. [Vol. I. General Introduction, Yoel, Amos, Hosea, and Zakharya 9–11. Vol. II. Yesaya, Obadya, and Mikah. Vol. III. Nahûm, Ssephanya, Habaqqûq, Zakhârya, Yéremya. Vol. IV. Hezekiel, Yesaya xl.–lxvi. Vol. V. Haggai, Zakharya, Malaki, Jona, Baruc, Daniel, Appendix and Index.] 5 vols. 8vo, cloth. 30s.

—— **COMMENTARY ON THE PSALMS.** Translated by the Rev. E. Johnson, M.A. 2 vols. 8vo, cloth. 12s.

—— **COMMENTARY ON THE BOOK OF JOB, with Translation.** Translated from the German by the Rev. J. Frederick Smith. 8vo, cloth. 6s.

HAUSRATH (Prof. A.). HISTORY OF THE NEW TESTAMENT TIMES. The Time of Jesus. Translated by the Revs. C. T. Poynting and P. Quenzer. 2 vols. 8vo, cloth. 12s.

The second portion of this work, "The Times of the Apostles," was issued apart from the Library, but in uniform volumes; *see* p. 19.

KEIM'S HISTORY OF JESUS OF NAZARA: Considered in its connection with the National Life of Israel, and related in detail. Translated from the German by Arthur Ransom and the Rev. E. M. Geldart. [Vol. I. Second Edition. Introduction, Survey of Sources, Sacred and Political Groundwork. Religious Groundwork. Vol. II. The Sacred Youth, Self-recognition, Decision. Vol. III. The First Preaching, the Works of

Jesus, the Disciples, and Apostolic Mission. Vol. IV. Conflicts and Disillusions, Strengthened Self-confidence, Last Efforts in Galilee, Signs of the Approaching Fall, Recognition of the Messiah. Vol. V. The Messianic Progress to Jerusalem, the Entry into Jerusalem, the Decisive Struggle, the Farewell, the Last Supper. Vol. VI. The Messianic Death at Jerusalem. Arrest and Pseudo-Trial, the Death on the Cross, Burial and Resurrection, the Messiah's Place in History, Indices.] Complete in 6 vols. 8vo. 36s.

(Vol. I. only to be had when a complete set of the work is ordered.)

KUENEN (Dr. A.). THE RELIGION OF ISRAEL TO THE FALL OF THE JEWISH STATE. By Dr. A. Kuenen, Professor of Theology at the University, Leyden. Translated from the Dutch by A. H. May. 3 vols. 8vo, cloth. 18s.

PFLEIDERER (O.). PAULINISM : A Contribution to the History of Primitive Christian Theology. Translated by E. Peters. 2nd Edition. 2 vols. 8vo, cloth. 12s.

—— PHILOSOPHY OF RELIGION ON THE BASIS OF ITS HISTORY. (Vols. I. II. History of the Philosophy of Religion from Spinoza to the Present Day ; Vols. III. IV. Genetic-Speculative Philosophy of Religion.) Translated by Prof. Allan Menzies and the Rev. Alex. Stewart. 4 vols. 8vo, cloth. 24s.

RÉVILLE (Dr. A.). PROLEGOMENA OF THE HISTORY OF RELIGIONS. With an Introduction by Prof. F. Max Müller. 8vo, cloth. 6s.

PROTESTANT COMMENTARY ON THE NEW TESTAMENT. With General and Special Introductions. Edited by Profs. P. W. Schmidt and F. von Holzendorff. Translated from the Third German Edition by the Rev. F. H. Jones, B.A. 3 vols. 8vo, cloth. 18s.

SCHRADER (Prof. E.). THE CUNEIFORM INSCRIPTIONS AND THE OLD TESTAMENT. Translated from the Second Enlarged Edition, with Additions by the Author, and an Introduction by the Rev. Owen C. Whitehouse, M.A. 2 vols. (Vol. I. not sold separately.) With a Map. 8vo, cloth. 12s.

ZELLER (Dr. E.). THE CONTENTS AND ORIGIN OF THE ACTS OF THE APOSTLES CRITICALLY INVESTIGATED. Preceded by Dr. Fr. Overbeck's Introduction to the Acts of the Apostles from De Wette's Handbook. Translated by Joseph Dare. 2 vols. 8vo, cloth. 12s.

THE CROWN THEOLOGICAL LIBRARY.

The volumes are uniform in size (crown octavo) and binding, but the price varies according to the size and importance of the work.

A Few Opinions of the Series.

Professor Marcus Dods: "By introducing to the English-speaking public specimens of the work of such outstanding critics and theologians, your 'Crown Theological Library' has done a valuable service to theological learning in this country."

Dr. John Watson: "The Library is rendering valuable service to lay theologians in this country, as well as to ministers."

Rev. Principal P. T. Forsyth: "As a whole it is an admirable series, and opens to the English reader at a low price some books which are of prime importance for religious thought."

Sir Edward Russell: "I have formed the highest opinion of this series. Each of the books is animated by a fine intelligent and at the same time devout spirit."

Rev. Principal D. L. Ritchie: "I have read many of the volumes in the 'Crown Library,' and I think it an admirable and useful series."

Rev. Professor A. E. Garvie: "I am very grateful for the publication of these volumes, as they bring within the reach of the English student, in a correct translation and at cheap price, important theological works, which otherwise would be accessible only to those familiar with French or German."

Rev. R. J. Campbell: "Your 'Crown Theological Library' is invaluable, and is doing excellent service for liberal Christianity."

Professor G. Currie Martin: "I think you are rendering a most valuable service to all serious students of theology by your publication of the 'Crown Theological Library.'"

Vol. I. **BABEL AND BIBLE.** By Dr. Friedrich Delitzsch, Professor of Assyriology in the University of Berlin. Authorised Translation. Edited, with an Introduction, by Rev. C. H. W. Johns. Crown 8vo, with 77 illustrations, cloth. 5s.

"This interestingly illustrated and well-made version of the Lectures should satisfy both scholars and general readers, though no doubt scholars will know best how to appreciate the high value of its arguments."—*Scotsman.*

Vol. II. **THE VIRGIN BIRTH OF CHRIST: An Historical and Critical Essay.** By Paul Lobstein, Professor of Dogmatics in the University of Strassburg. Translated by Victor Leuliette, A.K.C., B.-ès-L., Paris. Edited, with an Introduction, by Rev. W. D. Morrison, LL.D. Crown 8vo. 3s.

"It should be added that Lobstein falls behind no one of those who have refined the tone of modern controversy, that his attitude to those whose views he opposes is considerate, his own purpose constructive for faith, and his tone impressively reverent. Mr Leuliette's translation is in admirably clear and good English."—*Hibbert Journal.*

THE CROWN THEOLOGICAL LIBRARY—Continued.

Vol. III. **MY STRUGGLE FOR LIGHT**: Confessions of a Preacher. By R. Wimmer, Pastor of Weisweil-am-Rhein in Baden. Crown 8vo, cloth. 3s. 6d.

> Dr P. T. Forsyth, Principal of Hackney College.—"A beautiful translation of a beautiful book."

> "It is a book which will appeal to ministers who are anxious to preserve intellectual sincerity, and to thoughtful laymen who are turning over in their mind the deepest problems of religion. The author's spirit throughout the book reminds one of Martineau. The tone and style of the book are admirable."—Dr John Watson in *Christian Commonwealth.*

Vol. IV. **LIBERAL CHRISTIANITY**: Its Origin, Nature, and Mission. By Jean Réville, Professeur adjoint à la Faculté de Théologie Protestante de l'Université de Paris. Translated and edited by Victor Leuliette, A.K.C., B.-ès-L. Crown 8vo, cloth. 4s.

> "The book is a powerful, lucid and interesting restatement of the position of Protestantism in regard to modern advances in philosophy and science."—*Scotsman.*

Vol. V. **WHAT IS CHRISTIANITY?** By Adolf Harnack, Professor of Church History in the University, Berlin. Translated by Thomas Bailey Saunders. Crown 8vo. 5s.

> Prof. W. Sanday, of Oxford, in an examination of the work, says :—"I may assume that Harnack's book, which has attracted a good deal of attention in this country as in Germany, is by this time well known, and that its merits are recognised—its fresh and vivid descriptions, its breadth of view and skilful selection of points, its frankness, its genuine enthusiasm, its persistent effort to get at the living realities of religion."

Vol. VI. **FAITH AND MORALS.** By W. Herrmann, Professor of Systematic Theology at the University of Marburg; Author of "The Communion of the Christian with God." Crown 8vo, cloth. 5s.

> "A cordial welcome will be given the very readable translation by Mr Matheson and Mr Stewart."—*Spectator.*

Vol. VII. **EARLY HEBREW STORY.** A Study of the Origin, the Value, and the Historical Background of the Legends of Israel. By John P. Peters, D.D., Rector of St. Michael's Church, New York ; author of "Nippur, or Explorations and Adventures on the Euphrates." Crown 8vo, cloth. 5s.

> "These lectures are certainly of quite exceptional worth . . . . will not only interest the general reader, but will suggest much to the expert."—*British Weekly.*

THE CROWN THEOLOGICAL LIBRARY—Continued.

Vol. VIII. **BIBLE PROBLEMS AND THE NEW MATERIAL FOR THEIR SOLUTION.** A Plea for Thoroughness of Investigation, addressed to Churchmen and Scholars. By the Rev. T. K. Cheyne, D.Litt., D.D., Fellow of the British Academy ; Oriel Professor of Interpretation in the University of Oxford, and Canon of Rochester. Crown 8vo. 5s.

"The work is remarkably interesting and learned . . . . those who wish to understand what problems are likely to engage attention in the near future ought not to neglect the book."—*British Friend.*

Vol. IX. **THE DOCTRINE OF THE ATONEMENT AND ITS HISTORICAL EVOLUTION ; and RELIGION AND MODERN CULTURE.** By the late Auguste Sabatier, Professor in the University of Paris. Translated by Victor Leuliette, A. K. C., B.-ès-L. Crown 8vo. 4s. 6d.

". . . Both the studies in the volume are profoundly interesting ; marked everywhere by the piercing insight, philosophic grasp, and deep spirituality which are characteristic of this great and lamented Christian thinker."—*The Christian World.*

Vol. X. **THE EARLY CHRISTIAN CONCEPTION OF CHRIST : Its Value and Significance in the History of Religion.** By Otto Pfleiderer, D.D., Professor of Practical Theology in the University, Berlin. Crown 8vo. 3s. 6d.

"It would be difficult to name any recent English work which could compare with this brilliant essay, as a concise but lucid presentation of the attitude of the more advanced school of German theologians to the Founder of the Christian religion."—*Scotsman.*

Vol. XI. **THE CHILD AND RELIGION. Eleven Essays.** By Prof. Henry Jones, M.A., LL.D., University of Glasgow ; C. F. G. Masterman, M.A. ; Prof. George T. Ladd, D.D., LL.D., University of Yale ; Rev. F. R. Tennant, M.A., B.Sc., Hulsean Lecturer ; Rev. J. Cynddylan Jones, D.D. ; Rev. Canon Hensley Henson, M.A. ; Rev. Robert F. Horton, M.A., D.D. ; Rev. G. Hill, M.A., D.D. ; Rev. J. J. Thornton ; Rev. Rabbi A. A. Green ; Prof. Joseph Agar Beet, D.D. Edited by Thomas Stephens, B.A. Crown 8vo. 6s.

"No fresher and more instructive book on this question has been issued for years, and the study of its pages will often prove a godsend to many perplexed minds in the church and in the Christian home."—*British Weekly.*

Vol. XII. **THE EVOLUTION OF RELIGION : An Anthropological Study.** By L. R. Farnell, D.Litt., Fellow and Tutor of Exeter College, Oxford ; University Lecturer in Classical Archæology, etc., etc. Crown 8vo, cloth. 5s.

"It is one of the most valuable volumes that have appeared in this excellent series. He gives so clear and lucid a picture of the actual results of anthropology that his book is certainly the one we should put in the hands of students."—*Pall Mall Gazette.*

Vol. XIII. **THE HISTORY OF EARLY CHRISTIAN LITERATURE. The Books of the New Testament.** By H. von Soden, D.D., Professor of Theology in the University of Berlin. Translated by the Rev. J. R. Wilkinson, and edited by Rev. W. D. Morrison, LL.D. Crown 8vo, cloth. 5s.

Vol. XIV. **JESUS.** By Wilhelm Bousset, Professor of Theology in Göttingen. Translated by Janet Penrose Trevelyan, and edited by Rev. W. D. Morrison, LL.D. Crown 8vo. 4s.

"It is true the writers, von Soden and Bousset, have in the course of their papers said things that I regard as as nothing less than admirable. I very much doubt whether we have anything so admirable in English."—Rev. Dr. Sanday in the *Guardian.*

Vol. XV. **THE COMMUNION OF THE CHRISTIAN WITH GOD.** By Prof. Wilhelm Herrmann. Translated from the new German Edition by Rev. J. S. Stanyon, M.A., and Rev. R. W. Stewart, B.D., B.Sc. Crown 8vo, cloth. 5s.

Vol. XVI. **HEBREW RELIGION TO THE ESTABLISHMENT OF JUDAISM UNDER EZRA.** By W. E. Addis, M.A. Crown 8vo, cloth. 5s.

"It would be difficult to name a book better adapted to give the student a clear and reliable impression of the results of recent research into the origin and historical development of Hebrew religion."—*Scotsman.*

Vol. XVII. **NATURALISM AND RELIGION.** By Rudolf Otto, Professor of Theology in the University of Göttingen. Translated by J. Arthur Thomson, Professor of Natural History in the University of Aberdeen, and Margaret R. Thomson. Edited with an Introduction by Rev. W. D. Morrison, LL.D. Crown 8vo. 6s.

". . . A valuable survey, and a critical estimate of scientific theory and kindred ideas as they concern the religious view of the world. . . . It is well written, clear, and even eloquent."—*Expository Times.*

A Number of Works are under consideration, of which the following Volumes are in Active Preparation.

ESSAYS ON THE SOCIAL GOSPEL. By Professor Adolf Harnack, of Berlin, and Professor W. Herrmann, of Marburg.

THE RELIGION OF THE OLD TESTAMENT: Its Place among the Religions of the Nearer East. By Karl Marti, Professor of Old Testament Exegesis, Bern.

THE HIBBERT LECTURES.

Library Edition, demy 8vo, 10s. 6d. per volume. Cheap Popular Edition, 3s. 6d. per volume.

ALVIELLA (Count GOBLET D'). EVOLUTION OF THE IDEA OF GOD, ACCORDING TO ANTHROPOLOGY AND HISTORY. Translated by the Rev. P. H. Wicksteed. (Hibbert Lectures, 1891.) Cloth. 10s. 6d. Cheap Edition, 3s. 6d.

BEARD (Rev. Dr. C.). LECTURES ON THE REFORMATION OF THE SIXTEENTH CENTURY IN ITS RELATION TO MODERN THOUGHT AND KNOWLEDGE. (Hibbert Lectures, 1883.) 8vo, cloth. 10s. 6d. Cheap Edition, 3rd Edition, 3s. 6d.

DAVIDS (T. W. RHYS). LECTURES ON SOME POINTS IN THE HISTORY OF INDIAN BUDDHISM. (Hib. Lec., 1881.) 2nd Ed. 8vo, cloth. 10s. 6d. Cheap Ed., 3s. 6d.

DRUMMOND (Dr.) VIA, VERITAS, VITA. Lectures on Christianity in its most Simple and Intelligible Form. (The Hibbert Lectures, 1894.) 10s. 6d. Cheap Edition, 3s. 6d.

HATCH (Rev. Dr.). LECTURES ON THE INFLUENCE OF GREEK IDEAS AND USAGES UPON THE CHRISTIAN CHURCH. Edited by Dr. Fairbairn. (Hibbert Lectures, 1888.) 3rd Edition. 8vo, cloth. 10s. 6d. Cheap Edition, 3s. 6d.

KUENEN (Dr. A.). LECTURES ON NATIONAL RELIGIONS AND UNIVERSAL RELIGION. (The Hibbert Lectures, 1882.) 8vo, cloth. 10s. 6d. Cheap Edition, 3s. 6d.

MONTEFIORE (C. G.). ORIGIN AND GROWTH OF RELIGION AS ILLUSTRATED BY THE RELIGION OF THE ANCIENT HEBREWS. (The Hibbert Lectures, 1892.) 2nd Edition. 8vo, cloth. 10s. 6d. Cheap Edition, 3s. 6d.

PFLEIDERER (Dr. O.). LECTURES ON THE INFLUENCE OF THE APOSTLE PAUL ON THE DEVELOPMENT OF CHRISTIANITY. Translated by the Rev. J. Frederick Smith. (Hibbert Lectures, 1885.) 2nd Edition. 8vo, cloth. 10s. 6d. Cheap Edition, 3s. 6d.

RENAN (E.). ON THE INFLUENCE OF THE INSTITUTIONS, THOUGHT, AND CULTURE OF ROME ON CHRISTIANITY AND THE DEVELOPMENT OF THE CATHOLIC CHURCH. Translated by the Rev. Charles Beard. (Hibbert Lectures, 1880.) 8vo, cloth. 10s. 6d. Cheap Edition, 3rd Edition, 3s. 6d.

14 Henrietta Street, Covent Garden, London, W.C.

RENOUF (P. LE PAGE). ON THE RELIGION OF ANCIENT EGYPT. (Hibbert Lectures, 1879.) 3rd Edition. 8vo, cloth. 10s. 6d. Cheap Edition, 3s. 6d.

RHYS (Prof. J.). ON THE ORIGIN AND GROWTH OF RELIGION AS ILLUSTRATED BY CELTIC HEATHENDOM. (Hibbert Lectures, 1886.) 8vo, cloth. 10s. 6d. Cheap Edition, 3s. 6d.

RÉVILLE (Dr. A.). ON THE NATIVE RELIGIONS OF MEXICO AND PERU. Translated by the Rev. P. H. Wicksteed. (Hibbert Lectures, 1884.) 8vo, cloth. 10s. 6d. Cheap Edition, 3s. 6d.

SAYCE (Prof. A. H.). ON THE RELIGION OF ANCIENT ASSYRIA AND BABYLONIA. 4th Edition. (Hibbert Lectures, 1887.) 8vo, cloth. 10s. 6d. Cheap Ed., 3s. 6d

UPTON (Rev. C. B.). ON THE BASES OF RELIGIOUS BELIEF. (Hibbert Lectures, 1893.) Demy 8vo, cloth. 10s. 6d. Cheap Edition, 3s. 6d.

ALPHABETICAL LIST.

ADDIS (W. E.). HEBREW RELIGION. See Crown Theological Library, p. 13.

ALLIN (Rev. THOS.). UNIVERSALISM ASSERTED AS THE HOPE OF THE GOSPEL ON THE AUTHORITY OF REASON, THE FATHERS, AND HOLY SCRIPTURE. With a Preface by Edna Lyall, and a Letter from Canon Wilberforce. Crown 8vo. Sewed, 1s. 6d. net; cloth, 2s. 6d. net.

ALVIELLA (Count GOBLET D'). THE CONTEMPORARY EVOLUTION OF RELIGIOUS THOUGHT IN ENGLAND, AMERICA, AND INDIA. Translated from the French by the Rev. J. Moden. 8vo, cloth. 10s. 6d.

—— **EVOLUTION OF THE IDEA OF GOD.** See The Hibbert Lectures, p. 14.

ANNOTATED CATECHISM. A Manual of Natural Religion and Morality, with many practical details. 2nd Edition. Crown 8vo, cloth. 1s.

BAUR (F. C.). CHURCH HISTORY OF THE FIRST THREE CENTURIES. See Theological Translation Library, Old Series, p. 8.

—— **PAUL, THE APOSTLE OF JESUS CHRIST.** See Theological Translation Library, Old Series, p. 8.

BEARD (Rev. Dr. C.). THE UNIVERSAL CHRIST, AND OTHER SERMONS. Crown 8vo, cloth. 7s. 6d.

—— LECTURES ON THE REFORMATION OF THE SIXTEENTH CENTURY IN ITS RELATION TO MODERN THOUGHT AND KNOWLEDGE. See The Hibbert Lectures, p. 14.

BEEBY (Rev. C. E., B.D., Author of "Creed and Life"). DOCTRINE AND PRINCIPLES. Popular Lectures on Primary Questions. Demy 8vo, cloth. 4s. 6d.

BIBLE. Translated by Samuel Sharpe, being a Revision of the Authorised English Version. 6th Edition of the Old, 10th Edition of the New Testament. 8vo, roan. 5s. See also Testament.

BLEEK (F.). LECTURES ON THE APOCALYPSE. See Theological Translation Library, Old Series, p. 8.

BROADBENT (The late Rev. T. P., B.A.). THIRTEEN SERMONS, AN ESSAY, AND A FRAGMENT. With a Prefatory Note by Rev. Prof. J. Estlin Carpenter, M.A. Crown 8vo, cloth. 4s. net.

CAMPBELL (Rev. Canon COLIN). FIRST THREE GOSPELS IN GREEK. See Testament, New, p. 26.

CHANNING'S COMPLETE WORKS. Including "The Perfect Life," with a Memoir. Centennial Edition. 4to Edition. Cloth. 7s. 6d.

CHEYNE (Prof. T. K.). BIBLE PROBLEMS AND THE NEW MATERIAL FOR THEIR SOLUTION. See Crown Theological Library, p. 12.

CHILD AND RELIGION. Edited by Thomas Stephens, B.A. See Crown Theological Library, p. 12.

CHRISTIAN CREED (OUR). 2nd and greatly Revised Edition. Crown 8vo, cloth. 3s. 6d.

CLARK (ARCHD. JAS.). DE SUCCESSIONE APOSTOLICA NEC NON MISSIONE ET JURISDICTIONE HIERARCHIÆ ANGLICANÆ ET CATHOLICÆ. 8vo. (Georgetown, Guiana.) Cloth. 21s.

—— SEVEN AGES OF THE CHURCH; or, Exposition of the Apocalypse. Sewed. 1s.

COMMON PRAYER FOR CHRISTIAN WORSHIP: in Ten Services for Morning and Evening. 32mo, cloth. 1s. 6d. Also in 8vo, cloth. 3s.

CONWAY (MONCURE D.). CENTENARY HISTORY OF THE SOUTH PLACE ETHICAL SOCIETY. With numerous Portraits, a facsimile of the original MS. of the hymn, "Nearer, my God, to Thee," and Appendices. Crown 8vo, half vellum, paper sides. 5s.

DAVIDS (T. W. RHYS). LECTURES ON SOME POINTS IN THE HISTORY OF INDIAN BUDDHISM. See The Hibbert Lectures, p. 14.

DELITZSCH (F.). BABEL AND BIBLE. Two Lectures delivered before the Deutsche Orient-Gesellschaft in the presence of the German Emperor. See Crown Theological Library, p. 10. See also Harnack, A., "Letter to Preuss. Jahrbücher," p. 18.

DOBSCHÜTZ (E. VON). CHRISTIAN LIFE IN THE PRIMITIVE CHURCH. See Theological Translation Library, New Series, p. 4.

DRIVER (S. R.). See Mosheh ben Shesheth, p. 22.

DRUMMOND (JAMES, M.A., LL.D., Hon. Litt.D., Principal of Manchester College, Oxford). AN INQUIRY INTO THE CHARACTER AND AUTHORSHIP OF THE FOURTH GOSPEL. Demy 8vo, cloth. 10s. 6d.

> "This is a valuable book, the work of a liberal theologian of distinction and great influence."—Rev. R. J. CAMPBELL, in *Christian Commonwealth.*

> "The book is not only learned, but also reverent and spiritual in tone, and ought to find its way into the libraries of students of all shades of belief, as a very notable attempt to solve one of the most important of New Testament problems."—*Christian World.*

> "Of the spirit in which Dr. Drummond approaches the study of this work of a master mind, of the completeness and arrangement of the material, and of the temper in which the argument is conducted, it is impossible to speak too highly."—*Scotsman.*

—— **VIA, VERITAS, VITA.** See The Hibbert Lectures, p. 14.

—— **PHILO JUDÆUS.** See p. 29.

ECHOES OF HOLY THOUGHTS : Arranged as Private Meditations before a First Communion. 2nd Edition, with a Preface by Rev. J. Hamilton Thom. Printed with red lines. Fcap. 8vo, cloth. 1s.

EWALD (H.). COMMENTARY ON THE PROPHETS OF THE OLD TESTAMENT. See Theological Translation Library, Old Series, p. 8.

—— **COMMENTARY ON THE PSALMS.** See Theological Translation Library, Old Series, p. 8.

18 WILLIAMS & NORGATE'S

EWALD (H.). COMMENTARY ON THE BOOK OF JOB. *See* Theological Translation Library, Old Series, p. 8.

FIGG (E. G.). ANALYSIS OF THEOLOGY, NATURAL AND REVEALED. Crown 8vo, cloth. 6s.

FOUR GOSPELS (THE) AS HISTORICAL RECORDS. 8vo, cloth. 15s.

GILL (C.). THE EVOLUTION OF CHRISTIANITY. By Charles Gill. 2nd Edition. With Dissertations in answer to Criticism. 8vo, cloth. 12s.

—— **THE BOOK OF ENOCH THE PROPHET.** Translated from an Ethiopic MS. in the Bodleian Library, by the late Richard Laurence, LL.D., Archbishop of Cashel. The Text corrected from his latest Notes by Charles Gill. Re-issue, 8vo, cloth. 5s.

GOULD (Rev. S. BARING). LOST AND HOSTILE GOSPELS. An Account of the Toledoth Jesher, two Hebrew Gospels circulating in the Middle Ages, and Extant Fragments of the Gospels of the first Three Centuries of Petrine and Pauline Origin. Crown 8vo, cloth. 7s. 6d.

HARNACK (ADOLF). MONASTICISM: Its Ideals and History; and THE CONFESSIONS OF ST. AUGUSTINE. Two Lectures by Adolf Harnack. Translated into English by E. E. Kellett, M.A., and F. H. Marseille, Ph.D., M.A. Crown 8vo, cloth. 4s.

"The lectures impart to these old subjects a new and vivid interest which cannot but win this faithful version many admiring readers."—*Scotsman.*

"One might read all the ponderous volumes of Montalembert without obtaining so clear a view or so rare a judgment of this immense subject as are offered in these luminous pages. . . . The translation is excellent, and gives us Harnack in pure and vigorous English."—*Christian World.*

—— **LETTER to the "Preussische Jahrbücher" on the German Emperor's Criticism of Prof. Delitzsch's Lectures on "Babel and Bible."** Translated into English by Thomas Bailey Saunders. 6d. net.

—— **HISTORY OF DOGMA.** *See* Theological Translation Library, New Series, p. 5.

—— **WHAT IS CHRISTIANITY?** *See* Theological Translation Library, New Series, p. 6. *Also* Crown Theological Library, p. 11. *See* Saunders (T. B.), "Professor Harnack and his Oxford Critics," p. 25.

—— **EXPANSION OF CHRISTIANITY IN THE FIRST THREE CENTURIES.** *See* Theological Translation Library, p. 4.

HATCH (Rev. Dr.). LECTURES ON THE INFLUENCE OF GREEK IDEAS AND USAGES UPON THE CHRISTIAN CHURCH. *See* The Hibbert Lectures, p. 14.

HAUSRATH (Prof. A.). HISTORY OF THE NEW TESTAMENT TIMES. The Time of the Apostles. Translated by Leonard Huxley. With a Preface by Mrs Humphry Ward. 4 vols. 8vo, cloth. 42s. (Uniform with the Theological Translation Library, Old Series.)

—— **NEW TESTAMENT TIMES.** The Times of Jesus. *See* Theological Translation Library, Old Series, p. 8.

HEBREW TEXTS, in large type for Classes:
        Genesis. 2nd Edition. 16mo, cloth. 1s. 6d.
        Psalms. 16mo, cloth. 1s.
        Isaiah. 16mo, cloth. 1s.
        Job. 16mo, cloth. 1s.

HENSLOW (Rev. G.). THE ARGUMENT OF ADAPTATION ; or, Natural Theology reconsidered. 8vo, cloth. 1s.

—— **SPIRITUAL TEACHINGS OF BIBLE PLANTS; or, The Garden of God.** 8vo, cloth. 1s.

—— **THE AT-ONE-MENT ; or, The Gospel of Reconciliation.** 8vo, cloth. 1s.

—— **THE SPIRITUAL TEACHING OF CHRIST'S LIFE.** 8vo, cloth. 5s. net.

—— **CHRIST NO PRODUCT OF EVOLUTION.** 8vo, cloth. 1s.

HERFORD (R. TRAVERS, B.A.). CHRISTIANITY IN TALMUD AND MIDRASH. Demy 8vo, cloth. 18s. net.

CONTENTS :—Introduction. Division I. Passages from the Rabbinical Literature : A. Passages relating to Jesus. B. Passages relating to Minim, Minuth. Division II. General Results. Appendix containing the Original Texts of the Passages translated. Indices.

"His book (if he is right in his identification of the Minim) is a history of Judaising Christianity—the first independent and competent history written in English."—*Expository Times.*
"It must become at once the standard authority on its subject."—*Manchester Guardian.*
"It is no exaggeration to say that it will prove indispensable not only to scholars interested in Talmudic literature, but to all who study the subject of the evangelical tradition. It will introduce the reader into a new world—that of Jewish thought in the centuries after Christ."—*Cambridge Review.*

HERRMANN (W.). THE COMMUNION OF THE CHRISTIAN WITH GOD. *See* Theological Translation Library, New Series, p. 6.

HERRMANN (W.). FAITH AND MORALS. *See* Crown Theological Library, p. 11.

HIBBERT JOURNAL: A Quarterly Review of Religion, Theology, and Philosophy. Edited by L. P. Jacks and G. Dawes Hicks. Vol. I. Royal 8vo, 856 pp. Vol. II., 864 pp. Vol. III., 869 pp. Cloth. Each 12s. 6d. net. Annual Subscription, 10s. post free.

HOERNING (Dr. R.). THE KARAITE MSS., BRITISH MUSEUM. The Karaite Exodus (i. to viii. 5) in Forty-two Autotype Facsimiles, with a Transcription in ordinary Arabic type. Together with Descriptions and Collation of that and five other MSS. of portions of the Hebrew Bible in Arabic characters in the same Collection. Royal 4to, cloth, gilt top. 20s.

HUNTER (Rev. J., D.D.). THE COMING CHURCH. A Plea for a Church simply Christian. Cloth. 1s. 6d. net.

—— **CIVIC APATHY. A Sermon preached at Bechstein Hall, London, Sunday morning, 25th June 1905.** 6d. net.

JOHNSON (EDWIN, M.A.). THE RISE OF CHRISTENDOM. Demy 8vo, cloth. 7s. 6d.

—— **ANTIQUA MATER: A Study of Christian Origins.** Crown 8vo, cloth. 2s. 6d.

—— **THE RISE OF ENGLISH CULTURE.** Demy 8vo, cloth. 15s. net.

JONES (Rev. R. CROMPTON). HYMNS OF DUTY AND FAITH. Selected and Arranged. 247 pp. Fcap. 8vo, cloth. 2nd Edition. 3s. 6d.

—— **CHANTS, PSALMS, AND CANTICLES.** Selected and Pointed for Chanting. 18mo, cloth. 1s. 6d.

—— **ANTHEMS.** With Indexes and References to the Music. 18mo, cloth. 1s. 3d.

—— **THE CHANTS AND ANTHEMS.** Together in 1 vol., cloth. 2s.

—— **A BOOK OF PRAYER.** In Thirty Orders of Worship, with Additional Prayers and Thanksgivings. 18mo, cloth. 2s. 6d. With Chants, in 1 vol. 18mo, cloth. 3s.

KAUTZSCH (E.). AN OUTLINE OF THE HISTORY OF THE LITERATURE OF THE OLD TESTAMENT. With Chronological Tables for the History of the Israelites, and other Aids to the Explanation of the Old Testament. Reprinted from the "Supplement to the Translation of the Old Testament." By E. Kautzsch, Professor of Theology at the University of Halle. Edited by the Author. Translated by John Taylor, D. Lit., M.A., etc. Demy 8vo, cloth. 6s. 6d.

"This English translation . . . is likely to prove very acceptable to all those students who desire to see for themselves the view taken by the 'higher critics' of the growth of the Old Testament."—*The Guardian.*

"Dr. Taylor has rendered a great service to the English readers by his excellent translation of this important work."—*British Weekly.*

"As to matter, it is the work of a scholar who is not afraid of results suggested by fair research, but who never grasps at novelties merely for the sake of originality. In style and language, the book reads more like an original than a translation ; an original, too, which in its terseness of expression has escaped the prolix obscurity so commonly complained of in the writings of the author's country."—*Church Gazette.*

"A brief yet comprehensive statement of critical opinion respecting the order and origin of the Old Testament books."—*Methodist Times.*

KEIM'S HISTORY OF JESUS OF NAZARA. *See* Theological Translation Library, Old Series, p. 8.

KENNEDY (Rev. JAS.). BIBLICAL HEBREW. *See* p. 35.

KIRK (R. S.). SIDE-LIGHTS ON GREAT PROBLEMS OF HUMAN INTEREST. Crown 8vo, cloth. 1s.

KITTEL (R.). HISTORY OF THE HEBREWS. *See* Theological Translation Library, New Series, p. 6.

KUENEN (Dr. A.). LECTURES ON NATIONAL AND UNIVERSAL RELIGIONS. *See* The Hibbert Lectures, p. 14.

—— **THE RELIGION OF ISRAEL TO THE FALL OF THE JEWISH STATE.** *See* Theological Translation Library, Old Series, p. 9.

LOBSTEIN (P.). THE DOGMA OF THE VIRGIN BIRTH OF CHRIST. *See* Crown Theological Library, p. 10.

LODGE (Sir O.). LIFE AND MATTER. A Criticism of Professor Haeckel's "Riddle of the Universe." Fourth Impression. Crown 8vo, cloth. 2s. 6d. net.

MACAN (R. W.). THE RESURRECTION OF JESUS CHRIST. An Essay in Three Chapters. 8vo, cloth. 5s.

MACKAY (R. W.). SKETCH OF THE RISE AND PROGRESS OF CHRISTIANITY. 8vo, cloth. 6s.

MARCHANT (JAMES). THEORIES OF THE RESUR-RECTION OF JESUS CHRIST. Crown 8vo, stiff covers, 2s. net ; superior cloth binding, 3s.

MARTI (KARL). RELIGION OF THE OLD TESTA-MENT. *See* Crown Theological Library, p. 13.

MARTINEAU (Rev. Dr. JAMES). THE RELATION BETWEEN ETHICS AND RELIGION. An Address. 8vo, sewed. 1s.

—— **MODERN MATERIALISM : ITS ATTITUDE TO-WARDS THEOLOGY.** A Critique and Defence. 8vo, sewed. 2s. 6d.

MONTEFIORE (C. G.). ORIGIN AND GROWTH OF RELIGION AS ILLUSTRATED BY THE RELIGION OF THE ANCIENT HEBREWS. *See* The Hibbert Lectures, p. 14.

MOSHEH BEN SHESHETH'S COMMENTARY ON JEREMIAH AND EZEKIEL. Edited from a Bodleian MS., with a Translation and Notes, by S. R. Driver. 8vo, sewed. 3s.

MÜNSTERBERG (Prof. HUGO). THE AMERICANS. *See* p. 30.

NESTLE (E.). INTRODUCTION TO THE TEXTUAL CRITICISM OF THE GREEK NEW TESTAMENT. *See* Theological Translation Library, New Series, p. 7.

OTTO (R.). NATURALISM AND RELIGION. *See* Crown Theological Library, p. 13.

PERRIN (R. S.). THE EVOLUTION OF KNOWLEDGE. A Review of Philosophy. Crown 8vo, cloth. 6s.

PERSONAL AND FAMILY PRAYERS. 8vo, buckram. 1s. net.

PETERS (JOHN P.). EARLY HEBREW STORY. A Study of the Origin, the Value, and the Historical Background of the Legends of Israel. *See* Crown Theological Library, p. 11.

PFLEIDERER (Dr. O.). LECTURES ON THE IN-FLUENCE OF THE APOSTLE PAUL ON THE DEVELOPMENT OF CHRISTIANITY. *See* The Hibbert Lectures, p. 14.

—— PAULINISM : A Contribution to the History of Primitive Christianity. *See* Theological Translation Library, Old Series, p. 9.

—— PHILOSOPHY OF RELIGION ON THE BASIS OF ITS HISTORY. *See* Theological Translation Library, Old Series, p. 9.

—— THE EARLY CHRISTIAN CONCEPTION OF CHRIST : Its Significance and Value in the History of Religion. *See* Crown Theological Library, p. 12.

PLAIN COMMENTARY ON THE FIRST GOSPEL. By an Agnostic. 8vo, cloth. 14s.

POOLE (REG. LANE). ILLUSTRATIONS OF THE HISTORY OF MEDIÆVAL THOUGHT IN THE DEPARTMENTS OF THEOLOGY AND ECCLESI-ASTICAL POLITICS. 8vo, cloth. 10s. 6d.

PROTESTANT COMMENTARY ON THE NEW TES-TAMENT. *See* Theological Translation Library, Old Series. p. 9.

RENAN (E.). ON THE INFLUENCE OF THE INSTI-TUTIONS, THOUGHT, AND CULTURE OF ROME ON CHRISTIANITY AND THE DEVELOPMENT OF THE CATHOLIC CHURCH. *See* Hibbert Lectures, p. 14.

RENOUF (P. LE PAGE). ON THE RELIGION OF ANCIENT EGYPT. *See* Hibbert Lectures, p. 15.

RÉVILLE (A.). THE SONG OF SONGS, Commonly called the Song of Solomon, or the Canticle. Translated from the French. Crown 8vo, cloth. 1s. 6d.

RÉVILLE (A.). ON NATIVE RELIGIONS OF MEXICO AND PERU. *See* Hibbert Lectures, p. 15.

—— PROLEGOMENA OF THE HISTORY OF RE-LIGIONS. *See* Theological Translation Library, Old Series, p. 9.

RÉVILLE (JEAN). LIBERAL CHRISTIANITY. *See* Crown Theological Library, p. 11.

—— *See* also Sabatier's "Religions of Authority and Religion of the Spirit," p. 4.

RHYS (J.). ON THE ORIGIN AND GROWTH OF RELIGION AS ILLUSTRATED BY CELTIC HEATHENDOM. *See* Hibbert Lectures, p. 15.

RIX (HERBERT). A DAWNING FAITH; or, The World as a Spiritual Organism. Crown 8vo, cloth. 5s.

—— TENT AND TESTAMENT. A Camping Tour in Palestine, with some Notes on Scripture Sites. With 61 Illustrations, Frontispiece, and Maps. Demy 8vo, cloth. 8s. 6d. net.

ROBINSON (ALEX., M.A., B.D.). A STUDY OF THE SAVIOUR IN THE NEWER LIGHT. 2nd Edition. Revised and partly re-written. Demy 8vo, cloth. 7s. 6d.

—— OLD AND NEW CERTAINTY OF THE GOSPEL: A Sketch. Crown 8vo, cloth. 2s. 6d.

SABATIER (AUGUSTE). THE RELIGIONS OF AU-THORITY AND THE RELIGION OF THE SPIRIT. With a Memoir by Professor J. Réville. *See* Theological Translation Library, New Series, p. 4.

—— THE DOCTRINE OF THE ATONEMENT AND ITS HISTORICAL EVOLUTION; and RELIGION AND MODERN CULTURE. *See* Crown Theological Library, p. 12.

SADLER (Rev. Dr.). PRAYERS FOR CHRISTIAN WORSHIP. Crown 8vo, cloth. 3s. 6d.

—— CLOSET PRAYERS, Original and Compiled. 18mo, cloth. 1s. 6d.

SAUNDERS (T. BAILEY). PROFESSOR HARNACK AND HIS OXFORD CRITICS. Crown 8vo, cloth. 1s. 6d. net.

"It gives thoughtful and acutely reasoned support to the great historical student of Christianity who represents Berlin in theology against the pig-tailed opposition which Oxford has offered to his learning. A spirited piece of controversial writing, it cannot but prove stimulating to readers interested in modern divinity, no matter to which side of the debate their private preposses-sions incline them."—*Scotsman.*

"Mr. Saunders writes with sobriety and with a knowledge of the points at issue. Readers of 'Harnack and his Critics' will do well to read his comments."—*Sheffield Daily Telegraph.*

SAVAGE (M. J.). BELIEFS ABOUT THE BIBLE. 8vo, cloth. 7s. 6d.

SAYCE (A. H.). ON THE RELIGION OF ANCIENT ASSYRIA AND BABYLONIA. *See* Hibbert Lectures, p. 15.

SCHRADER (E.). CUNEIFORM INSCRIPTIONS AND THE OLD TESTAMENT. *See* Theological Translation Library, Old Series, p. 9.

SEVERUS (Patriarch of Antioch). THE SIXTH BOOK OF THE SELECT LETTERS OF SEVERUS, PATRIARCH OF ANTIOCH, in the Syriac Version of Athanasius of Nisibis. Edited and translated by E. W. Brooks. Vol. I. (Text), Part 1, and Vol. II. (Translation), Part 1. 2 vols. 8vo, cloth. 42s. net. Vol. I. (Text), Part 2, and Vol. II. (Translation), Part 2. 2 vols. 8vo, cloth. 42s. net. *See* Text and Translation Society, p. 38.

SHARPE (SAMUEL). HISTORY OF THE HEBREW NATION AND ITS LITERATURE. With an Appendix on the Hebrew Chronology. 5th Edition. Crown 8vo, cloth. 4s. 6d.

—— **CRITICAL NOTES ON THE AUTHORISED ENGLISH VERSION OF THE NEW TESTAMENT.** 2nd Edition. 12mo, cloth. 1s. 6d.

SMITH (MARTIN R.). WHAT I HAVE TAUGHT MY CHILDREN. 2nd Edition, Revised. Crown 8vo, cloth. 3s. 6d.

SODEN (H. von, D.D.). THE HISTORY OF EARLY CHRISTIAN LITERATURE. *See* Crown Theological Library, p. 13.

THE STATUTES OF THE APOSTLES. The hitherto unedited Ethiopic and Arabic Texts. Edited, with an Introduction and Translations of the Ethiopic, Arabic, and Coptic Texts, by Rev. G. Horner, M.A. With an Appendix—a recently discovered variant of the Coptic Text. 18s. net.

TAYLER (Rev. JOHN JAMES). AN ATTEMPT TO ASCERTAIN THE CHARACTER OF THE FOURTH GOSPEL, especially in its Relation to the First Three. 2nd Edition. 8vo, cloth. 5s.

TAYLOR (Rev. C.). THE DIRGE OF COHELETH IN ECCLES. XII. DISCUSSED AND LITERALLY INTERPRETED. 8vo, cloth. 3s.

TAYLOR (Rev. Dr. J.). THE MASSORETIC TEXT AND THE ANCIENT VERSIONS OF THE BOOK OF MICAH. Crown 8vo, cloth. 5s.

—— *See also* Kautzsch, "Outline," p. 21.

TEN SERVICES OF PUBLIC PRAYER, with Special Collects. 8vo, cloth, 3s. ; or 32mo, cloth, 1s. 6d.

—— **PSALMS AND CANTICLES.** 8vo, cloth. 1s. 6d.

—— **PSALMS AND CANTICLES,** with Anthems. 8vo, cloth. 2s.

TEN SERVICES OF PUBLIC PRAYER, taken in Substance from the Common Prayer for Christian Worship, with a few additional Prayers for particular Days. 8vo, cloth, 2s. 6d. ; or 32mo, cloth, 1s.

TESTAMENT, THE NEW. TISCHENDORF (C.). NOVUM TESTAMENTUM GRÆCE. 3 vols. 8vo. 70s. net.

—— **CAMPBELL (Rev. Canon COLIN, M.A., D.D.). THE FIRST THREE GOSPELS IN GREEK.** Arranged in parallel columns. 2nd Edition, Revised. Crown 8vo, cloth. 5s. net.

UPTON (C. B.). ON THE BASES OF RELIGIOUS BELIEF. *See* Hibbert Lectures, p. 15.

VICKERS (J.). THE REAL JESUS: a Review of his Life, Character, and Death, from a Jewish Standpoint. Crown 8vo. 6s.

—— THE CRUCIFIXION MYSTERY. Crown 8vo, cloth. 3s. 6d.

VIZARD (P. E.). PRAYERS, NEW AND OLD. New Edition. Printed at the Chiswick Press. Crown 8vo, buckram. 1s. net.

VOYSEY (Rev. C.). THE SLING AND THE STONE. Vol. VIII. On the Lord's Prayer, 8vo, cloth. 3s. 6d. Vol. IX. The Fatherhood of God. Sermon on the Mount, etc. 8vo, cloth. 7s. 6d. Vol. X. Revelation tested on Moral Grounds, etc. 8vo, cloth. 10s. 6d.

—— THEISM AS A SCIENCE OF NATURAL THE-OLOGY AND NATURAL RELIGION. 2s. 6d.

—— THEISTIC PRAYER BOOK. 3rd Edition. 12mo, cloth. 3s. 6d.

WEIR (T. H., B.D.). A SHORT HISTORY OF THE HEBREW TEXT OF THE OLD TESTAMENT. By Thomas H. Weir, Assistant to the Professor of Oriental Languages in the University of Glasgow. Crown 8vo, sewed, 5s. ; cloth, 6s.

WEIZSÄCKER (C. von). THE APOSTOLIC AGE. 2 vols. See Theological Translation Library, New Series, p. 7.

WERNLE (Paul). THE BEGINNINGS OF CHRIS-TIANITY. 2 vols. 8vo. See Theological Translation Library, New Series, p. 4.

WICKSTEED (Rev. P. H.). THE ECCLESIASTICAL INSTITUTIONS OF HOLLAND, treated with Special Reference to the Position and Prospects of the Modern School of Theology. A Report presented to the Hibbert Trustees, and published by their direction. 8vo, sewed. 1s.

WIMMER (R.). MY STRUGGLE FOR LIGHT: Con-fessions of a Preacher. See Crown Theological Library, p. 11.

WRIGHT (Rev. C. H. H.). BOOK OF GENESIS IN HEBREW TEXT. With a critically revised Text, various Readings, and Grammatical and Critical Notes. Demy 8vo. 3s. 6d.

—— **BOOK OF RUTH IN HEBREW TEXT.** With a critically revised Text, various Readings, including a new Collation of Twenty-eight Hebrew MSS., and a Grammatical and Critical Commentary; to which is appended the Chaldee Targum. Demy 8vo. 7s. 6d.

—— **DANIEL AND HIS PROPHECIES.** Demy 8vo, cloth. 7s. 6d.

—— **DANIEL AND ITS CRITICS.** A Critical and Grammatical Commentary with Appendix. Demy 8vo, cloth. 7s. 6d.

WRIGHT (G. H. BATESON). THE BOOK OF JOB. A new critically revised Translation, with Essays on Scansion, Date, etc. 8vo, cloth. 6s.

—— **WAS ISRAEL EVER IN EGYPT?** or, A Lost Tradition. By G. H. Bateson Wright, D.D., Queen's College, Oxford; Headmaster Queen's College, Hong-Kong; Author of "A Critical Revised Translation of the Book of Job." 8vo, art linen. 7s. 6d.

WRIGHT (W. ALDIS), Edited by, and Dr S. A. HIRSCH. A COMMENTARY ON THE BOOK OF JOB. From a Hebrew MS. in the University Library, Cambridge. Med. 8vo, cloth. 21s. net.

ZELLER (E.). CONTENTS AND ORIGIN OF THE ACTS OF THE APOSTLES. *See* Theological Translation Library, Old Series, p. 9.

14 Henrietta Street, Covent Garden, London, W.C.

II. Philosophy, Psychology.

BACON (ROGER), THE "OPUS MAJUS" OF. Edited, with Introduction and Analytical Table, by John Henry Bridges, Fellow of Royal College of Physicians, sometime Fellow of Oriel College. Complete in 3 vols., 31s. 6d. ; Vol. III. sold separately, 7s. 6d.

BREWSTER (H. B.). THE THEORIES OF ANARCHY AND OF LAW. A Midnight Debate. Crown 8vo, parchment. 5s.

—— **THE PRISON.** A Dialogue. Crown 8vo, parchment. 5s.

—— **THE STATUETTE AND THE BACKGROUND.** Crown 8vo, parchment. 4s.

COLLINS (F. H.). AN EPITOME OF THE SYNTHETIC PHILOSOPHY. By F. Howard Collins. With a Preface by Herbert Spencer. 5th Edition. The Synthetic Philosophy Completed. 8vo, cloth. 21s.

DENNYS (EDWARD N.). THE ALPHA; or, The First Mental Principle and Truth-Guide to General Well-Being and Progress: A Revelation but no Mystery. 6th Edition. With a Portrait of the Author. Crown 8vo, cloth. 3s. 6d.

DRUMMOND (Dr.). PHILO JUDÆUS; or, The Jewish Alexandrian Philosophy in its Development and Completion. By James Drummond, LL.D., Principal of Manchester New College, Oxford. 2 vols. 8vo, cloth. 21s.

HODGSON (S. H.). PHILOSOPHY AND EXPERIENCE. An Address delivered before the Aristotelian Society. 8vo, sewed. 2s.

—— **THE REORGANISATION OF PHILOSOPHY.** Address. 8vo, sewed. 1s.

LAURIE (Professor SIMON). ETHICA: or, The Ethics of Reason. By Scotus Novanticus. 2nd Edition. 8vo, cloth. 6s.

—— **METAPHYSICA NOVA ET VETUSTA: A Return to Dualism.** 2nd Edition. Crown 8vo, cloth. 6s.

LODGE (Sir O.). LIFE AND MATTER. See Religion, p. 21.

MACKENZIE (MALCOLM). SOCIAL AND POLITICAL DYNAMICS. An Exposition of the Function of Money as the measure of Contract, Trade, and Government, viewed from the Principles of Natural Philosophy and Jurisprudence, in refutation of Economic Dogmas. Demy 8vo, cloth. 10s. 6d.

MIND: A Quarterly Review of Psychology and Philosophy. Nos. 1-64. 1876-90. 8vo, each 3s. Vols. III.-XVI. in cloth, each 13s. New Series, Nos. 1-32, each 3s.; 33 and after, 4s. Vols I.-VIII., each 13s. Vols. IX.-XIV., each 17s. Annual Subscription, post free, 12s.

MÜNSTERBERG (HUGO, Professor of Psychology at Harvard University). THE AMERICANS. Translated by Edwin B. Holt, Ph.D., Instructor at Harvard University. Royal 8vo, cloth. 12s. 6d. net.

PERRIN (R. S.). EVOLUTION OF KNOWLEDGE, THE. A Review of Philosophy. *See* Religion, p. 22.

PIKLER (JUL.). THE PSYCHOLOGY OF THE BELIEF IN OBJECTIVE EXISTENCE. Part I. 8vo, cloth. 4s. 6d.

PROCEEDINGS OF THE ARISTOTELIAN SOCIETY FOR THE SYSTEMATIC STUDY OF PHILOS-OPHY. Proceedings. Vol. I., 4 Nos., 1890-91. 8vo, 12s. Discontinued after Vol. III. Part 2. Or each Part separately. Vol. I. No. 1, 2s. 6d.; No. 2, 2s. 6d.; No. 3, Part 1, 1s. 6d.; Part 2, 2s.; No. 4, Part 1, 1s. 6d.; Part 2, 2s. Vol. II. No. 1, Part 1, 1s. 6d.; Part 2, 2s.; No. 2, Part 1, 1s. 6d.; Part 2, 2s.; No. 3, Part 1, 2s.; Part 2, 2s. Vol. III. Part 1, 2s. 6d.; Part 2, 2s. NEW SERIES, Vols. I.-VI. Demy 8vo, buckram, each 10s. 6d. net.

ROBERTSON (G. C.). PHILOSOPHICAL REMAINS OF GEORGE CROOM ROBERTSON, Grote Professor of Mind and Logic, University College, London. With a Memoir. Edited by Alexander Bain, LL.D., Emeritus Professor of Logic, Aberdeen, and T. Whittaker, B.A. (Oxon.). With Portrait. Med. 8vo, cloth. 9s. net.

SALEEBY (C. W., M.D., F.R.S.). INDIVIDUALISM AND COLLECTIVISM. Crown 8vo, cloth. 2s.

SCHURMAN (J. GOULD). KANTIAN ETHICS AND THE ETHICS OF EVOLUTION. 8vo, cloth. 5s.

—— **THE ETHICAL IMPORT OF DARWINISM.** Crown 8vo, cloth. 5s.

SCRIPTURE (EDWARD W., Ph.D.). STUDIES FROM THE YALE PSYCHOLOGICAL LABORATORY. Vols. I.-VI., each 4s. 2d. net.

SMITH (H. W.). THE GARDEN OF LIFE. Flowers of Thought on Culture, Conduct, and Character for every day in the year, gathered and arranged by H. W. Smith. Crown 8vo, cloth gilt. 5s. net.

SPENCER (HERBERT). AN AUTOBIOGRAPHY. 2 vols. demy 8vo. With Portraits. Green buckram, gilt top. 28s. net.

> "It is not too much to say that we close this book, the most interesting, and certainly one of the most important we have ever opened, feeling better, wiser, and humbler for having thus hastily read it."—*Academy.*

> "It is a book for all men and for all time. In its pages the thinker may trace, step by step, the synthesis of synthetic philosophy. Here the poet will find not only a worthy inspiration, but a possibly surprising vein of sympathy. The statesman, the inventor, the litterateur, the man of theory, and the man of practice will find alike, within the covers of these two massive volumes, an almost inexhaustible treasury of interest and constructive thought. There is suggestion and instruction for all the world, and an almost indefinable fascination—whether it be due to the mere intrinsic beauty of the picture itself, or to the dignity of its execution, or to the sense of its almost laborious faithfulness, or to the combined attraction of all three."—*St. James's Gazette.*

—— A SYSTEM OF SYNTHETIC PHILOSOPHY—

Vol. I. **First Principles.** With an Appendix and a Portrait. Finally revised. New Edition, large crown 8vo, cloth. 7s. 6d.

Vols. II. and III. **The Principles of Biology.** 6th Thousand. 8vo, cloth. Revised and greatly enlarged. Vols. I. and II. 18s. each.

Vols. IV. and V. **The Principles of Psychology.** 5th Thousand. 2 vols. 8vo, cloth. 36s.

Vol. VI. **The Principles of Sociology.** Vol. I. Part 1, The Data of Sociology; Part 2, The Inductions of Sociology; Part 3, Domestic Institutions. 4th Thousand, revised and enlarged. 8vo, cloth. 21s.

Vol. VII. **The Principles of Sociology.** Vol. II. Part 4, Ceremonial Institutions; Part 5, Political Institutions. 3rd Thousand. 8vo, cloth. 18s.

Vol. VIII. **The Principles of Sociology.** Vol. III. Part 6, Ecclesiastical Institutions; Part 7, Professional Institutions; Part 8, Industrial Institutions. 2nd Thousand. 8vo, cloth. 16s.

Vol. IX. **The Principles of Ethics.** Vol. I. Part 1, The Data of Ethics; Part 2, The Inductions of Ethics; Part 3, The Ethics of Individual Life. 2nd Thousand. 8vo, cloth. 15s.

Vol. X. **The Principles of Ethics.** Vol. II. Part 4, Justice; Part 5, Negative Beneficence; Part 6, Positive Beneficence; Appendices. Demy 8vo, cloth. 12s. 6d.

Also to be had separately :

SPENCER (HERBERT). DATA OF ETHICS. Reset uniform with popular edition of " First Principles." Sewed, 2*s.* 6d. net. ; cloth. 3*s.* net.

—— **JUSTICE.** Being Part 4 of the Principles of Ethics. 2nd Thousand. 8vo, cloth. 6*s.*

Other Works.

—— **THE STUDY OF SOCIOLOGY.** Library Edition (21st Thousand), with a Postscript. 8vo, cloth. 10*s.* 6*d.*

—— **EDUCATION : Intellectual, Moral, and Physical.** Cheap Edition. Entirely reset. 46th Thousand. Crown 8vo, cloth. 2*s.* 6*d.*

—— **ESSAYS : Scientific, Political, and Speculative.** A new Edition, rearranged, with additional Essays. 3 vols. 8vo, cloth. (Each 10*s.*) 30*s.*

—— **SOCIAL STATICS.** Abridged and revised, together with "The Man *v.* The State." 8vo, cloth. 10*s.*

—— **VARIOUS FRAGMENTS.** Uniform in Library binding. Demy 8vo, cloth. Enlarged Edition. 6*s.*

—— **FACTS AND COMMENTS.** Demy 8vo, cloth. 6*s.*

—— **THE MAN *versus* THE STATE.** 14th Thousand. Sewed. 1*s.*

—— **A REJOINDER TO PROFESSOR WEISMANN.** Sewed. 6*d.*

—— **REASONS FOR DISSENTING FROM THE PHIL-OSOPHY OF M. COMTE.** Sewed. 6*d.*

—— **DESCRIPTIVE SOCIOLOGY; or, Groups of Socio-logical Facts.** Compiled and abstracted by Professor D. Duncan of Madras, Dr. Richard Scheppig, and James Collier. Folio, boards.

No. 1. English. 18*s.*
No. 2. Ancient American Races. 16*s.*
No. 3. Lowest Races, Negritto Races, Polynesians. 18*s.*
No. 4. African Races. 16*s.*
No. 5. Asiatic Races. 18*s.*
No. 6. American Races. 18*s.*
No. 7. Hebrews and Phœnicians. 21*s.*
No. 8. The French Civilisation. 30*s.*

New volumes in preparation.

SPENCER (HERBERT). COLLINS (F. H.). AN EPITOME OF THE SYNTHETIC PHILOSOPHY. By F. Howard Collins. Being a Digest of Mr. Herbert Spencer's Works. 5th Edition, the Synthetic Philosophy Completed. With a Preface by Herbert Spencer. 8vo, cloth. 21*s.*

—— **DREY (S.). HERBERT SPENCER'S THEORY OF RELIGION AND MORALITY.** By Sylvan Drey. 8vo, sewed. 1*s.*

—— —— **A THEORY OF LIFE DEDUCED FROM THE EVOLUTION PHILOSOPHY.** Demy 8vo, sewed. 1*s.*

SPINOZA: Four Essays. By Professors Land, Van Vloten, and Kuno Fischer, and by E. Renan. Edited by Professor Knight, of St. Andrews. Crown 8vo, cloth. 5*s.*

STUDIES FROM THE YALE PSYCHOLOGICAL LABORATORY. Edited by Professor E. W. Scripture. With many Illustrations. 8vo, sewed. 4*s.* 2*d.* each net. Vol. I. 1892–93, 100 pages. Vol. II. 1894, 124 pages. Vol. III. 1895, 110 pages. Vol. IV. 1896, 141 pages. Vol. V. 1897, 105 pages. Vol. VI. 1898, 105 pages.

WUNDT (WILHELM). OUTLINES OF PSYCHOLOGY. Translated, with the co-operation of the Author, by Charles Hubbard Judd, Ph.D., Instructor in the Wesleyan University. 2nd Enlarged Edition. Demy 8vo, cloth. 8*s.* net.

III. Oriental Languages, Literature, and History.

ABHIDHANARATNAMALA (THE) OF HALÂYUDHA.
A Sanskrit Vocabulary (120 pp.). Edited, with a Sanskrit-English Glossary (180 pp.), by Dr. T. Aufrecht. 8vo, cloth. (Published at 18s.) 10s.

AVESTI, PAHLAVI, and ANCIENT PERSIAN STUDIES in Honour of the late SHAMS-UL-ULAMA DASTUR PESHOTANJI BEHRAMJI SANJANA, M.A., Ph.D. Paper cover, 12s. 6d. net; cloth, 13s. 6d. net.

BERNSTEIN and KIRSCH. SYRIAC CHRESTOMATHY AND LEXICON (Chrestomathia Syriaca cum Lexico). 2 vols. in 1. 8vo, cloth boards. 7s. 6d. I. Chrestomathia, separately. Sewed. 3s.

DAVIDS (T. W. RHYS). LECTURES ON SOME POINTS IN THE HISTORY OF INDIAN BUDDHISM. *See* The Hibbert Lectures, p. 14.

DELITZSCH (Prof. F.). ASSYRIAN GRAMMAR. With Paradigms, Exercises, Glossary, and Bibliography. Translated by the Rev. Prof. A. R. S. Kennedy. Crown 8vo, cloth. 15s.

—— **THE HEBREW LANGUAGE VIEWED IN THE LIGHT OF ASSYRIAN RESEARCH.** Demy 8vo, cloth. 4s.

—— **BABEL AND BIBLE.** *See* Crown Theological Library, p. 10.

DIETTRICH (GUSTAV). DIE MASSORAH DER ÖSTLICHEN UND WESTLICHEN SYRER IN IHREN ANGABEN ZUM PROPHETEN JESAIA nach fünf Handschriften des British Museum in Verbindung mit zwei Tractaten über Accente. Sewed. 8s. 6d. net.

DÎPAVAMSA (THE): A Buddhist Historical Record in the Pali Language. Edited, with an English Translation, by Dr. H. Oldenberg. 8vo, cloth. 21s.

> The "Dîpavamsa" is the most ancient historical work of the Ceylonese; it contains an account of the ecclesiastical history of the Buddhist Church, of the conversion of the Ceylonese to the Buddhist faith, and of the ancient history of Ceylon.

ERMAN'S EGYPTIAN GRAMMAR. Translated, under Professor Erman's supervision, by J. H. Breasted, Professor of Egyptology in the University of Chicago. Crown 8vo, cloth. 18s.

EVANS (GEORGE). AN ESSAY ON ASSYRIOLOGY. With 4to Tables of Assyrian Inscriptions. 8vo, cloth. 5s.

FAIZULLAH-BHAI (Shaikh, B.D.). A MOSLEM PRESENT. Part I., containing the famous poem of Al-Busaree. With an English Version and Notes. 8vo, cloth. 4s.

—— **AN ESSAY ON THE PRE-ISLAMITIC ARABIC POETRY,** with special reference to the Seven Suspended Poems. 8vo, sewed. 4d.

FLINDERS PETRIE PAPYRI. See Cunningham Memoirs, vols. 8, 9, and 11, p. 48.

FRANKFURTER (Dr. O.). HANDBOOK OF PALI : Being an Elementary Grammar, a Chrestomathy, and a Glossary. 8vo, cloth. 16s.

FUERST (Dr. JUL.). HEBREW AND CHALDEE LEXICON TO THE OLD TESTAMENT. 5th Edition, improved and enlarged. Translated by Rev. Dr. Samuel Davidson. Royal 8vo, cloth. 21s.

HARDY (R. SPENCE). MANUAL OF BUDDHISM IN ITS MODERN DEVELOPMENT. Translated from Singhalese MSS. 2nd Edition, with a complete Index and Glossary. 8vo, cloth. 21s.

HEBREW TEXTS. Large type. 16mo, cloth.

> Genesis. (2nd Edition. Baer and Delitzsch's Text.) 1s. 6d.
> Psalms. 1s.
> Job. 1s.
> Isaiah. 1s.

KENNEDY (Rev. JAS.). INTRODUCTION TO BIBLICAL HEBREW, presenting Graduated Instruction in the Language of the Old Testament. By James Kennedy, B.D., Acting Librarian in the New College, and one of the additional Examiners in Divinity at the University, Edinburgh. 8vo, cloth. 12s.

—— **STUDIES IN HEBREW SYNONYMS.** Demy 8vo, cloth. 5s.

LYALL (C. J., M.A., K.C.I.E.). ANCIENT ARABIAN POETRY, CHIEFLY PRÆ-ISLAMIC. Translations, with an Introduction and Notes. Fcap. 4to, cloth. 10s. 6d.

MACHBEROTH ITHIEL. By Yehuda ben Shelomoh Alcharizi. Edited from the MS. in the Bodleian Library, by Thomas Chenery, M.A. 8vo, cloth. 3s.

MILANDA PANHO, THE: Being Dialogues between King Milanda and the Buddhist Sage Nāgasena. The Pali Text, edited by V. Trenckner. 440 pp. 8vo, sewed. 21s. See also "Pali Miscellany."

MOSHEH BEN SHESHETH'S COMMENTARY ON JEREMIAH AND EZEKIEL. See p. 22.

MUSS-ARNOLT (W.). A CONCISE DICTIONARY OF THE ASSYRIAN LANGUAGE (Assyrian—English—German). By W. Muss-Arnolt. Completed in 19 parts. Each 5s. net.

NEW HEBREW SCHOOL of POETS of the SPANISH-ARABIAN EPOCH. Selected Texts with Introduction, Notes, and Dictionary. Edited by H. Brody, Ph.D., Rabbi in Nachod (Bohemia), and K. Albrecht, Ph.D., Professor in Oldenburg (Grand Duchy). English translation of the Introduction, etc., by Mrs Karl Albrecht. Cloth. 7s. 6d. net.

NÖLDEKE (THEODOR, Professor of Oriental Languages in the University of Strassburg). COMPENDIOUS SYRIAC GRAMMAR. With a Table of Characters by Julius Euting. Translated (with the sanction of the author) from the second and improved German Edition by Rev. James A. Crichton, D.D. Royal 8vo. 18s. net.

—— DELECTUS VETERUM CARMINUM ARABI-CORUM GLOSSARIUM CONFECIT A. MULLER. Crown 8vo, cloth. 7s. 6d.

NORRIS (E.). ASSYRIAN DICTIONARY. Intended to further the Study of the Cuneiform Inscriptions of Assyria and Babylonia. Vols. I. to III. 4to, cloth. Each 28s.

OLDENBERG (Prof. H.). BUDDHA: His Life, his Doctrine, his Order. By Dr. Hermann Oldenberg, Professor at the University of Berlin. Translated by W. Hoey, M.A. 8vo, cloth gilt. 18s.

PALI MISCELLANY. By V. Trenckner. Part I. The Introductory Part of the Milanda Panho, with an English Translation and Notes. 8vo, sewed. 4s.

PLATTS (J. T.). A GRAMMAR OF THE PERSIAN LANGUAGE. By John T. Platts, Hon. M.A. (Oxon.), Teacher of Persian in the University of Oxford ; late Inspector of Schools in the Central Provinces of India. Part I. Accidence. Broad crown 8vo. 10s. 6d.

RENOUF (P. LE PAGE). LECTURES ON THE RELIGION OF ANCIENT EGYPT. See Hibbert Lectures, p. 15.

SADI. THE GULISTAN (ROSE GARDEN) OF SHAIK SADI OF SHIRAZ. A new Edition of the Persian Text, with a Vocabulary, by F. Johnson. Square royal 8vo, cloth. 15s.

SAYCE (Prof. A. H.). LECTURES ON THE RELIGIONS OF ANCIENT BABYLONIA AND SYRIA. See the Hibbert Lectures, p. 15.

SCHRADER (E.). THE CUNEIFORM INSCRIPTIONS AND THE OLD TESTAMENT. See Theological Translation Library, Old Series, p. 9.

SHIHĀB AL DIN. FUTŪH AL-HABASHAH ; or, The Conquest of Abyssinia. By Shināb al Din Ahmad B. 'Abd al Kādir B. Sālim B. 'Uthman. Edited, from an Arabic MS., by S. Arthur Strong. Part I. 8vo, sewed. 3s. net.

SOCIN (Dr. A.). ARABIC GRAMMAR. Paradigms, Literature, Exercises, and Glossary. 2nd Edition. Translated from the 3rd German Edition by the Rev. Prof. A. R. S. Kennedy, D.D. Crown 8vo, cloth. 8s. 6d.

—— **KEY FOR TRANSLATING THE GERMAN EXERCISES IN ABOVE GRAMMAR.** Sewed. 1s. 6d.

SÖRENSEN (S., Ph.D.), Compiled by. AN INDEX TO THE NAMES IN THE MAHABHARATA. With short explanations. Royal 4to, in twelve parts, which are not sold separately, at 7s. 6d. per part net. Parts I. and III. now ready.

STATUTES, THE, OF THE APOSTLES. The hitherto unedited Ethiopic and Arabic Texts, with translations of Ethiopic, Arabic, and Coptic Texts, by G. Horner, M.A. See p. 26.

TEXT AND TRANSLATION SOCIETY. *Established for the purpose of editing and translating Oriental Texts chiefly preserved in the British Museum.*

Volumes already issued—

THE SIXTH BOOK OF THE SELECT LETTERS OF SEVERUS, PATRIARCH OF ANTIOCH, in the Syriac Version of Athanasius of Nisibis. Edited and translated by E. W. Brooks, M.A. Vol. I. Text, Parts I. and II. Vol. II. Translation, Parts I. and II. 84*s*. net.

THE CANONS OF ATHANASIUS OF ALEX-ANDRIA, in Arabic, Ethiopic, and Coptic. Edited and Translated by Prof. W. Riedel (Griefswald) and W. E. Crum. 21*s*. net.

A RABBINIC COMMENTARY ON THE BOOK OF JOB, contained in a unique MS. at Cambridge. Edited, with Translation and Commentary, by W. Aldis Wright, LL.D. 21*s*. net.

———

TURPIE (Dr. D. McC.). MANUAL OF THE CHALDEE LANGUAGE. Containing Grammar of the Biblical Chaldee and of the Targums, and a Chrestomathy, with a Vocabulary. Square 8vo, cloth. 7*s*.

VINAYA PITAKAM : One of the Principal Buddhist Holy Scriptures. Edited in Pali by Dr. H. Oldenberg. 5 vols. 8vo, cloth. Each 21*s*.

WALLIS (H. W.). THE COSMOLOGY OF THE RIG-VEDA : An Essay. 8vo, cloth. 5*s*.

IV. Modern Languages & Literature.

A complete list of Messrs. Williams & Norgate's Educational Publications on Modern Languages may be had on application.

ABBOTSFORD SERIES OF THE SCOTTISH POETS.
Edited by George Eyre-Todd. I. Early Scottish Poetry; II. Mediæval Scottish Poetry; III. Scottish Poetry of the Sixteenth Century. Price of each vol., 3*s.* 6*d.* ; large paper, 5*s.* net. IV. Scottish Ballad Poetry. 5*s.* ; large paper, half-morocco, Roxburghe, 7*s.* 6*d.* net. V. Scottish Poetry of the Seventeenth Century. 5*s.* ; large paper, half-morocco, Roxburghe, 7*s.* 6*d.* net. Vol. VI. Scottish Poetry of the Eighteenth Century. Vol. I. 3*s.* 6*d.* ; large paper, half-morocco, Roxburghe, 5*s.* net. Vol. II. cloth, 5*s.* ; large paper, half-morocco, 7*s.* 6*d.* net.

ARMY SERIES OF FRENCH AND GERMAN NOVELS.
Edited, with short Notes, by J. T. W. Perowne, M.A.

This series is equally well adapted for general reading, and for those preparing for the Army, Oxford and Cambridge Certificates, and other Examinations—in fact, for all who wish to keep up or improve their French and German. The notes are as concise as possible, with an occasional etymology or illustration to assist the memory. The books selected being by recent or living authors, are adapted for the study of most modern French and German.

LE COUP DE PISTOLET, etc. Prosper Merimée. 2*s.* 6*d.*

" A book more admirably suited to its purpose could not be desired. The Editors deserve to be congratulated."—*National Observer.*

" The first two volumes are an excellent choice, and we advise any one, whether candidate or lay, to purchase the volume of Merimée."—*Journal of Education.*

VAILLANTE. Jacques Vincent. 2*s.* 6*d.*

" The books are well got up, and in *Vaillante* an excellent choice has been made."—*Guardian.*

" The notes are few and brief, but all are helpful. The story itself is a delightful one."—*Scotsman.*

AUF VERLORNEM POSTEN AND NAZZARENA DANTI. Johannes v. Dewall. 3*s.*

" The two stories by Johannes v. Dewall are well suited for their purpose; the style and diction are not too difficult for those whose acquaintance with German is not extensive, and ample explanatory annotation is provided."—*Saturday Review.*

" Well printed, well bound, and annotated just sufficiently to make the reading of them sure as well as easy."—*Educational Times.*

ARMY SERIES—Continued.

CONTES MILITAIRES. A. Daudet. 2s. 6d.

"These stories are mainly culled from a series called *Contes du Lundi*, originally contributed by their author to the *Figaro*. Written at fever heat immediately after the great 1870 war, they show Daudet's power in many ways at its highest. . . . We therefore do more than recommend—we urge all readers of French to get the stories in some form, and the present one is both good and cheap. The paper is excellent, and the type clear and bold. . . . A neat map of Paris will assist the reader in following the movement of the stories."—*The Schoolmaster.*

"The choice is an exceptionally good one, and the notes are excellent."—*Guardian.*

ERZÄHLUNGEN. E. Höfer. 3s.

"The series has brought fascinating examples of fiction under the eyes of English readers in a neat and handy form. Besides having the military flavour, they are models of style."—*Scotsman.*

ATKINSON (ROBERT, M.A., LL.D.). THE PASSIONS AND HOMILIES FROM LEABHAR BREAC. With an Introductory Lecture on Irish Lexicography. 958 pp. Todd Lecture Series, Vol. II. 8vo, sewed. Pages 1–34 out of print; pages 35–958, 6s.

BAYLDON (Rev. G.). ICELANDIC GRAMMAR. An Elementary Grammar of the Old Norse or Icelandic Language. 8vo, cloth. 7s. 6d.

BOÏELLE (JAS.). FRENCH COMPOSITION THROUGH LORD MACAULAY'S ENGLISH. Edited, with Notes, Hints, and Introduction, by the late James Boïelle, B.A. (Univ. Gall.), Officier d'Académie, Senior French Master, Dulwich College, etc., etc. Crown 8vo, cloth. Vol. I. Frederick the Great. 3s. Vol. II. Warren Hastings. 3s. Vol. III. Lord Clive. 3s.

—— *See* Victor Hugo, "Les Misérables" and "Notre Dame."

BOOK OF BALLYMOTE (THE). A Collection of Pieces in the Irish Language, dating from the end of the Fourteenth Century. Now published in Photo-Lithography from the Original Manuscript in the Library of the Royal Irish Academy. With Introduction, Analysis of Contents, and Index, by Robert Atkinson, M.A., LL.D., Professor of Sanskrit and Comparative Philology in the University of Dublin; Secretary of Council, Royal Irish Academy.

The Book of Ballymote contains numerous articles of interest to the scholar and to the antiquary. The original portion consists of—Genealogical Lists; Histories and Legends; a fragment of the Brehon Laws; a copy of the *Dindsenchas*; Treatise on Grammatical Topics, etc. The other portion contains translations from Latin originals: the Destruction of Troy, the Wandering of Ulysses, the Story of the Æneid, and the life of Alexander the Great.

In imperial folio, reproduced by Photo-Lithography. Half-morocco, Roxburghe, cloth sides. £5, 5s. (200 copies only printed.)

BOOK OF LEINSTER (THE), sometime called The Book of Glendalough. A Collection of Pieces in the Irish Language, compiled in part about the middle of the Twelfth Century. From the original MS. in Trinity College, Dublin. With Introduction, Analysis of Contents, and Index, by Robert Atkinson, M.A., LL.D., Professor of Sanskrit and Comparative Philology in the University of Dublin ; Secretary of Council, Royal Irish Academy. In imperial folio, on toned paper, with a Photograph of a page of the Original. Half-roan, Roxburghe, cloth sides. £6, 6s. (200 copies only printed.)

DELBOS (L.). NAUTICAL TERMS IN ENGLISH AND FRENCH AND FRENCH AND ENGLISH. With Notes and Tables. For the use of Naval Officers and Naval Cadets. By Leon Delbos, M.A., of H.M.S. *Britannia*, Dartmouth. 4th Edition, thoroughly revised and considerably enlarged, with additional Plates. Crown 8vo, cloth. 7s. 6d. net.

EUGENE'S STUDENT'S COMPARATIVE GRAMMAR OF THE FRENCH LANGUAGE, with an Historical Sketch of the Formation of French. For the use of Public Schools. With Exercises. By G. Eugène-Fasnacht, late French Master, Westminster School. 23rd Edition, thoroughly revised. Square crown 8vo, cloth, 5s. ; or separately, Grammar, 3s. ; Exercises, 2s. 6d.

GOETHE (W. v.). ANNOTATED TEXTS. *See* Educational Catalogue.

HAGMANN (J.G., Ph.D.). REFORM IN PRIMARY EDUCATION. Translated from Second German Edition by R. H. Hoar, Ph.D., and Richmond Barker, M.A. Cr. 8vo, cl., 2s. 6d. net.

HOGAN (E.). CATH RUIS NA RIG FOR BOINN. With Preface, Translation, and Indices ; also a Treatise on Irish Neuter Substantives, and a Supplement to the Index Vocabulorum of Zeuss's "Grammatica Celtica." Todd Lecture Series, Vol. IV. 8vo, sewed. 3s. 6d.

—— **THE LATIN LIVES OF THE SAINTS AS AIDS TOWARDS THE TRANSLATION OF IRISH TEXTS AND THE PRODUCTION OF AN IRISH DICTIONARY.** By Edmund Hogan, S.J., F.R.U.I., M.R.I.A., Royal Irish Academy's Todd Professor of Celtic Languages. Todd Lecture Series, Vol. V. 2s. 6d.

—— **THE IRISH NENNIUS FROM L. NA HUIDRE, AND HOMILIES AND LEGENDS FROM L. BREAC.** Alphabetical Index of Irish Neuter Substantives. Todd Lecture Series, Vol. VI. 2s. 6d.

HUGO (VICTOR). LES MISÉRABLES : Les Principaux Episodes. Edited, with Life and Notes, by the late J. Boïelle. 2 vols. 6th Edition. Crown 8vo, cloth. Each 3s. 6d.

HUGO (VICTOR). NOTRE DAME DE PARIS. Adapted for the use of Schools and Colleges. By the late J. Boïelle. 2 vols. 2nd Edition. Crown 8vo, cloth. Each 3s.

LEABHAR BREAC. The "Speckled Book," otherwise styled, "The Great Book of Dun Doïghre": a Collection of Pieces in Irish and Latin, transcribed towards the close of the Fourteenth Century. "The oldest and best Irish MS. relating to Church History now preserved" (*G. Petrie*). Now first published, from the original MS. in the Royal Irish Academy's Library. In imperial folio, on toned paper. In one vol., half-calf, £4, 4s. (200 copies only printed.)

LEABHAR NA H-UIDHRI. A Collection of Pieces in Prose and Verse, in the Irish Language, transcribed about A.D. 1100; the oldest volume now known entirely in the Irish language, and one of the chief surviving native literary monuments—not ecclesiastical—of ancient Ireland; now for the first time published, from the original in the Library of the Royal Irish Academy, with account of the Manuscript, description of its contents, index, and facsimiles in colours. In folio on toned paper, half-calf. £3, 3s. (200 copies only printed.)

LILJA (The Lily). An Icelandic Religious Poem. By Eystein Asgrimson. Edited, with Translation, Notes, and Glossary, by E. Magnusson. Crown 8vo, cloth extra. 10s. 6d.

LODGE (Sir O.). SCHOOL TEACHING AND SCHOOL REFORM. A Course of Four Lectures on School Curricula and Methods, delivered to Secondary Teachers and Teachers in Training at Birmingham during February 1905. 3s.

   "The work of a sensible iconoclast, who does not pull down for the sake of mere destruction, but is anxious to set up something more worthy in place of the mediævalism he attacks."—*Outlook.*

   "Let me commend this wise volume not only to teachers but to all concerned in national education. And especially to the politician. Half an hour with Sir Oliver Lodge would make him realise that there are problems on the inner side of the school door not dreamt of in his philosophy—would make him feel that the more he knows of these the better will he be able wisely to handle those others about which he is glibly talking every day."—Dr MACNAMARA in the *Daily Chronicle.*

MAORI. NEW AND COMPLETE MANUAL OF MAORI CONVERSATIONS. Containing Phrases and Dialogues on a variety of Topics, together with a few general rules of Grammar, and a comprehensive Vocabulary. 4s. net. *See also* Williams.

NIBELUNGENLIED. "The Fall of the Nibelungens," otherwise "The Book of Kriemhild." An English Translation by W. N. Lettsom. 4th Edition. 8vo, cloth. 5s.

O'GRADY (STANDISH H.). SILVA GADELICA (I.-XXXI.). A Collection of Tales in Irish, with Extracts illustrating Persons and Places. Edited from MSS. and translated. 2 vols. royal 8vo, cloth. 42s. Or separately, Vol. I., Irish Text; and Vol. II., Translation and Notes. Each vol. 21s.

OORDT (J. F. VAN, B.A.). CAPE DUTCH. Phrases and Dialogues, with Translations, preceded by short Grammatical Notes. Crown 8vo, cloth. 2s. 6d. net.

PHILLIPPS (V., B.A.). A SHORT SKETCH OF GERMAN LITERATURE, for Schools. By Vivian Phillipps, B.A., Assistant Master at Fettes College, Edinburgh. 2nd Edition, revised. Pott 8vo, cloth. 1s.

ROGET (F. F.). AN INTRODUCTION TO OLD FRENCH. History, Grammar, Chrestomathy, and Glossary. 2nd Edition. Crown 8vo, cloth. 6s.

—— **FIRST STEPS IN FRENCH HISTORY, LITERATURE, AND PHILOLOGY.** For Candidates for the Scotch Leaving Certificate Examinations, the various Universities Local Examinations, and the Army Examinations. 4th Edition. Crown 8vo, cloth. 5s.

—— *See also* Voltaire.

ROSING (S.). ENGLISH-DANISH DICTIONARY. New Edition. Large 8vo, strongly bound, half-roan. 11s. 6d.

SCHILLER (F. VON). THE BALLADS AND SHORTER POEMS. Translated into English Verse by Gilbert Clark. Fcap. 8vo, cloth. 5s.

—— **ANNOTATED TEXTS.** *See* Educational Catalogue.

STOKES (WHITLEY). OLD IRISH GLOSSARIES. Cormac's Glossary. O'Davoran's Glossary. A Glossary to the Calendar of Oingus the Culdee. Edited, with an Introduction and Index. 8vo, cloth. 10s. 6d.

—— **THE CREATION OF THE WORLD.** A Mystery in Ancient Cornish. Edited, with Translations and Notes. 8vo, cloth. 6s.

—— **ON THE FELIRE OF ŒNGUS.** Vol. I., Part 1. Trans. R.I.A.'s Irish MSS. Series. 4to, sewed. 6s.

—— **THE LIFE OF ST. MERIASEK.** A Cornish Drama. Edited, with Translation and Notes. Royal 8vo. One 8vo facsimile. Cloth. 5s.

STOKES (WHITLEY). BRETON GLOSSES AT OR-LEANS. Edited by W. Stokes. 8vo, sewed. 1s.

—— **OLD IRISH GLOSSES AT WUERZBURG AND CARLSRUHE.** Edited by W. Stokes. 8vo, sewed. 3s. 6d.

SULLIVAN (W. K.). CELTIC STUDIES FROM THE GERMAN OF EBEL. With an Introduction on the Roots, Stems, and Derivatives, and on Case-endings of Nouns in the Indo-European Languages. 8vo, cloth. 10s.

TODD LECTURE SERIES (Royal Irish Academy)—

Vol. I. Part 1. **Mesca Ulad; or, The Intoxications of the Ultonians.** Irish Text, with Translation and Notes, by W. M. Hennesy. 8vo, sewed. 1s. 6d.

Vol. II. **Leabhar Breac, Passions and Homilies from.** Irish Text, Translation, and Glossary, with Lecture on Irish Lexicography, by Dr. R. Atkinson. 8vo, cloth. Part 1, pages 1–34, out of print. Part 2, pages 35–958, 6s.

Vol. III. **The Codex Palatino-Vaticanus.** No. 830. Texts, Translations, and Indices, by B. MacCarthy, D.D. 8vo, sewed. 2s. 6d.

Vol. IV. **Cath Ruis na Rig for Boinn.** With Preface, Translation, Indices, a Treatise on Irish Neuter Substantives, and a Supplement to the Index Vocabulorum of Zeuss's "Grammatica Celtica." By E. Hogan. 8vo, sewed. 3s. 6d.

Vol. V. **The Latin Lives of the Saints as aids towards the Translation of Irish Texts and the Production of an Irish Dictionary.** By Edmund Hogan, S.J., F.R.U.I., M.R.I.A., Royal Irish Academy's Todd Professor of the Celtic Languages. 2s. 6d.

Vol. VI. **The Irish Nennius from L. Na Huidre, and Homilies and Legends from L. Breac.** Alphabetical Index of Irish Neuter Substantives. By Edmund Hogan, S.J., F.R.U.I., M.R.I.A., Royal Irish Academy's Todd Professor of the Celtic Languages. 2s. 6d

VELASQUEZ. LARGER SPANISH DICTIONARY. Composed from the Dictionaries of the Spanish Academy, Terreros and Salva. Spanish-English and English-Spanish. 1279 pp., triple columns. 2 vols. in 1. Imp. 8vo, cloth. 24s.

VIGA GLUMS SAGA. Translated from the Icelandic, with Notes and an Introduction, by Sir Edmund Head, Bart. Fcap. 8vo, cloth. 5s.

WEISSE (T. H.). SYSTEMATIC CONVERSATIONAL EXERCISES FOR TRANSLATING INTO GERMAN, adapted to his Grammar. New Edition. Crown 8vo, cloth. (Key, 5s. net.) 3s. 6d.

WEISSE (T. H.). A SHORT GUIDE TO GERMAN IDIOMS: being a Collection of the Idioms most in use. With Examination Papers. 3rd Edition. Cloth. 2s.

WERNER'S ELEMENTARY LESSONS IN CAPE DUTCH (AFRIKANDER TAAL). By A. Werner and G. Hunt. 16mo, cloth. 1s. 6d.

> "We most cordially recommend this book to anyone going out to settle in South Africa. . . . The dialogues and exercises are admirably planned."—*Reformer.*

> "To those outward bound such a book is sure to be useful."—*Practical Teacher.*

WILLIAMS (The Right Rev. W. L., D.C.L.). A DICTIONARY OF THE NEW ZEALAND LANGUAGE. 4th Edition. Edited by the Right Rev. Bishop W. L. Williams, with numerous additions and corrections. Demy 8vo, cloth. 12s. 6d.

—— **LESSONS IN MAORI.** 3rd Edition. Fcap. 8vo, cloth. 3s.

YELLOW BOOK OF LECAN. A Collection of Pieces (Prose and Verse) in the Irish Language, in part compiled at the end of the Fourteenth Century ; now for the first time published from the original Manuscript in the Library of Trinity College, Dublin, by the Royal Irish Academy. With Introduction, Analysis of Contents, and Index, by Robert Atkinson. 30 and 468 pp. (Royal Irish Academy's Irish facsimiles.) Large post folio, 1896, half-roan, Roxburghe, cloth sides. £4, 4s.

ZOEGA (G. T.). ENGLISH-ICELANDIC DICTIONARY. 8vo, cloth. 6s. net.

ZOMPOLIDES (Dr. D.). A COURSE OF MODERN GREEK ; or, The Greek Language of the Present Day. I. The Elementary Method. Crown 8vo, cloth. 5s.

V. Science.

ABRAHAM (P. S.). LEPROSY: A Review of some Facts and Figures. 8vo. 1s.

ANNETT (H. E., M.D., D.P.H.), J. EVERETT DUTTON, M.B., B.Ch., and J. H. ELLIOTT, M.D., Toronto. REPORT OF THE MALARIA EXPEDITION TO NIGERIA (1900). Part I. Malarial Fever, etc. (Liverpool School of Tropical Medicine, Memoir III.). 10s. 6d. Part II. Filariasis (Liverpool School of Tropical Medicine, Memoir IV.). *Out of print separately, but is contained in the Thompson-Yates Laboratory Reports, Vol. IV., Part I. Price 20s.*

BASTIAN (H. CHARLTON, M.A., M.D., F.R.S.). STUDIES IN HETEROGENESIS. With 825 Illustrations from Photomicrographs. Royal 8vo, cloth. 31s. 6d.

BENTHAM and HOOKER. GENERA PLANTARUM AD EXEMPLARIA IMPRIMIS IN HERBARIIS KEWENSIBUS SERVATA DEFINITA. Auctoribus G. Bentham et J. D. Hooker. 3 vols., £8, 2s. Vol. I. (not sold separately). Vol. II., 56s. Vol. III. (Parts 1 and 2), 56s.; or separately, Part 1, 24s.; Part 2, 32s.

BERGMANN (Prof. E. von, M.D.). A SYSTEM OF PRACTICAL SURGERY. Edited by William T. Bull, M.D. In five imperial 8vo volumes, containing 4174 pages, with 1976 illustrations in the text, and 102 superb full-page plates in colours and monochrome. Extra cloth, £6, 6s.; half-leather, marble sides and edges, £7, 7s.; half-morocco, £8, 8s.

"We regard it as a valuable exposition of modern surgery. The main characteristics of the system are the fulness with which the subjects are treated and the wealth of illustrations. Many of these are in colours, and are very successful examples of colour-printing. The vast majority of the articles are very good, but we desire especially to praise those on Injuries of the Head and Diseases of the Breast."—*Lancet.*

BERZELIUS (JÖNS JAKOB) and SCHŒNBEIN (CHRISTIAN FREDERICK). LETTERS, 1836-1847. Edited by George W. A. Kahlbaum. Translated by Francis V. Darbishire and N. V. Sidgwick. Crown 8vo, cloth. 3s.

BOYCE (RUBERT, M.B., F.R.S.). THE ANTI-MALARIA MEASURES AT ISMAILIA. (Liverpool School of Tropical Medicine, Memoir XII.) Price 1s.

—— **YELLOW FEVER PROPHYLAXIS IN NEW OR-LEANS, 1905.** (Liverpool School of Tropical Medicine, Memoir XIX.) 5s. net.

BOYCE (RUBERT), A. EVANS, M.R.C.S., and H. H. CLARKE, M.A., B.C. REPORTS ON THE SANITATION AND ANTI-MALARIAL MEASURES IN PRACTICE AT BATHURST, CONAKRY, AND FREETOWN (1905). (Liverpool School of Tropical Medicine, Memoir XIV.) With 8 Plates. 5s.

BRUCE (ALEX., M.A., M.D., F.R.C.P.E., F.R.S.E.). A TOPOGRAPHICAL ATLAS OF THE SPINAL CORD. Fcap. folio, half-leather. £2, 2s. net.

CATON (R., M.D., F.R.C.P., J.P.). HOW TO LIVE. A Simple Manual of Hygiene for the Older Pupils in Primary Schools. 3d.

CHAPMAN (E. J., Ph.D.). MINERAL SYSTEMS. With Outline of an attempted Classification of Minerals in Natural Groups. Crown 8vo, cloth. 2s. 6d.

COOKE (M. C.). MYCOGRAPHIA SEU ICONES FUNGORUM. Figures of Fungi from all parts of the World. Vol. I. (in 6 Parts, each 12s. 6d.). 406 coloured Plates. Royal 8vo, cloth. 80s.

—— **ILLUSTRATIONS OF BRITISH FUNGI (HYMENOMYCETES).** In 8 vols. 1198 coloured Plates. Royal 8vo, cloth gilt. £30, 5s. 6d.

—— **BRITISH DESMIDS.** A Supplement to "British Freshwater Algæ." 66 coloured Plates. 8vo, cloth. 52s. 6d.

—— **HANDBOOK OF AUSTRALIAN FUNGI.** With 36 Plates. 8vo, cloth. £2.

—— *See* also "Grevillea."

CUNNINGHAM MEMOIRS—
1. **Cubic Transformations.** By John Casey, LL.D. 4to, sewed. 2s. 6d.
2. **On the Lumbar Curve in Man and the Apes.** By D. J. Cunningham, M.D. 13 Plates. 4to, sewed. 5s.
3. **New Researches on Sun-heat, Terrestrial Radiation, etc.** By Rev. Samuel Haughton, M.A., M.D. 9 Plates. 4to, sewed. 1s. 6d.
4. **Dynamics and Modern Geometry.** A New Chapter in the Theory of Screws. By Sir Robert S. Ball, LL.D. 4to, sewed. 2s.
5. **The Red Stars.** Observations and Catalogue. New Edition. Edited by Rev. T. Espin, M.A. 4to, sewed. 3s. 6d.
6. **On the Morphology of the Duck Tribe and the Auk Tribe.** By W. K. Parker, F.R.S. 9 Plates. 4to, sewed. 3s. 6d.
7. **Contribution to the Surface Anatomy of the Cerebral Hemispheres.** By D. J. Cunningham, M.D. With a Chapter upon Cranio-Cerebral Topography by Victor Horsley, M.B., F.R.S. 4to, sewed. 8s. 6d.

8. **On the Flinders Petrie Papyri.** Part I. Out of Print.
9. **On the Flinders Petrie Papyri.** Part II. With 18 Autotypes. 4to, sewed. 42s. net. Appendix to 8 and 9. 5s. net.

10. **The Decorative Art of British New Guinea.** A Study in Papuan Ethnography. By Alfred C. Haddon, M.A. With 12 Plates, and numerous other Illustrations. 4to, sewed. 14s. net.

11. **On the Flinders Petrie Papyri.** With Transcriptions, Commentaries, and Index. By John P. Mahaffy, D.D., and Prof. J. Gilbert Smyly. With 7 Autotypes. 4to, sewed. 42s. net.

DITTMAR (Prof. W.). CHEMICAL ARITHMETIC. Part I. A Collection of Tables, Mathematical, Chemical, and Physical, for the use of Chemists, etc. 8vo, cloth. 6s. net.

—— **EXERCISES IN QUANTITATIVE CHEMICAL ANALYSIS, with a short Treatise on Gas Analysis.** 8vo, cloth. 10s. 6d.

DURHAM (H. E., M.A., M.B., F.R.C.S.), and the late WALTER MYERS, M.B. REPORT OF THE YELLOW FEVER EXPEDITION TO PARA (1900). (Liverpool School of Tropical Medicine, Memoir VII.) 4to, 7s. 6d.

DUTTON (J. E., M.B., Ch.B.). REPORT OF THE MALARIA EXPEDITION TO THE GAMBIA. (Liverpool School of Tropical Medicine, Memoir X.) 4to. 10s. 6d. net.

—— **and JOHN L. TODD, B.A., M.D., C.M., M'Gill. FIRST REPORT OF THE TRYPANOSOMIASIS EXPEDITION TO SENEGAMBIA (1902).** (Liverpool School of Tropical Medicine, Memoir XI.) 4to. 10s. 6d. net.

—— —— **RAPPORT SUR L'EXPÉDITION AU CONGO 1903-5.** Price 5s.

—— —— **THE NATURE OF HUMAN TICK-FEVER IN THE EASTERN PART OF THE CONGO FREE STATE.** (Liverpool School of Tropical Medicine, Memoir XVII.) 4to. With Map, 4 Plates, and 9 Temperature Charts. Price 7s. 6d. net.

FARADAY and SCHŒNBEIN, LETTERS OF, 1836-1862. With Notes, Comments, and References to Contemporary Letters. Edited by George W. A. Kahlbaum and Francis V. Darbishire, with Portraits of Faraday and Schoenbein in Photogravure. Demy 8vo, cloth. 13s. net.

FASCICULI MALAYENSES. Anthropological and Zoological results of an Expedition to Perak and the Siamese Malay States, 1901–1902, undertaken by Nelson Annandale and Herbert C. Robinson. 4to. Now ready. Anthropology, Part I., 15s. Part IIA. 10s. net. Zoology, Vol. I., Parts I., II., III., and Appendix. 52s. Supplement (Itinerary), 5s.

GILES (Lieut-Col.). **GENERAL SANITATION AND ANTI-MALARIAL MEASURES IN SEKONDI, THE GOLDFELDS, AND KUMASSI, AND A COMPARISON BETWEEN THE CONDITIONS OF EUROPEAN RESIDENCE IN INDIA.** (Liverpool School of Tropical Medicine, Memoir XV.) 4to. Price 7s. 6d. net.

GREVILLEA : A Record of Cryptogamic Botany and its Literature. Edited by M. C. Cooke. Parts. 8vo. Each 1s. 6d. Plates. Vols. I.–XVIII. In 9 vols. Cloth (each 14s.). £6, 6s.

HARNACK (AXEL). **INTRODUCTION TO THE ELEMENTS OF THE DIFFERENTIAL AND INTEGRAL CALCULUS.** From the German. Royal 8vo, cloth, 10s. 6d.

HOFF (J. H. VAN'T). **STUDIES IN CHEMICAL DYNAMICS.** Revised and enlarged by Dr. Ernst Cohen, Assistant in the Chemical Laboratory of the University of Amsterdam. Translated by Thomas Ewan, M.Sc., Ph.D., Demonstrator of Chemistry in the Yorkshire College, Leeds. Royal 8vo, cloth. 10s. 6d.

JOHNSTONE (J.). **BRITISH FISHERIES: Their Administration and their Problems.** A short account of the Origin and Growth of British Sea Fishery Authorities and Regulations. 10s. 6d. net.

JONES (J. T. SHARE-). **SURGICAL ANATOMY OF THE HORSE.** To be completed in 4 Parts. With above 100 Illustrations, a number being in colour. Price per part, 15s. net, sewed; cloth, 16s. 6d. net. Part I. ready.

JOURNAL OF THE FEDERATED MALAY STATES MUSEUMS. Issued Quarterly. Single numbers, 1s. 6d. net. Subscription, 5s. per annum.

JOURNAL OF THE LINNEAN SOCIETY. Botany. At various prices. Index to Journal (Botany), 20s. **Zoology.** At various prices. General Index to the first 20 vols. of the Journal (Zoology) and the Zoological portion of the Proceedings, 20s.

JOURNAL OF THE ROYAL MICROSCOPICAL SOCIETY, containing its transactions and Proceedings, with other Microscopical information. Bi-monthly. Previous to 1893 at various prices; after that date bi-monthly, each 6s. net.

JOURNAL OF THE QUEKETT MICROSCOPICAL CLUB. Nos. 1–26, 1s. net; Nos. 27–31, 2s. 6d. net. 1893, No. 32, and following Nos., half-yearly, 3s. 6d. net.

LIVERPOOL MARINE BIOLOGY COMMITTEE. MEMOIRS ON TYPICAL BRITISH MARINE PLANTS AND ANIMALS. Edited by W. A. Herdman, D.Sc., F.R.S. All demy 8vo, stiff boards.

1. **Ascidia.** By W. A. Herdman. With 5 Plates. Price 2s. net.
2. **Cardium.** By J. Johnstone, Fisheries Assistant, University College, Liverpool. With 7 Plates. Price 2s. 6d. net.

3. **Echinus.** By Herbert Clifton Chadwick, Curator of the Port Erin Biological Station. With 5 Plates. Price 2s. net.

4. **Codium.** By R. J. Harvey Gibson, M.A., F.L.S., Professor of Botany in University College, Liverpool, and Helen P. Auld, B.Sc., With 3 Plates. Price 1s. 6d. net.

5. **Alcyonium.** By Sydney J. Hickson, M.A., D.Sc., F.R.S., Beyer Professor of Zoology in Owens College, Manchester. With 3 Plates. Price 1s. 6d. net.

6. **Lepeophtheirus and Lernea.** By Andrew Scott, Resident Fisheries Assistant at the Peel Hatchery. With 5 Plates. 2s. net.

7. **Lineus.** By R. C. Punnett, B.A., with 4 Plates. 2s. net.

8. **Pleuronectes.** By Frank J. Cole, Jesus College, Oxford, Lecturer in the Victoria University, Demonstrator of Zoology, University, Liverpool, and James Johnstone, B.Sc. Lond., Fisheries Assistant, University, Liverpool. With 11 Plates. 7s. net.

9. **Chondrus.** By Otto V. Darbishire, Owens College, Manchester. With 7 Plates. 2s. 6d. net.

10. **Patella (the Common Limpet).** By J. R. Ainsworth Davis, M.A., Professor of Zoology in the University College of Wales, Aberystwyth, and H. J. Fleure, B.Sc., Fellow of the University of Wales. With 4 Plates. 2s. 6d. net.

11. **Arenicola (the Lug-Worm).** By J. H. Ashworth, D.Sc., Lecturer in Invertebrate Zoology in the University of Edinburgh. With 8 Plates. Price 4s. 6d. net.

12. **Gammarus.** By Margaret Cussans, B.Sc., Zoological Department, University of Liverpool. With 4 Plates. 2s. net.

13. **Anurida.** By A. D. Imms, B.Sc. (Lond.). With 7 Plates. Price 4s. net.

LIVERPOOL MARINE BIOLOGY COMMITTEE. FIFTH REPORT UPON THE FAUNA OF LIVERPOOL BAY AND THE NEIGHBOURING SEAS. Written by the Members of the Liverpool Marine Biology Committee and other Naturalists; and edited by W. A. Herdman, D.Sc., F.R.S., Professor of Natural History, the University, Liverpool. Demy 8vo, cloth. 12 Plates. 8s. 6d. net.

MEMOIRS OF THE LIVERPOOL SCHOOL OF TROPICAL MEDICINE.

I. **Ross (R.)** Malarial Fever: Its Cause, Prevention, and Treatment. 8vo. 2s. 6d.

II. **Ross (R.), H. E. Annett, and E. E. Austen.** Report of the Malaria Expedition to Sierra Leone (1899). 4to. 21s.

III. **Annett (H. E.), J. E. Dutton, and J. H. Elliott.** Report of the Malaria Expedition to Nigeria (1900). I. Malarial Fever. 4to. 10s. 6d.

LIVERPOOL SCHOOL OF TROPICAL MEDICINE—continued.

IV. Annett (H. E.), J. E. Dutton, and J. H. Elliott. Report of the Malaria Expedition to Nigeria (1900). II. Filariasis. 4to. [This is out of print separately, but is also contained in the Report of the Thompson-Yates Laboratories, Vol. IV. Part 1. Price 20s.]

V. Ross (R.) and M. L. Taylor. Progress Reports of the Campaign against Mosquitoes in Sierra Leone. Part I. 1901. With a Letter from Dr. Daniels regarding the results arrived at to date. 8vo. 1s. Part II. 1902. 8vo. 1s.

VI. [Not issued yet.]

VII. Durham (H. E.) and W. Myers. Report of the Yellow Fever Expedition to Para (1900). 4to. 7s. 6d.

VIII. Taylor (M. L.). Report on the Sanitary Conditions of Cape Coast Town. 8vo. 1s.

IX. Ross (R.). Report on Malaria at Ismailia and Suez. 8vo. 1s.

X. Dutton (J. E.). Report of the Malaria Expedition to the Gambia. 4to. 10s. 6d. net.

XI. Dutton (J. E.) and J. L. Todd. First Report of the Trypanosomiasis Expedition to Senegambia (1902). 4to. 10s. 6d. net. [Also contained in Thompson-Yates Laboratories Reports, V. 2.]

XII. Boyce (R.). The Anti-Malaria Measures at Ismailia. 8vo. 1s.

XIII. Dutton (J. E) and J. L. Todd. Reports of the Trypanosomiasis Expedition to the Congo (1903-1904). With a Comparison of the Trypanosomes of Uganda and the Congo Free State by H. W. Thomas, M.D. M'Gill, and Stanley F. Linton, B.Sc., M.B. Liverpool; and a Note on Tsetse Flies by E. E. Austen, Zoological Department, British Museum. Paper covers. 15s.

XIV. Boyce (Rubert, M.B., F.R.S.), Arthur Evans, M.R.C.S., H. Herbert Clarke, M.A., B.C., Cantab. Report on the Sanitation and Anti-Malarial Measures in practice in Bathurst, Conakry, and Freetown (1905). 4to. 8 Plates. Price 5s.

XV. Giles (Lieut.-Colonel). General Sanitation and Anti-Malarial Measures in Sekondi, the Goldfields, and Kumassi, and a Comparison between the Conditions of European Residence in India. 4to. Price 7s. 6d. net.

XVI. Thomas (H. Wolferstan, M.D., M'Gill) and Anton Breinl, M.U.Dr., Prag. Trypanosomes, Trypanosomiasis, and Sleeping Sickness : Pathology and Treatment. 4to. 6 Plates (5 coloured) and 7 Charts. Price 12s. 6d. net.

XVII. Dutton (J. Everett, M.B.) and John L. Todd, B.A., M.D., M'Gill. The Nature of Human Tick-Fever in the Eastern Part of the Congo Free State. 4to. With Map, 4 Plates, and 9 Temperature Charts. Price 7s. 6d. net.

LIVERPOOL SCHOOL OF TROPICAL MEDICINE—continued.

XVIII.—1. Dutton (J. Everett, M.B.) and John L. Todd, B.A., M.D., C.M., M'Gill. Gland Palpation in Human Trypanosomiasis ; and 2. The Distribution and Spread of "Sleeping Sickness" in the Congo Free State. With 4 Maps (2 colours) and 4 Plates. 3. Newstead (R., A.L.S., F.E.S.) and John L. Todd, B.A., M.D., C.M., M'Gill. A New Dermanyssid Acarid. With 1 Plate. 4. Newstead (R., A.L.S., F.E.S.). Another New Dermanyssid Acarid. With 1 Plate. 5. Stephens (J. W. W., M.D., Cantab.) and R. Newstead, A.L.S., F.E.S. Anatomy of the Proboscis of Biting Flies. With 6 Plates. Imp. 8vo. Price 7s. 6d. net.

XIX. Boyce (Rubert, M.B., F.R.S.). Yellow Fever Prophylaxis in New Orleans in 1905. Imp. 8vo. Maps and 6 Plates. Price 5s. net.

XX.—1. Dutton (J. Everett, M.B.) and John L. Todd, B.A., M.D. La prophylaxie de la Malaria dans les principaux postes de l'Etat Indépendant du Congo. With 4 Maps, and 4 Illustrations. Imp. 8vo. 2. Breinl (Anton, M.D.) and A. Kinghorn, M.B. The Animal Reactions of the Spirochæta of African "Tick Fever." Imp. 8vo. 3. Breinl (Anton, M.D.). The Specific Nature of the Spirochæta of African "Tick Fever." Imp. 8vo. Price 5s.

XXI. Runcorn Research Laboratories. An Experimental Study of the Parasite of the African "Tick Fever." Note on a new Spirochæta found in a Mouse. Comparison between the Trypanosomes, and other articles. 4to. 7s. 6d. net.

NOTES ON SANITARY CONDITIONS OBTAINING IN PARA. By the Members of the Yellow Fever Expedition. (Published by the Liverpool School of Tropical Medicine.) 1s.

OTTO (RUDOLF). NATURALISM AND RELIGION. See Crown Theological Library, p. 13.

PALLIN (Capt. W. A., F.R.C.V.S.). A TREATISE ON EPIZOOTIC LYMPHANGITIS. Second Edition. Demy 8vo, cloth. 3s. 6d. net. ; 3s. 9d. post free. Nearly 100 pages, 17 full-page Plates.

PATERSON (ANDREW MELVILLE, M.D., Derby Professor of Anatomy in the University of Liverpool, Hunterian Professor at the Royal College of Surgeons of England). THE HUMAN STERNUM. Three Lectures delivered at the Royal College of Surgeons, England, November 1903. With 10 Plates. Crown 4to. 10s. net.

PIDDINGTON (HENRY). THE SAILORS' HORN-BOOK FOR THE LAW OF STORMS. Being a Practical Exposition of the Theory of the Law of Storms, and its uses to Mariners of all Classes in all Parts of the World. Shown by transparent Storm Cards and useful Lessons. 7th Ed. Demy 8vo, cloth. 10s. 6d.

PRAY (Dr.). **ASTIGMATIC LETTERS.** Printed on Mill-board, size 22 by 14 inches. 1s.

PROCEEDINGS OF THE OPTICAL CONVENTION, No. 1, 1905. Crown 4to, cloth. 10s. net.

RANSOM (W. H., M.D., F.R.S., F.R.C.P.). **THE IN-FLAMMATION IDEA IN GENERAL PATHOLOGY.** Demy 8vo, cloth. 7s. 6d.

REPORTS OF THE THOMPSON-YATES AND JOHN-STON LABORATORIES. Demy 4to, with Illustrations. Vol. I. 1898-9. 10s. 6d. Vol. II. 1898-9. 25s. Vol. III. Part 1. 1900. 7s. 6d. Vol. III. Part 2. 1901. 12s. 6d. Vol. IV. Part I. 1901. 20s. Vol. IV. Part 2. 1902. 21s. New Series. Vol. V. Part 1. 1903. Limp, 20s.; cloth, 21s. Vol. V. Part 2. 1903. Limp, 12s. 6d.; cloth, 13s. 6d. Vol. VI. Part 1. 1905. Limp, 12s. 6d.; cloth, 13s. 6d. Vol. VI. Part 2. 15s. Vol. VII. Part 1. 10s. 6d.

ROSS (RONALD, C.B., F.R.S., etc., Major I.M.S. (retired)). **MALARIAL FEVER**: Its Cause, Prevention, and Treatment. (Liverpool School of Tropical Medicine, Memoir I.) 8vo, cloth. 2s. 6d.

—— H. E. ANNETT, M.D., D.P.H., and E. E. AUSTEN **REPORT OF THE MALARIA EXPEDITION TO SIERRA LEONE** (1899). (Liverpool School of Tropical Medicine, Memoir II.) 4to. 21s.

—— **FIRST PROGRESS REPORT OF THE CAMPAIGN AGAINST MOSQUITOES IN SIERRA LEONE** (1901). With a Letter from Dr. Daniels regarding the results arrived at to date. (Liverpool School of Tropical Medicine, Memoir V. 1.) 1s.

—— **SECOND PROGRESS REPORT OF THE CAM-PAIGN AGAINST MOSQUITOES IN SIERRA LEONE** (1902). By M. Logan Taylor, M.B. (Liverpool School of Tropical Medicine, Memoir V. 2.) 1s.

—— **REPORT ON MALARIA AT ISMAILIA AND SUEZ.** (Liverpool School of Tropical Medicine, Memoir IX.) 1s.

SANG'S LOGARITHMS. A new Table of Seven-place Logarithms of all Numbers continuously up to 200,000. 2nd Edition. Royal 8vo, cloth. 21s.

SCHŒNBEIN. CORRESPONDENCE WITH FARA-DAY. See Faraday.

—— **CORRESPONDENCE WITH BERZELIUS.** See Berzelius.

**SCHREBER (D. G. M.). MEDICAL INDOOR GYMNAS-
TICS,** or a System of Hygienic Exercises for Home Use, to be
practised anywhere, without apparatus or assistance, by young and
old of either sex, for the preservation of health and general activity.
Revised and Supplemented by Rudolf Graefe, M.D. With a
large plate and 45 illustrations in the text. Royal 8vo, cloth.
3*s.* net.

> "The exercises described, when efficiently used, will undoubtedly be of value
> in strengthening and developing the muscular system. The descriptions of the
> exercises and the figures in the text are excellent."—*Physician and Surgeon.*
>
> "Well worthy of the attention of those who go in for regular physical train-
> ing as a means for the preservation of health."—*Scotsman.*
>
> "A very sensible little treatise."—*Glasgow Herald.*

**SCHROEN (L.). SEVEN-FIGURE LOGARITHMS OF
NUMBERS** from 1 to 108,000, and of Sines, Cosines,
Tangents, Cotangents to every 10 Seconds of the Quad-
rant. With a Table of Proportional Parts. By Dr. Ludwig
Schroen, Director of the Observatory of Jena, etc., etc. 5th
Edition, corrected and stereotyped. With a description of the
Tables by A. De Morgan, Professor of Mathematics in University
College, London. Imp. 8vo, cloth, printed on light green paper.
9*s.*

SNELLEN'S OPHTHALMIC TEST TYPES. Best Types
for the Determination of the Acuteness of Vision. 14th Edition,
considerably augmented and improved. 8vo, sewed. 4*s.* Single
Sheets: E T B, M O V, B D E, ɰ ɰ ɰ, and Large Clock Sheet.
8*d.* each. Small Clock Sheet and R T V Z. 4*d.* each.

—— **ASTIGMATIC TEST CHART.** Long folio, varnished,
mounted on rollers. 2*s.* net.

**SONNTAG (C. O.). A POCKET FLORA OF EDIN-
BURGH AND THE SURROUNDING DISTRICT.**
A Collection and full Description of all Phanerogamic and the
principal Cryptogamic Plants, classified after the Natural System,
with an artificial Key and a Glossary of Botanical Terms. By the
late C. O. Sonntag, the Royal High School, Edinburgh; formerly
Secretary of the Microscopical Society of Glasgow, etc. Fcap. 8vo,
limp cloth, round corners, with Map of the Environs of Edinburgh.
3*s.* 6*a.* net.

SPENCER (W. G.). INVENTIONAL GEOMETRY. With
a Preface by Herbert Spencer. 8vo, cloth. 1*s.*

—— **A SYSTEM OF LUCID SHORTHAND.** With a
Prefatory Note by Herbert Spencer. Cloth. 1*s.*

STEPHENS (J. W. W., M.D. Cantab., D.P.H.) and S. R. CHRISTOPHERS, M.B. Vict., I.M.S. PRACTICAL STUDY OF MALARIA AND OTHER BLOOD PARA-SITES. (Published for the Liverpool School of Tropical Medicine). 8vo, cloth. 2nd Edition. 12s. 6d. net.

TAYLOR (M. LOGAN, M.B., Ch.B.). REPORT ON THE SANITARY CONDITIONS OF CAPE COAST TOWN. (Liverpool School of Tropical Medicine, Memoir VIII.) 8vo. 1s.

—— REPORT OF THE CAMPAIGN AGAINST THE MOSQUITOES IN SIERRA LEONE. See Ross and Taylor.

THOMAS (H. WOLFERSTAN, M.D., M'GILL) and ANTON BREINL, M.U.Dr., Prag. TRYPANOSOMES, TRYPANOSOMIASIS, AND SLEEPING SICKNESS: PATHOLOGY AND TREATMENT. 4to. (Liverpool School of Tropical Medicine, Memoir XVI.) 6 Plates (5 coloured) and 7 Charts. Price 7s. 6d. net.

TRANSACTIONS OF THE EPIDEMIOLOGICAL SOCIETY OF LONDON. New Series. Vol. XXIII. Session 1903-1904. Demy 8vo, cloth. 6s. net. The earlier volumes of the New Series, I.-XXII., are still obtainable. Price 6s. net each. Commemoration Volume, containing an account of the Foundation of the Society and of the Commemoration Dinner, together with an Index of the papers read at its meetings between 1855 and 1900. 8vo, cloth. 5s. net.

TRANSACTIONS OF THE ROYAL SOCIETY OF EDINBURGH. Vol. XXXVIII. Part 1, 40s. Part 2, 25s. Part 3, 30s. Part 4, 7s. 6d. Vol. XXXIX. Part 1, 30s. Part 2, 19s. Part 3, 43s. Part 4, 9s. Vol. XL. Part 1, 25s. General Index to First Thirty-four Volumes (1783-1888), with History of the Institution. 4to, cloth. 21s.

TRANSACTIONS OF THE ROYAL IRISH ACADEMY, DUBLIN. Vols. I.-XX. 4to. £22, 5s. 6d. Vols. XXI.-XXXI. Various prices.

TRANSACTIONS OF THE ROYAL DUBLIN SOCIETY. Various volumes at various prices.

VEGA. LOGARITHMIC TABLES OF NUMBERS AND TRIGONOMETRICAL FUNCTIONS. Translated from the 40th, or Dr. Bremiker's Edition, thoroughly revised and enlarged, by W. L. F. Fischer, M.A., F.R.S., Fellow of Clare College, Cambridge, ; Professor of Natural Philosophy in the University of St. Andrews. 75th Stereotyped Edition. Royal 8vo, cloth. 7s.

VI. Miscellaneous.

ANTHROPOLOGY—SOCIOLOGY—MYTHOLOGY—
BIBLIOGRAPHY—BIOGRAPHY, ETC.

AVEBURY (Lord, D.C.L., F.R.S., etc.) (Sir John Lubbock).
PREHISTORIC TIMES, as Illustrated by Ancient Remains and the Manners and Customs of Modern Savages.
6th Edition, revised, with 239 Illustrations, a large number of which are specially prepared for this Edition. Demy 8vo, cloth, gilt tops. 18s.

" To anyone who wishes to obtain a succinct conspectus of the present state of knowledge on the subject of early man, we recommend the perusal of this comprehensive volume."—*Jour. Brit. Archæolog. Assoc.*

" The fact that this well-known standard work has reached a sixth edition is evidence of its value to ethnologists and archæologists. The many and beautiful illustrations are most helpful in better understanding the plain but accurate letterpress. Lord Avebury is to be congratulated on the new edition, which is sure to further popularise a fascinating subject for investigation by cultured people."—*Science Gossip.*

" It is necessary to compare the present volume with the fifth edition in order to see how much it has been improved. The illustrations to this sixth edition are immeasurably superior to the fifth."—*Knowledge.*

BIBLIOGRAPHICAL REGISTER. Published Quarterly. 6d. net ; 2s. 2d. per annum post free. Nos. 1–3 ready.

BLACKBURN (HELEN). WOMEN'S SUFFRAGE. A Record of the Women's Suffrage Movement in the British Isles, with a Biographical Sketch of Miss Becker. Portraits. Crown 8vo, cloth. 6s.

—— *See also* Vynne, Nora, and Blackburn, " Women under the Factory Acts."

BROWN (ROBERT, Jun., F.S.A.). SEMITIC INFLUENCE IN HELLENIC MYTHOLOGY. With special reference to the recent mythological works of the Right Hon. Prof. Max Müller and Mr. Andrew Lang. Demy 8vo, cloth. 7s. 6d.

—— **RESEARCHES INTO THE ORIGIN OF THE PRIMITIVE CONSTELLATIONS OF THE GREEKS, PHŒNICIANS, AND BABYLONIANS.** With a large map of the Northern Hemisphere as viewed at Phœnicia 1200 B.C., and other maps. 2 vols. demy 8vo, cloth. 10s. 6d. each.

—— **MR. GLADSTONE AS I KNEW HIM, and other Essays.** Demy 8vo, cloth. 7s. 6d.

CATALOGUE OF THE LONDON LIBRARY, St James's Square. By C. T. Hagberg Wright, LL.D., etc. xiv + 1626 pp. 4to, cloth. 42s. net. **Supplement I.,** 1902-3. Buckram, 1 vol., 196 pp. 5s. net. **Supplement II.** 198 pp. 1903-4. Buckram. 5s. net. **Supplement III.** 1904-5. 5s. net.

"The present catalogue is essentially a working catalogue. . . . The general level of accuracy in the printing and editing of the work appears to us to be an unusually high one. . . . We heartily applaud the work, both as a landmark in library land, and as a monument standing upon a firm foundation of its own.' —*The Times.*

CURTIN (JEREMIAH). CREATION MYTHS OF PRIMITIVE AMERICA IN RELATION TO THE RELIGIOUS HISTORY AND MENTAL DEVELOP-MENT OF MANKIND. Contains twenty long myths taken down word for word by Mr. Curtin from Indians who knew no religion or language but their own, and many of whom had not seen a white man until they had attained years of maturity. With an elaborate Introduction and Notes. Demy 8vo, cloth. 10s. 6d. net.

DIETRICHSON (L.). MONUMENTA ORCADICA. The Norsemen in the Orkneys, and the Monuments they have left, with a Survey of the Celtic (Pre-Norwegian) and Scottish (Post-Norwegian) Monuments on the Islands. With original drawings and some Chapters on St Magnus' Cathedral, Kirkwall, by Johan Meyer, Architect. Demy 4to, cloth. £3 net.

ENGELHARDT (C.). DENMARK IN THE EARLY IRON AGE. Illustrated by recent Discoveries in the Peat-Mosses of Slesvig. 33 Plates (giving representations of upwards of a thousand objects), Maps, and numerous other Illustrations on wood. 1866. 4to, cloth. 31s. 6d.

GOLDAMMER (H.). THE KINDERGARTEN. A Guide to Fröbel's Method of Education. 2 vols. in 1. 120 pp. of Illustrations. 8vo, cloth. 10s. 6d.

HARRISON (A., D.Sc.). WOMEN'S INDUSTRIES IN LIVERPOOL. An Inquiry into the Economic Effects of Legislation regulating the Labour of Women. 8vo. 3s.

HENRY (JAMES). ÆNEIDEA; or, Critical, Exegetical and Æsthetical Remarks on the Æneis. With a personal collation of all the first-class MSS., and upwards of 100 second-class MSS., and all the principal editions. Vol. I. (3 Parts), Vol. II. (3 Parts), Vol. III. (3 Parts), Vol. IV. (1 Part). Royal 8vo, sewed. £2, 2s. net.

HERBERT (Hon. A.). THE SACRIFICE OF EDUCA-TION TO EXAMINATION. Letters from "All Sorts and Conditions of Men." Edited by Auberon Herbert. Half-cloth boards. 2s.

58   **WILLIAMS & NORGATE'S**

HERBERT (Hon. A.). WINDFALL AND WATERDRIFT. Verse Miniatures. Square 12mo, cloth limp, gilt tops. 2s.

—— **and WAGER (HAROLD). BAD AIR AND BAD HEALTH.** Dedicated to Professor Clifford Allbutt. Reprinted from the "Contemporary Review." 8vo, cloth, 1s. 6d. ; sewed, 1s.

JOHNSON (E.). THE RISE OF ENGLISH CULTURE. With a brief account of the Author's Life and Writings. Demy 8vo, cloth. 15s. net.

KIEPERT'S NEW ATLAS ANTIQUUS. Twelve Maps of the Ancient World, for Schools and Colleges. Third hundred thousand. 12th Edition, with a complete Geographical Index. Folio, boards. 6s. Strongly bound in cloth. 7s. 6d.

—— **WALL-MAPS OF THE ANCIENT WORLD—**

Wall-map of Ancient Italy. Italia antiqua. For the study of Livy, Sallust, Cicero, Dionysius, etc. Scale 1 : 800,000. Mounted on rollers, varnished. 20s.

General Wall-map of the Old World. Tabula orbis terrarum antiqui ad illustrandam potissimum antiquissimi ævi usque ad Alexandrum M. historiam. For the study of ancient history, especially the history of the Oriental peoples : the Indians, Medes, Persians, Babylonians, Assyrians, Egyptians, Phœnicians, etc. Scale 1 : 5,400,000. Mounted on rollers, varnished, 20s.

General Wall-map of the Roman Empire. Imperii Romani tabula geographica. For the study of the development of the Roman Empire. Scale 1 : 300,000. Mounted on rollers, varnished. 24s.

Wall-map of Ancient Latium. Latii Veteris et finitimarum regionum tabula. For the study of Livy, Dionysius, etc. Scale 1 : 125,000. With supplement : Environs of Rome. Scale 1 : 25,000. Mounted on rollers, varnished. 18s.

Wall-map of Ancient Greece. Græciæ Antiquæ tabula. For the study of Herodotus, Thucydides, Xenophon, Strabo, Cornelius Nepos, etc. Scale 1 : 500,000. Mounted on rollers, varnished. 24s.

Wall-Map of the Empires of the Persians and of Alexander the Great. Imperia Persarum et Macedonum. For the study of Herodotus, Xenophon, Justinian, Arian, Curtius. Scale 1 : 300,000. Mounted on rollers and varnished. 20s.

Wall-Map of Gaul, with portions of Ancient Britain and Ancient Germany. Galliæ Cisalpinæ et Transalpinæ cum partibus Britanniæ et Germaniæ tabula. For the study of Cæsar, Justinian, Livy, Tacitus, etc. Scale 1 : 1,000,000. Mounted on rollers and varnished. 24s.

KIEPERT'S WALL-MAPS OF THE ANCIENT WORLD—Contd.

Wall-Map of Ancient Asia Minor. Asiæ Minoris Antiquæ Tabula. For the study of Herodotus, Xenophon, Justinian, Arian, Curtius, etc. Scale 1 : 800,000. Mounted on rollers and varnished. 20s.

LAING and HUXLEY. PREHISTORIC REMAINS OF CAITHNESS. By Samuel Laing, Esq., with Notes on the Human Remains by Th. H. Huxley, F.R.S. 150 Engravings. 8vo, cloth. 4s. 6d.

MARCKS (ERICH, Professor of Modern History at the University of Leipzig). ENGLAND AND GERMANY: Their Relations in the Great Crises of European History, 1500–1900. Demy 8vo, stiff wrapper. 1s.

MUIR (RAMSAY) and EDITH M. PLATT. A HISTORY OF MUNICIPAL GOVERNMENT IN LIVERPOOL. From the Earliest Times to the Municipal Reform Act of 1835. 4to, cloth. 21s. net.

OTIA MERSEIANA. The Publication of the Arts Faculty of the University of Liverpool, Vols. I.–III. 8vo. 1899–1903. Each 10s. 6d.

PEDDIE (R. A.). PRINTING AT BRESCIA IN THE FIFTEENTH CENTURY. A List of the Issues. 5s. net.

ST. CLAIR (GEORGE, Author of "Creation Records," "Buried Cities and Bible Countries," etc.). MYTHS OF GREECE EXPLAINED AND DATED. An Embalmed History from Uranus to Perseus, including the Eleusinian Mysteries and the Olympic Games. Demy 8vo. 2 vols. 16s.

SCHLOSS (DAVID F.). METHODS OF INDUSTRIAL REMUNERATION. 3rd Edition, revised and enlarged. Crown 8vo, cloth. 7s. 6d.

"In its new as in its old form the book is well nigh indispensable to the student who desires to get some insight into the actual facts about the various methods of industrial remuneration, and the degree of success with which they have been applied in the various trades."—*Manchester Guardian.*
"More useful than ever to the students of the labour problem."—*Political Science Quarterly.*

SPENCER (HERBERT). AN AUTOBIOGRAPHY. *See* p. 31.

—— **PRINCIPLES OF SOCIOLOGY.** *See* p. 31.

—— **STUDY OF SOCIOLOGY.** *See* p. 32.

—— **DESCRIPTIVE SOCIOLOGY.** *See* p. 32.

STEPHENS (GEORGE). PROFESSOR BUGGE'S STUDIES ON NORTHERN MYTHOLOGY EXAMINED. Illustrations. 8vo, cloth. 8s.

—— THE RUNES, WHENCE CAME THEY? 4to, sewed. 6s.

—— OLD NORTHERN RUNIC MONUMENTS. Vol. IV. Folio. 20s. net.

VEILED FIGURE (THE), and Other Poems. Large post 8vo, buckram, gilt, cover designed by Mr. T. Blake Wirgman. 2s. 6d.

VYNNE (NORA) and HELEN BLACKBURN, and with the Assistance of H. W. ALLASON. WOMEN UNDER THE FACTORY ACTS. Part 1. Position of the Employer. Part 2. Position of the Employed. Crown 8vo, cloth. 1s. net.

WELD (A. G.). GLIMPSES OF TENNYSON AND OF SOME OF HIS FRIENDS. With an Appendix by the late Bertram Tennyson. Illustrated with Portraits in photogravure and colour, and with a facsimile of a MS. poem. Fcap. 8vo, art linen. 4s. 6d. net.

" This is a delightful little book, written by one who has all the qualifications for the task—the opportunities of observation, the interest of relationship, and the sympathetic and appreciative temper. . . . We do not attempt to criticise, but only to give such a description as will send our readers to it."—*Spectator*.

" Everyone who reads the book will understand Tennyson a little better, and many will view him in a new aspect for the first time."—*Daily Chronicle*.

" It is quite worthy of a place side by side with the larger ' Life.' "—*Glasgow Herald*.

LIST OF PERIODICALS, REVIEWS, AND TRANSACTIONS AND PROCEEDINGS OF LEARNED SOCIETIES

PUBLISHED BY WILLIAMS & NORGATE.

THE HIBBERT JOURNAL: A Quarterly Review of Religion, Theology, and Philosophy. Single numbers, 2*s*. 6*d*. net. Subscription, 10*s*. per annum, post free.

"There is, for English readers at least, no existing medium for expression of free-thought in this best sense ; and should anything but success await the venture of publishing 'The Hibbert Journal,' we shall confess painful surprise. . . . It will be a reflection on our theological and philosophical students if they do not show full appreciation of a journal so admirably planned and so strongly commenced. . . . For the form of the journal we have nothing but praise, the print being large and the margins ample. We have never with more sincerity wished well to a new undertaking ; and should it fulfil its undoubted possibilities, 'The Hibbert Journal' must be of immense service to all serious and progressive students of the subjects with which it deals."—*Christian World*.

THE LIBERAL CHURCHMAN. Single numbers, 1*s*. net ; 1*s*. 2*d*. post free. Issued half-yearly, January and July.

THE ENGLISHWOMAN'S REVIEW OF SOCIAL AND INDUSTRIAL QUESTIONS. Edited by Antoinette M. Mackenzie. Issued quarterly on 15th January, April, July, and October. Price 1*s*. Per annum, 4*s*. 6*d*., post free.

JOURNAL OF THE FEDERATED MALAY STATES MUSEUMS. Issued quarterly. Single numbers, 1*s*. 6*d*. net. Subscription, 5*s*. per annum.

JOURNAL OF THE ROYAL MICROSCOPICAL SOCIETY, containing its Transactions and Proceedings, with other Microscopical Information. Bi-monthly. 6*s*. net. Yearly subscriptions, 37*s*. 6*d*., post free.

JOURNAL OF THE QUEKETT MICROSCOPICAL CLUB. Issued half-yearly, April and November. Price 3*s*. 6*d*. net. 7*s*. 6*d*. per annum, post free.

---

14 Henrietta Street, Covent Garden, London, W.C.

LINNEAN SOCIETY OF LONDON. Journal of Botany and Journal of Zoology. Published irregularly at various prices.

ROYAL SOCIETY OF EDINBURGH. Transactions. Issued irregularly at various prices.

LIVERPOOL MARINE BIOLOGY COMMITTEE. Memoirs. I.-XII. already published at various prices. Fauna of Liverpool Bay. Fifth Report written by Members of the Committee and other Naturalists. Cloth. 8s. 6d. net. *See* p. 50.

LIVERPOOL UNIVERSITY INSTITUTE OF COMMERCIAL RESEARCH IN THE TROPICS. Quarterly Journal. Numbers, 2s. net.

MEMOIRS OF THE LIVERPOOL SCHOOL OF TROPICAL MEDICINE. *See* p. 50.

ROYAL ASTRONOMICAL SOCIETY. Memoirs and Monthly Notices. Yearly volumes at various prices.

ROYAL IRISH ACADEMY. Transactions and Proceedings issued irregularly; prices vary. Cunningham Memoirs. Vols. I.-X. already issued at various prices.

ROYAL DUBLIN SOCIETY. Transactions and Proceedings. Issued irregularly at various prices.

REPORTS OF THE THOMPSON-YATES LABORATORIES. *See* p. 53.

TRANSACTIONS OF THE EPIDEMIOLOGICAL SOCIETY OF LONDON. *See* p. 55.

PRINTED BY NEILL AND CO., LTD., EDINBURGH.

9290 096

APR ~~30 1985~~

~~OCT 81 1985~~

DEC 81 1938

ACME
~~BINDING~~ CO., INC.

JUL 1 0 1984

100 CAMBRIDGE STREET.
CHARLESTOWN, MASS.

CPSIA information can be obtained
at www.ICGtesting.com
Printed in the USA
BVHW072155280619
552220BV00010B/247/P